The Politically Incorrect Guide™ to
the Constitution

The Politically Incorrect Guide™ to
the Constitution

Kevin R. C. Gutzman, J.D., Ph.D.

Since 1947
REGNERY
PUBLISHING, INC.
An Eagle Publishing Company

Library of Congress Cataloging-in-Publication Data
Gutzman, Kevin Raeder Constantine, 1963–
  The politically incorrect guide to the constitution / Kevin R. C. Gutzman.
      p. cm.
  Includes bibliographical references and index.
  ISBN-13: 978-1-59698-505-6
  1. Constitutional law—United States. 2. Constitutional history—United States. 3. United States. Supreme Court. 4. Judges—United States. I.
Title.
  KF4550.Z9G88 2007
  342.7302—dc22

                                        2007013954

Published in the United States by
Regnery Publishing, Inc.
One Massachusetts Avenue, NW
Washington, DC 20001
www.regnery.com

10 9 8 7

Books are available in quantity for promotional or premium use. Write to Director of Special Sales, Regnery Publishing, Inc., One Massachusetts Avenue NW, Washington, DC 20001, for information on discounts and terms or call (202) 216-0600.

To Lorie,
Who makes all things new again,
and everything seem possible.

CONTENTS

Contents

INTRODUCTION

Few subjects in American life are so thoroughly mystified, so completely surrounded by a myth of incomprehensibility, as the United States Constitution. From its earliest days, its exponents—chiefly lawyers and judges, but with a helping of other politicians, journalists, and authors of various kinds thrown in—have trained the people at large to believe that only the few, the specially trained "elite," can understand it. If court rulings "interpreting" the Constitution defy common sense, well, that must be because common sense is so . . . common.

In introductory lessons about America's federal government, students are introduced to the ideas of "republicanism," "limited government," and "federalism." Republicanism refers to a system in which policymakers are chosen through popular elections. Limited government and federalism are simply two sides of the same coin. They are different ways of understanding a system in which the states came first, delegated some carefully enumerated powers to a central government, and retained the rest for themselves.

But in what sense is our federal government limited? What remains of the idea that power over almost all significant issues is retained by the states? Why is it, in other words, that issues such as homosexual sodomy, abortion, and affirmative action—not to mention prayer in schools and the outcome of the 2000 presidential election in Florida—are decided by federal judges? What ever happened to republicanism, limited government, and federalism?

In recent decades, numerous judges—and particularly the Platonic guardians on the Supreme Court—have undertaken to use the Constitution as a blank check allowing them to write into American law their own ideas of "the evolving standards of decency that mark the progress of a maturing society," as Chief Justice Earl Warren put it in *Trop v. Dulles* (1958). Note the allusion to Darwin's theory of evolution here: if the judges' conceptions of decency differ from those of all their predecessors, then today's judges must be *superior* to their predecessors, because they have "evolved" within their "maturing" society. And of course, if the judges' ideas differ from those of the majority of the electorate, that only shows how much further the judges have evolved and how superior they really are.

This is not to say that every federal judge, or every judge on the Supreme Court, fancies himself a Platonic guardian. But it is to say that judges face few constraints on foisting their own views on the people as "constitutional law." Yet for a judge today disinclined to legislate "constitutional law," the obstacles to self-restraint are formidable. First, he will have to deal with the criticism, and, if he is consistent, eventually with the derision of the media, of politicians, and of legal academics. Second, and perhaps more important, he will have to escape from the mode of thought inculcated in him by his legal education.

For a century now, instruction in American law schools has focused on the "case method." Prospective lawyers do not study the continental, English, and colonial antecedents of the federal Constitution. Neither do they read the records of the Philadelphia Convention of 1787, where the Constitution was written, or the ratification debates that led to its implementation. Instead, they imbibe the latest opinions on constitutional matters from the courts, and particularly from the Supreme Court. Those opinions, and not the Constitution's text as understood by the people when they ratified it, are what law schools teach as "constitutional law."

This "law" is the product, to a large degree, of the political preferences (refracted through the constitutional "theories") of judges and lawyers. It has almost nothing to do with history or with the original understanding of particular provisions. Thus, asked by a student why his constitutional law class would not be reading any of *The Federalist*, a famous constitutional law professor at an elite law school responded that *The Federalist* had nothing to do with constitutional law. The sad thing is that the professor was right, because today's "constitutional law" is not constitutional at all.

Even "originalist" judges' application of the Constitution to real cases, as we will see, is far removed from Thomas Jefferson's test of the Constitution's meaning: "the true sense in which it was adopted by the States, that in which it was advocated by its friends." Jeffersonian judges have seldom dominated the Supreme Court—certainly not in the last three-quarters of a century.

This book's goal is to explain how the Constitution was understood in the first place and then to chronicle the federal courts' history of dealing with it. It will show how we went from the Constitution's republican federal government, with its very limited powers, to an unrepublican judgeocracy with limitless powers. The approach is historical—to see the Constitution as we should see it, in its original context, as it was originally understood, and to chart, over the course of two centuries, how we got from there to here. Perhaps more than anything else, *The Politically Incorrect Guide™ to the Constitution* provides further illustration of the old adage that "absolute power corrupts absolutely."

Chapter One

WHAT MADE THE CONSTITUTION: REVOLUTION AND CONFEDERATION

W hy do we have a federal constitution, anyway? Before we can understand the Constitution's meaning, we have to have an idea of its purpose. There were twenty-six British colonies in the New World when the American Revolution began. They had distinct histories, and they had been founded for distinct purposes, at distinct times, by distinct groups of people.

The British government essentially displayed an attitude of "benign neglect" toward the American colonies, including the thirteen that ultimately joined together in 1775 to fight for their rights. It did not, for the most part, legislate regarding their internal affairs, and it did not tax them internally.

Each of the colonies had its own government, including a governor and an assembly with a representative element. The colonists grew accustomed to considering their colonial governments as analogous to the British government in England: the British had their king, House of Lords, and House of Commons (made up of elected members), while Virginia, for example, had its appointed governor, its Council, and its House of Burgesses (the first elective assembly in the New World).

Colonial charters, which described how the government of a particular colony worked, often included guarantees to the colonists of their rights. Thus, Virginia's charter said that King James I's colonists there would have

Guess what?

- The American colonists fought to rid themselves of an intrusive government they couldn't control. (Does that remind you of nine unelected oracles in robes?)

- The Articles of Confederation were not designed to create a new nation, but to protect the rights of the states that were joined as the United States.

all the rights of his subjects in England. When one governor of colonial Virginia left office, a new one, with a new commission, replaced him. These commissions often included new guarantees of the colonists' English rights. People in Virginia—the first, largest, and most populous colony—sanguinely enjoyed their ongoing status as Englishmen.

The trouble begins...

Well, not *entirely* as Englishmen: they had no representation in Parliament and after the middle of the seventeenth century could not export goods from Virginia without transshipment through England. This regulation of commerce, as it was called in those days, seemed a small price to pay for inclusion in the British Empire—which benefited colonists and denizens of the home islands alike.

None of this is to suggest, however, that there was never conflict between the colonies and England over events in the New World. There certainly was. In the 1750s, Virginians bridled at the attempt of one of their governors to charge them for land patents in the Pistole Fee Controversy. The elected House of Burgesses insisted to the royally appointed governor that he had no authority to tax the colonists and that this new fee amounted to a tax. In the end, the governor backed down.

The real theoretical difficulty arose in the 1760s when Britain won the Seven Years' War (1756–1763), which in America was called the French and Indian War (1754–1763). This first world war had begun with a skirmish started by a young Virginia militia major named George Washington. Victory in the war proved a mixed blessing for Great Britain.

On one hand, the British had seized much of France's colonial empire, including Canada. On the other, they had done so chiefly through the invention of modern deficit finance, which allowed them to buy the latest warships in numbers the French (who had far more men and natural resources than Britain) could not match.

So, in the end, Britain had acquired a greater empire and a huge debt. While people throughout the Empire (including in the thirteen American colonies) celebrated their victory, the question arose: what was to be done about the debt?

The period 1763–1775 was marked by repeated British efforts to get some money, any money, out of the colonists to help service the new imperial debt. While the colonists had willingly provided men and money, along with various supplies, to the war effort, they proved unwilling to be taxed directly. As the New York Assembly put it in a 1764 petition to the British House of Commons, New Yorkers had been willing to provide money when asked to do so, and even to provide more than had been requested, but they would not accept being taxed by a legislature—the British Parliament—in which they were not represented.

At first, arguments against Parliament's taxing the colonies were presented in a conciliatory way. After all, the colonists were British and

Holy Pistole!

In 1752, Lieutenant Governor Robert Dinwiddie tried to charge a pistole—a coin valued at a little more than one English pound—for signing any land patent. The governor's signature had always been required, but no governor had ever tried to charge for it. Virginians were outraged and created the slogan "Liberty, Property, and No Pistole" in protest. Dinwiddie claimed that the pistole fee was his prerogative as the king's representative, but the people argued that it was a tax on them without the consent of their elected representatives in the General Assembly. Dinwiddie said the colonists were "much inflam'd ... with republican Principles" and wondered if they were becoming a threat to his royal authority because they had been allowed to govern themselves for too long.[1]

enthusiastically patriotic. It was only yesterday that they had won the first world war against Britain's most powerful rival. They were persuaded that the unwritten British constitution was the world's finest. They had defeated papist France, with its absolute monarchy, because they were free—and, many believed, because God favored their Protestant nation.

But the colonists would not pay taxes to a Parliament they had not elected. They protested, they boycotted, they bullied representatives of the Crown, and they organized a congress, the Stamp Act Congress, to speak formally for them. But the British, for their part, would not respond to the Congress. King George III believed that the colonies must be either subject to the King-in-Parliament or independent; he would make them comply.

In the course of the 1760s and 1770s, Britain sent home New York's legislature, reorganized Massachusetts's government, closed Boston's port, restricted access to trial by jury, and adopted various other laws intended to make it easier to tax the colonists. The colonists' response was a more and more heartfelt "No!"

"If this be treason, make the most of it"

In Virginia, a young member of the House of Burgesses named Patrick Henry offered his colleagues a set of resolutions. He wanted the elected representatives of America's most important colony to go on record in opposition to the Stamp Act of 1765—a British tax measure—and he wanted them to do it in a radical way.

Henry's resolutions against the Stamp Act, later known as the Virginia Stamp Act Resolves, said that Virginians had always had, from their colony's settlement, "all the privileges and immunities" of "the people of Great Britain." Virginia's two royal charters of the seventeenth century, Henry pointed out, had made that guarantee. Moreover, Virginians had always "enjoyed the right of being thus governed by their own Assembly in the article of taxes and internal police."

Henry would have had the Burgesses resolve that "the General Assembly of this colony, together with his Majesty... have... the only exclusive right and power to lay taxes and imposts upon the inhabitants of this colony; and that every attempt to vest such power in any other person or persons whatever... is illegal, unconstitutional, and unjust, and has a manifest tendency to destroy British as well as American freedom." Along this same line, he insisted that "his Majesty's liege people, the inhabitants of this colony, are not bound to yield obedience to any law or ordinance whatever, designed to impose any taxation whatsoever upon them, other than the laws or ordinances of the General Assembly aforesaid." His final proposed resolution held that "any person who shall, by speaking or writing, assert or maintain that any person or persons, other than the General Assembly of this colony, have any right or power to impose or lay any taxation on the people here, shall be deemed an enemy to his Majesty's colony."

This was stern stuff. To be recognized as an enemy to the colony opened the door to punishment for treason. Clearly, Patrick Henry—who would dominate Virginia politics for decades to come—believed that Virginians' chief right was the right to govern themselves through their General Assembly. Yet his was still a minority position in America, even among Virginia's political elite.

Reflecting most colonists' hope for reconciliation, the Stamp Act Congress of 1765 adopted far more restrained language. Led by Pennsylvania's conservative statesman John Dickinson, the Congress began by saying that the congressmen (from nine of the colonies) loved

What a Patriot Said

PIG

"Let those flatter who fear, it is not an American art."

Thomas Jefferson,
A Summary View of the Rights of British America

the king and his family. Next, they said that the colonists had all the *duties* of Englishmen. Only then did they get around to insisting that they had the *rights* of Englishmen. After explaining that they insisted on traditional English rights, including the right to be taxed only by their own representatives, this first American congress closed by saying that the resolves had been adopted out of duty, to call to the king's attention a budding threat to the British constitution.

In the wake of colonial boycotts, intimidation of stamp agents, and formal protests, the British repealed the Stamp Act in 1766. They then passed a new law, the Declaratory Act, in which they claimed authority to legislate for the colonies "in all cases whatsoever."

Britain's Parliament here followed the line of thinking laid out by the all-time leading British legal scholar, Sir William Blackstone. In his four-volume 1765 book, *Commentaries on the Laws of England*, Blackstone explained a concept called "sovereignty."

In every society, Blackstone wrote, there must be a sovereign. It could be an individual, a committee, an assembly, or any other type of organization, but there had to be one. That sovereign had ultimate authority—its decisions were final. It had to be unitary—its power could not be shared or limited in any way. And in the British Empire, that sovereign was Parliament.

In the Declaratory Act, then, Parliament did not claim anything new. In England, if you favored liberty, you favored parliamentary sovereignty. The historical alternative, after all, had been royal sovereignty, and Britain's constitution had resolved against it.

Jefferson stakes out America's rights

In 1774, a Virginia planter named Thomas Jefferson spelled out the colonists' position in very fiery language. It followed a decade of contention between Parliament and the colonists, a decade marked by increasingly ham-fisted British measures like the Coercive Acts against Massachusetts and increasingly pugnacious responses by a growing American opposition.

Jefferson's pamphlet came to be known as *A Summary View of the Rights of British America*. Building on a tradition of insistence on local self-government peculiar to Virginia, and borrowing especially from his mentor in constitutional matters, Richard Bland, Jefferson flung the gauntlet at King George's feet.

You, King George, he said, are merely a functionary put in your office for our good, "no more than the chief officer of the people." And if you ever ceased to serve our purposes, we would be justified in replacing you. "Let those flatter who fear," Jefferson said, "it is not an American art."

According to Jefferson's version of colonial history, the colonies in North America had been founded by Britons exercising their natural right to emigrate. Once they had emigrated to a land still unsettled, they had had a right to establish new civil societies. The British Empire, Jefferson claimed, could be a happy one if its constituent parts—the various

Portrait of a Patriot

Thomas Jefferson (1743–1826) was the clearest expositor among leading figures of the original understanding of the Constitution. Jefferson did not participate in drafting or ratifying the Constitution, except insofar as he influenced James Madison to agree to work for a bill of rights in the first Congress. Yet his 1791 memorandum to President George Washington regarding the constitutionality of the Bank Bill laid out the most cogent of arguments in favor of a respectful (opponents say "strict") construction of constitutional language, and his 1798 Kentucky Resolutions summarized the state sovereignty version of the Constitution in its most powerful form. Jefferson's 1801 electoral triumph swept his Republicans into power for a quarter-century and more, on the basis, he said, of the state sovereignty position.[2]

dominions—were kept in balance. Only the king was in a position to ensure that that happened. As Jefferson had it, each part of the Empire—Connecticut, Virginia, Great Britain, Jamaica, and so on—had its own local legislature. The only political institution they had in common was the Crown: their common monarch, George III.

In case the legislature of one part of the Empire should try to coerce another part of the Empire into surrendering some of its rights, Jefferson said, it was incumbent upon King George to intervene. He could veto Parliament's legislation if it violated colonists' rights, and Jefferson seemed to be threatening the king to act on the colonists' behalf.

Jefferson's view of the British Empire: A federation of independent states

Jefferson's vision of the British Empire in 1774 featured a strong federal element; that is, to his way of thinking there was no national government ruling the whole Empire, but instead provincial assemblies in each of the king's dominions. In reference to the British Parliament's suspension of New York's assembly, Jefferson referred to the latter as a "free and independent legislature" and equated it in that sense to Parliament.

And what was Parliament? According to Jefferson, it was "a body of men foreign to our constitutions, and unacknowledged by our laws." George III maintained a common foreign and defense policy for the Empire. But in matters of local import, the people, through their elected assemblies, should rule themselves.

In common with other educated men of the eighteenth century, Jefferson was well versed in the classical Greek and Latin authors. For him, as for the Greeks, freedom was local self-government. He closed his *Summary View* with the claim that "the god who gave us life gave us liberty at the same time; the hand of force may destroy, but cannot disjoin them."

George III should "interpose . . . to establish fraternal love and harmony thro' the whole empire."

How did the king respond? He never accepted the American colonists' constitutional claims. He subscribed instead to the theory described by Blackstone in 1765: Parliament was sovereign throughout the Empire, which meant that its authority could not be limited or divided. The colonists might insist that Britain's constitution did not grant Parliament the power to tax them or deprive them of the right to trial by jury, but the king held that Parliament could legislate for everyone in the British Empire "in all cases whatsoever." Parliamentary sovereignty left no room for an assertion of individual or colonial rights.

Gunsmoke—and fear of domestic tyranny

The fighting began at Lexington, Massachusetts, on April 19, 1775. Still, only a minority of colonists thought of independence as desirable. It was a daunting prospect: a declaration of independence meant war, which the colonists might well lose.

Even if they won, the colonists would have a victorious army and a conquering general, which had always been a formula for military dictatorship as a precursor to monarchy. And leaving the British Empire would mean being outside the protective tariff wall behind which the British economy had developed, instead of inside it, where the colonies had become so prosperous.

Early in 1776, however, Thomas Paine published his pamphlet *Common Sense*. He moved the majority of his fellow colonists from the Loyalist and undecided columns into the Patriot camp.

On May 15, 1776, Virginia's ruling revolutionary convention, the May Convention, adopted three resolutions:

1. Virginia must have a declaration of rights.

2. Virginia must have a republican constitution.

3. Virginia must seek federal relations with such other colonies as wanted them and alliances with whichever foreign powers would enter into them.

The delegates then ran a Continental Union flag up the flagpole at the old Virginia capitol in Williamsburg. As James Madison wrote that night, Virginia had established its independence!

But alone. And, as Benjamin Franklin famously put it in another context, the Patriots must all hang together, or they would surely all hang separately. So the Virginia Convention (Virginia's ruling body in the Revolution's early days, as the last royal governor had fled the colony) instructed Virginia's representatives in the Second Continental Congress to secure a declaration of American independence.

A state is a state is a . . . country

The Congress was, as Massachusetts's John Adams put it, a meeting place of ambassadors. In fact, the word *congress* had always denoted assemblies of the representatives of sovereigns—as in the case of the Congress of Westphalia in the seventeenth century. It made sense, then, when Virginia's Richard Henry Lee stood up to move, in language given to him by the Virginia Convention, that Congress should declare "that these United Colonies are, and of right ought to be, free and independent states, that they are absolved from all allegiance to the British Crown, and that all political connection between them and the state of Great Britain is, and ought to be, totally dissolved."

Like the word *congress*, the word *state* had a meaning in the eighteenth century that may be lost on us today. For a Virginia congressman to say that Virginia was a state was to put it on par not with Brittany in France or Yorkshire in England, but with France and England. Congress responded by appointing a committee to draft a declaration of independence.

The chairman of the committee, John Adams, had long been the leading spokesman (a tireless pest, really) for independence. As Adams admired *A Summary View of the Rights of British America*, he asked Thomas Jefferson to write the first draft of the Declaration. Adams and Ben Franklin made slight alterations to it before the committee presented it to the whole Congress.

And what did the Declaration declare? That the colonies were independent states. Politicians and historians have made a habit of fixating on the second paragraph of the Declaration, which includes a restatement of Richard Bland's account of the origin and just powers of government (including the statement "We hold these truths to be self-evident..."). They say that America was founded on that. But it wasn't.

The Old Dominion Paves the Way

Virginia established its independence on May 15, 1776—long before the Declaration of American Independence.

In instructing Richard Henry Lee and his colleagues to secure a declaration of independence, the Virginia Convention did not tell them to concoct a new theory of government. (The same held true for the other states' representatives.) The first three sections of the Declaration—which explained why King George III's stewardship had been found wanting—had no legal effect. That portion of the Declaration was what lawyers call "hortatory" language: like a statutory preamble, it was the predicate for the effective section—the one that proclaimed the states independent.

In the Declaration's culminating fourth section, Congress declared the colonies to be "free and independent states" and claimed for them the right to do everything that free countries could do. They were the sovereign equivalents of Russia, Sweden, and Spain. (Okay, maybe San Marino and Monaco, but you get the idea.) As the war progressed, they continued to behave as if they were. They guarded their sovereignty carefully, never giving to Congress authority that they might be unable to reclaim.

In 1777, Congress sent out to the states for their ratification the Articles of Confederation, America's first federal constitution. It began by saying, "Articles of Perpetual Union between the states of . . ." and listed the states, from north to south. Article I said, in full, "The Stile [sic] of this Confederacy shall be 'The United States of America.'" Article II added, "Each state retains its sovereignty, freedom, and independence, and every power, jurisdiction, and right, which is not by this Confederation expressly delegated to the United States, in Congress assembled."

This language is, under the circumstances, entirely unsurprising. It would have been surprising if they had said anything else. The United States were states, and they had joined together. The fact that their union had no set end date, in part because the length of the war could not be foreseen, was denoted by calling it "perpetual." (In those days treaties between European states often purported to be "perpetual." This did not mean that neither side could bring a treaty agreement to an end, but that there was no built-in sunset provision.) The express reservation of each state's undelegated powers was a hedge against arrogation of power by

What a Patriot Said

"America was conquered, and her settlements made, and firmly established, at the expence of individuals, and not of the British public. Their own blood was spilt in acquiring lands for their settlement, their own fortunes expended in making that settlement effectual; for themselves they fought, for themselves they conquered, and for themselves alone they have right to hold."

Thomas Jefferson, *A Summary View of the Rights of British America*

the Confederation. After all, the new Congress under the Articles was to have an army, so it might well be tempted to intrude on the states' prerogatives. It was for this reason that Article II noted that sovereignty—indivisible final authority—remained in the states.

According to Article III of the Confederation, the thirteen states entered into this formal relationship "for their common defense, the security of their liberties, and their mutual and general welfare." In keeping with the federal (not national) nature of the new government, Article V provided that each state's congressional delegation would have one vote. This provision would not have made sense if the thirteen states had been one nation, or if their people had been one people. As they were thirteen distinct states, each equally sovereign, however, it made sense for them each to carry equal weight in the federal councils. (Here again, we must recall that the word *state* in the eighteenth century connoted a sovereign entity on the order of Spain or France, not a province like Andalusia or Dauphiné.)

Articles VI and VII bound the states to wage war and carry on diplomacy only through the Confederation. Article VIII said that the expenses of the war would be paid out of a common treasury into which the states would contribute on the schedule Congress set, but it left to the states the task of deciding what taxation scheme to employ to raise their contributions. As the colonists had insisted that Great Britain allow the states sovereignty over taxes, it was incumbent on them to practice what they preached in their own confederation.

Article IX established procedures for resolving boundary disputes and other matters that might easily have brought the states to blows. It also provided that the Congress could not take major steps such as coining money, borrowing money, appointing a commander in chief, and making war unless nine states agreed to do so. Not majority rule but a supermajority was required for doing any of those things.

Article XIII, finally, required the consent of all the states to any amendment of the Articles. Again, while the constitution of a national government could, presumably, be amended by a national majority, a *federal* constitution, such as the Articles of Confederation created, required the agreement of all the constituent parts—all the states. This last article also included the Congress's thanks to "the Great Governor of the World" (no, not the UN) for the states' ratification. It said that it was effective on the "ninth day of July in the Year of our Lord One Thousand Seven Hundred and Seventy-Eight."

To anyone familiar with the form of the dispute between the colonists and the mother country over the previous decade, the various elements of the Articles of Confederation described above cannot be surprising. The colonists had insisted for years that their colonial legislatures alone, not the British Parliament, could tax them. When Parliament had insisted that it alone was sovereign, and that sovereignty was ultimate power, the colonies had responded by locating sovereignty in their colonial legislatures. The colonists saw themselves as defending their traditional English rights. They believed that to defend their traditional rights from an overweening British Parliament it was necessary for the colonies to declare themselves "free and independent states." Now, in order to formalize the military alliance that was fighting the Revolution, they opted not to merge their thirteen societies into one, but to cooperate so much as seemed necessary to win the war.

Chapter Two

FEDERALISM VS. NATIONALISM AT THE PHILADELPHIA CONVENTION

W hile the Revolution absorbed much of the attention of the Continental Congresses, and later the Confederation Congress, other issues demanded attention as well during the 1770s and 1780s. Among those was the pressing need to provide some type of governance for the larger colonies' western lands.

The boundary of English settlement at the end of the French and Indian War in 1763 was, essentially, the peaks of the Appalachian Mountains. In fact, King George III issued a proclamation that year banning his subjects from settling beyond those peaks. He did not want further difficulties with the Indians who had sided with the French during the war.

For many wealthy colonists, this royal decree came as a great shock. From John Hancock in Massachusetts to Ben Franklin and the Morrises in the middle states, from George Washington, Thomas Jefferson, Patrick Henry, and George Mason in Virginia to the Laurenses in South Carolina, many wealthy people owned land claims beyond the Appalachians. And the king had made those claims worthless.

Thus one of the first things the elite class did upon independence was resuscitate its land titles—or at least, its purported land titles. As it turned out, the colonies' inland claims often overlapped, and so did the titles the great men thought they owned.

Guess what?

- In the Treaty of Paris ending the Revolution, King George III recognized the independence not of a single American nation, but of *thirteen* "states" (eighteenth-century-speak for "nations").

- The delegates rejected attempts by monarchists and nationalists in the Philadelphia Convention of 1787 to create a national (rather than a federal) government.

So far as Virginia was concerned, what we now call the Midwest belonged to it. In fact, colonial Virginia included not just today's Virginia, but also West Virginia, Kentucky, Ohio, Michigan, Indiana, Illinois, Wisconsin, and part of Minnesota. Augusta County, the western county that took in that vast expanse, was the biggest county in history.

When Congress sent the Articles of Confederation to the states for their ratification in 1777, twelve ratified. But Maryland held out. Why? Marylanders said that they would never agree to join in a permanent confederation with Virginia so long as it maintained its enormous western land claims.

Congress periodically attempted to resolve the title disputes and the boundary issues. However, Virginia congressmen, including George Mason, James Madison, and James Monroe, responded that there was nothing in the Articles of Confederation giving Congress authority to say anything about anyone's land titles in Virginia—or about the extent of Virginia's western claims. That being the case, they said, they would not even discuss the matter in Congress.

Once again, the history of the Revolution demonstrates that the revolutionaries understood their states to be sovereign, their "nations" to be . . . their states. If America as a whole had been a nation, and if the Confederation Congress had been a national legislature, such questions should have been resolved by a majority vote. But sovereignty lay in the states. That was the first principle of American government.

A constitution for the "United States"

Even before the Articles finally went into effect in 1781, numerous figures in politics and the military were agitating for a further strengthening of the federal center. These people took the name "Federalists." Their efforts ultimately resulted in adoption of the federal Constitution of 1788.

Why did the Federalists want a strengthened federation? Mostly because they thought the Revolutionary War had exposed the shortcomings of the Continental and Confederation Congresses. The Continental Army and the various state military units seemed perpetually short of men, money, and supplies. The Federalists leapt to the (false) conclusion that if the thirteen newborn states had had a difficult time in obtaining credit from European monarchies and bankers to fight a war against the greatest power in the world, it must have been because the Articles of Confederation were inadequate!

The Federalists invented a litany of complaints about the state and federal governments of the revolutionary decade. They are familiar to students of history today, because historians—who tend almost unanimously to side with the Federalists in this dispute—have been echoing them ever since.

If states were slow to pay their requisitions, then, it must have been because they were selfish and unpatriotic. Federalists claimed that only a stronger government could solve the "problem" of a government that just barely had enough money and coercive power to do what it was intended to do and did not have the resources to do much of anything else. (What a wonderful problem!)

But the Federalist version leaves out some important facts. For instance, the total amount of voluntary state contributions supposedly owed to the Confederation by the states in 1788 exceeded the amount of gold and silver (that is, money) in the entire United States! And political scientist Keith L. Dougherty has demonstrated that the states actually contributed more to the war effort than any rational choice model would predict.

A Book You're Not Supposed to Read

Collective Action under the Articles of Confederation by Keith L. Dougherty; New York: Cambridge University Press, 2001.

Federalists in the Continental and Confederation Congresses repeatedly attempted to get the states to cede more power to Congress. In each case, they were unsuccessful: Americans from New Hampshire to Georgia simply refused. They did not want to trade one distant, unaccountable authority in the British Parliament for another in a more powerful American Congress. Especially heroic on this score was little Rhode Island, which refused to ratify a tariff amendment when all twelve other states did. Virginia responded by repealing its ratification, and for Federalists, that was the last straw.

The campaign for a stronger federal government grew—even when King George III admitted defeat. But he admitted defeat to the "sovereign and independent states." As Article I of the Treaty of Paris put it, "His Britannic Majesty acknowledges the said United States, viz., New Hampshire, Massachusetts Bay, Rhode Island and Providence Plantations, Connecticut, New York, New Jersey, Pennsylvania, Delaware, Maryland, Virginia, North Carolina, South Carolina, and Georgia, to be free, sovereign and independent States; that he treats with them as such, and for himself, his heirs and successors, relinquishes all claims to the Government, propriety and territorial rights of the same, and every part thereof." Note that King George was required by the terms of the treaty not to admit that "America" was independent or that "the United States" was independent, but that the thirteen named states were independent.

Interestingly, in Article V, the American commissioners undertook on behalf of Congress to implore the states to restore confiscated rights and property to Loyalists. This provision, which never bore the fruit the British hoped for, recognized the constitutional situation of the American states—independent not only of Great Britain, but also of each other. Article VII said that there would be a "perpetual" peace between Great Britain and the United States—which meant that the treaty did not have a fixed expiration date.

Reforming the Confederation

In 1785, the states of Maryland and Virginia appointed delegates to a conference to meet at George Washington's home, Mount Vernon, on the Potomac River. Their task was to negotiate an arrangement for sharing the river—establishing each state's navigation and taxing rights. The conference failed—Virginia's delegates didn't show—but a new meeting was set for the following year at Annapolis. This time, the goal was a reform of the Confederation.

When only five states sent delegates to the Annapolis Convention of 1786, leading figures like Alexander Hamilton of New York and James Madison of Virginia called for a new convention to take place the following summer in Philadelphia.

Why would a new convention meet in 1787? The Federalists told the state governments that its purpose would be to propose amendments to the Articles of Confederation. Rhode Island, which had no interest in

Portrait of a Patriot

Alexander Hamilton (1757–1804), a native of Nevis, was among the most significant figures in American constitutional history. His monarchist musings in the Philadelphia Convention (in which he represented New York) did not have much effect on the shape of the Constitution. In support of ratification, he organized the series of newspaper essays that ultimately came to be known as *The Federalist*, which formed the nub of the Federalist case in New York, writing more than half the essays. In time, the series would form the backbone of nationalist interpretation of the Constitution. As secretary of the treasury under Washington, Hamilton enunciated the clearest argument ever made for a liberal (loose) construction of the Constitution. He was killed by a political enemy, Vice President Aaron Burr, in an 1804 duel.[1]

strengthening the Confederation, did not send a delegation. New York, where Governor George Clinton and the majority of the legislature were skeptical of the Federalists, sent a moderately pro-reform three-man delegation. (Nationalist Alexander Hamilton received an appointment, but his friend and political ally John Jay missed out.)

In Virginia, which agreed to send a delegation to help propose amendments, Richard Henry Lee and Patrick Henry—long the dominant voices in the all-powerful General Assembly—stayed home. Lee confided that he did not think the convention likely to do work he approved; Henry, more prone to offer up a memorable line, later said he "smelt a rat."

Legal Latinisms

Senate: from the Latin *senatus*, the great national council of the Roman people. The federal government and most of the states have legislative bodies so named.[2]

Why? There was a little history behind it. Congress had been receptive, in 1785–1786, when John Jay assured it that he could negotiate an agreement with Spain that would grant the states valuable trade concessions in the Caribbean. All he needed to offer in return, he said, was an American commitment to forgo use of the Mississippi River (which then belonged to Spain) for twenty-five years. Under the Articles of Confederation, nine states needed to agree to any treaty, but Congress authorized Jay to negotiate the agreement anyway, despite the objections of the five southern states.

According to James Madison, this move by Congress converted Patrick Henry from "the Champion of the federal cause" to a lukewarm advocate at best. If Mississippi navigation rights were actually surrendered, Madison said, Henry would become an outright opponent.

The year 1787 also saw the Confederation Congress adopt its most significant legislative initiative, the Northwest Ordinance. In that law, Congress provided that states could be carved out of Virginia's former trans–Ohio River territory (what we now call the Midwest). Among other things, it said in Section 13 that once they had been organized, the new states would be admitted to the Union on an equal footing with the original states. The federal principle—the principle of state equality—would guide their incorporation into the United States.

A vision of national government: The Virginia Plan

James Madison spent several months researching the history of confederations before the Philadelphia Convention met. He found much to encourage his desire for a stronger federation. He decided, in fact, to push for the abandonment of America's federal experiment.

Madison, a veteran of many legislative battles in Virginia and in Congress, encouraged his fellow Virginia delegates—Governor Edmund Randolph, George Washington, and George Mason among them—to arrive in Philadelphia several days early. If the Old Dominion presented its plan at the beginning of the convention, he thought, that blueprint would guide the convention's deliberations.

Thus, when the Philadelphia Convention opened, its first acts were to install George Washington as president of the convention, to vote to close the doors so that the public would not know what was being discussed, and to take up the constitutional proposals on which the Virginians had agreed. Those provisions came to be called the Virginia Plan.

The Virginia Plan was the outline of a national government. It would have substituted a central government with all the power national officials could want for the federal government of the Confederation. This was a type of government to which the people were known to be averse—which explains why the Philadelphia Convention operated in secret, and why its minutes, like James Madison's famous notes, were kept secret for decades after the event.

Fortunately for us, there were delegates to the Convention who kept notes of what was said up to the point of their departure. Most notable are those of New York delegate Robert Yates, one-time chief justice of the Empire State. He tells us that Virginia's governor, Edmund Randolph, explained the Virginia proposals' rationale with three resolutions:

> 1. Resolved, That a union of the States merely federal, will not accomplish the objects proposed by the articles of the confederation, namely, common defence, security of liberty, and general welfare. 2. Resolved, That no treaty or treaties among any of the States as sovereign, will accomplish or secure their common defence, liberty, or welfare. 3. Resolved, That a national government ought to be established, consisting of a supreme judicial, legislative, and executive.

As Yates explains matters, another delegate objected at that point that the goal of the Convention was to propose amendments to the Confederation, not to create a national government. If it adopted the first two resolutions, then, the Convention would be at an end. When asked what the third resolution meant by the word "supreme," the answer was that the states should yield when they conflicted with the federal government. Six states voted for that resolution, which was thus temporarily adopted. Over the following days, the Convention adopted resolutions about a "national" legislature and a "national" executive. The limit of the Convention's nationalism in its early days was reached when James Wilson of Pennsylvania proposed multi-state districts for the Senate and the Convention rejected his proposal.

Monarchists and nationalists and federalists—oh my!

It may be useful to note at this point that there were three parties in the Convention. The first was a monarchist party, the chief exemplar of which was New York's Alexander Hamilton. The monarchists were intent on wiping the states from the map and substituting one unitary govern-

Portrait of a Patriot

George Mason (1725–1792) was one of the towering figures in American constitutional history. His Virginia Declaration of Rights (1776), the first American bill of rights, provided a template—and in many cases language—for the other states', the federal, the French, the UN, and numerous other bills of rights. Mason played an extremely significant role in the Philadelphia Convention that wrote the Constitution, including helping to defeat efforts to draft a national—in lieu of a federal—constitution and insisting that the assent of nine states be required for ratification. He also proposed that the House of Representatives initiate all money bills, that Congress be able to ban slave importation, that export taxes be banned, that lawmakers not be able to hop into plush positions in other branches, and that the House resolve electoral college deadlocks. Mason played a key role in devising the procedure for overriding presidential vetoes, and his refusal to sign the Constitution, coupled with his resounding insistence that it not be ratified until a bill of rights was added, helped spur Federalists to pledge to submit a bill of rights to the states in the first Congress.

ment for the entire continent. In the Convention, Hamilton made a famous speech in which he avowed his admiration for the British constitution and said that while the American people were not prepared to assimilate their government to the British model so closely as he could wish, he owed it to himself to speak frankly. He called for a president with a life term, senators with life terms, and appointment of governors by the president—all in the manner of Great Britain. Hamilton here displayed two of his outstanding characteristics: candor and intellectual brilliance. Many delegates, we are told, thought very highly of Hamilton's learned disquisition, although none joined him in his characteristic near-suicidal frankness.

The second party consisted of nationalists, people who—without ever avowing admiration for the monarchical form—wanted to push centralization as far as reasonably could be hoped. These people hoped to establish a centralized government largely dominated by their own states. Most prominent among these was Virginia's James Madison, long Hamilton's coadjutor in the Federalist cause, whose work the Virginia Plan chiefly was. In the wake of the Convention, Madison would be greatly dismayed by the discrepancy between what he had wanted and what the Convention had yielded. He repeatedly acted in positions of high public trust over the next four decades to bring the federal regime into consonance with his proposals—even to the extent of arguing that the Constitution meant what the Convention had squarely decided that it should not mean. We will return to the topic of Madison's peculiar role in American constitutional history again and again.

Finally, there was a cohort in the Convention of members insistent on proposing a reinforcement of the central government while maintaining the primary place of the states in the American polity—a truly federal, rather than national, government. They would have their way in the short run. In time, however, "constitutional law" would undo their victory almost completely.

Early in the Convention, the committee of the whole house very narrowly agreed to create a national government with a national executive, a national legislative, and a national judicial branch. It also agreed that the national legislature ought to be empowered to legislate in all cases to which the separate states might be incompetent and all areas in which the harmony of the states might be interrupted by separate state legislation. In addition, it decided that the national legislature should have a veto over state laws it considered contrary to the articles of union. At this early stage in the convention, the committee of the whole also decided that the national judiciary should have power to decide all cases affecting the "national peace and harmony."

How do we know these things? We can extract them from the record of deliberations provided by two of the delegates, Maryland's Luther

Martin—who first provided the three-party classification of the delegates given above—and New York's Robert Yates. In addition, we have the journal of the Convention. As the Philadelphia Convention early on decided to create a national government with an overwhelmingly powerful national legislature and a very strong national judiciary, and as by the end of the Convention it had produced a federal constitution without either of those features, we are on firm ground in concluding that the change was no accident.

The Constitution as finally referred to Congress by the Convention featured a federal legislative body, or Congress, without either the sweeping legislative authority or the veto over state laws earlier proposed by the advocates of a national government (and supported, through the summer, by the theoretical monarchists). We know that this decision was a carefully considered one because delegate James Madison of Virginia repeatedly implored the other delegates to restore the congressional veto of state laws, only to see his arguments repeatedly rejected.

Rather than wiping the states off the map, the Convention made their continued existence essential to the selection of members of Congress. First, members of the House of Representatives would be elected by voters eligible to vote for members of the relevant state legislatures. No state, no representatives. And as for senators, they would not be selected by the president (as Hamilton, following the model of the British House of Lords, would have preferred) or by the lower house of Congress (as Madison and the Virginia nationalists proposed), but were to be chosen by the state legislatures.

Madison was very unhappy that the new Congress, like the old ones, would be federal, not national. He confided to Thomas Jefferson on

Legal Latinisms

Veto: Latin for "I forbid." A refusal by the president or a governor to sign into law a bill that has been passed by a legislature. Unlike the British royal veto, American vetoes can be overridden by super-majority vote.

October 24, 1787, that he feared the ongoing state role in federal policy-making meant that the new government would be too responsive to the people's whims. This new government would be inadequate to nationalist aims, just as the old one had been. (Madison had also broached the idea that Congress should be empowered to sic the U.S. Navy on states that did not comply with national commands. The Convention rejected that idea too.)

There were other provisions displeasing to the monarchist-nationalist coalition as well. Instead of saying "Congress may legislate as it will" or "Congress may legislate in any area to which it considers the states incompetent," the final Constitution carefully hedged congressional power.

In Article I, Section 8 the draft Constitution included a list of congressional powers. Virtually all of them were related to foreign affairs and trade. They were also few and provided little wiggle room for expansion. And in the course of the ratification dispute of 1787–1788, Federalists from north to south promised to take a tightly constricted view of constitutional interpretation.

The judiciary article of the Constitution also lived up to the hopes of the delegates favoring a federal over a national structure. Instead of giving federal courts power to hear any cases Congress wanted them to hear (that is, cases "affecting the national peace and harmony"), as the Hamilton-Madison, monarchist-nationalist coalition had proposed, the Convention restricted federal courts' jurisdiction in two ways. First, the Constitution did not require that there be any federal trial courts at all. In fact, Madison would promise in the ratification debate in Virginia that the new government would try to get along without them. Only if that experiment failed, he said, would federal trial courts be created.

The Constitution also provided a list of the kinds of cases Congress might authorize federal courts to decide—which meant, as lawyers understood things in those days, that Congress could not authorize

Portrait of a Patriot

James Madison (1751–1836) played a major role in assembling the Philadelphia Convention but had a checkered constitutional record thereafter. In the Convention, Madison attempted to create a national, instead of federal, government with military power to attack states that did not comply with federal mandates, a Congress with unlimited legislative powers and a veto on state legislation, and courts with unlimited jurisdiction. He soon knuckled under to Virginian pressure for amendments, but he intentionally provided amendments without serious effect. As a congressman, he enunciated a strict constructionist reading of the Constitution in 1791, but he flip-flopped on congressional authority to charter banks in 1816. His Bonus Bill Veto Message (1817) sounded like the Madison of 1791, as did his criticism of Marshall's *McCulloch v. Maryland* decision, but his confused response to nullification was both disingenuous and destructive. Madison was as unpredictable an oracle as the Pythia at ancient Delphi.

federal courts to decide any other kinds of cases. Instead of a national judiciary, in other words—one with power to hear any case that came to hand—Article III created a *federal* judiciary and left most judicial power in the state governments.

Not coincidentally, the various contentious issues roiling the American political waters today—flag burning, abortion, state government recognition of religion (say through public prayer), and homosexual marriage—are not among those the federal courts were given power to decide by the federal Constitution written in Philadelphia. Had the Hamilton-Madison axis had its way, the federal courts' purview would have been greater. But the point is that the Hamilton-Madison axis did not prevail, and the Constitution the people ultimately ratified gives the federal courts no scope to interfere in or rule on these issues. Nor did the Federalists, when they advocated ratifying the Constitution, pretend otherwise.

This might surprise those "educated" in modern "constitutional law." But it should not surprise anyone familiar with the factors leading to the

American Revolution. After all, the people who advocated, in the 1760s and 1770s, a national authority to bind the states "in all cases whatsoever" were called Tories or monarchists, and they lost.

The Patriots, on the other hand, had argued for home rule, for the right of the individual states to govern themselves through their elected representatives. They had won the Revolution. And then they won in Philadelphia. But, alas, the fight was not over.

Chapter Three

SELLING THE CONSTITUTION

The arguments that were made for ratifying the Constitution are yet another subject most law students aren't taught. But these arguments are vital to the so-called original understanding—the real meaning—of the Constitution.

By law, Congress had to send any amendment to the Articles of Confederation to the states to be ratified. So even though the Philadelphia Convention was proposing more than an amendment, it sent the proposed new constitution to Congress, which forwarded it to the states for their consideration.

A rocky road

Even before the Philadelphia Convention ended, many delegates returned to their states to organize opposition to the proposed constitution. They were bolstered when three prominent delegates, who had stayed to the end of the Convention on September 17, 1787, refused to sign the Convention's final product: the unamended Constitution.

Among these non-signers was Virginia's governor, Edmund Randolph, who had presented the Virginia Plan at the beginning of the Convention. Randolph had many criticisms of the new Constitution, including that Congress's powers were not well enough defined, that the boundary

Guess what?

🪶 Virginia's state constitution of 1776 was the first American constitution (and the first written constitution adopted by the people's representatives in the history of the world).

🪶 There was nothing in the Declaration of Independence, the Articles of Confederation, or the ratification process of the federal Constitution that created a national (rather than a federal) government.

between state and federal authority was not clearly demarcated, that the federal courts' jurisdiction had not been sufficiently circumscribed, and that there was no bill of rights in the Constitution guarding traditional rights of Englishmen against federal infringement. (Many states had their own bills of rights.)

Randolph's fellow Virginia delegate George Mason also refused to sign the Constitution, and for similar reasons. Mason had argued that the Constitution should ban the importation of slaves immediately and that a congressional super-majority should be required for passage of any tariff law; otherwise, he said, the northern majority in Congress would abuse the South to favor the North's interests—as it had tried to do in changing John Jay's negotiating instructions with Spain in 1786. A deal between New England and Deep South delegates on these issues defeated Mason's positions—to the everlasting detriment of the country.

Of more concern to Mason, however, was the omission of a bill of rights. Mason was the chief author of Virginia's state constitution of 1776—the first American constitution and, more significant, the first written constitution adopted by the people's representatives in the history of the world. As chairman of the committee that drafted that constitution, Mason had also played the leading role in drafting the 1776 Virginia Declaration of Rights, which—in the manner of the English Glorious Revolution of 1688—set traditional rights of Englishmen in stone before the new republican constitution based on them was adopted. Mason, a self-described "man of 1688," insisted that basic rights had to be protected first.

When he raised the issue of a bill of rights in Philadelphia, however, Mason was rebuffed. A bill of rights was unnecessary, his fellow delegates insisted. This new government would have only the powers the Constitution gave it. As the Constitution was not going to give Congress power to infringe on the freedoms of speech, the press, or petition, the right to keep and bear arms, or any of the other English-descended rights Amer-

Framers vs. Ratifiers

We hear a lot about the "framers" of the Constitution. But who were they? The framers were the people who wrote the Constitution; what they did had no legal effect at all. The ratifiers, on the other hand, were the people who put the Constitution into effect; it was their act that made it binding, and their understanding that is significant. Just as today we don't care what some congressman's legal counsel thought when writing a legal provision, but look instead at the congressman's own understanding of and intent regarding it, so when it comes to the Constitution, what matters is not what the draftsmen thought they were doing, but what the people with legal power to put it into effect thought they were doing.

icans had always taken for granted, it would have no such power. There was no need, then, to provide against it.

Mason was not persuaded. As Madison wrote, he left Philadelphia in a very ill humor.

Federalists battle Republicans over the Bill of Rights

Advocates of ratification took the name "Federalists," while their opponents—particularly in Virginia—called themselves "Republicans." Federalists called Republicans "Anti-Federalists," however, and historians, never slow to take sides, have been nearly unanimous in calling Republican opponents of ratification "Anti-Federalists."

The chief issue in dispute in the ratification campaign was whether the proposed constitution would be consistent with the state-centered constitutionalism that the Patriots had fought for during the Revolution. Federalists insisted it would, while Republicans feared it would not.

What a Patriot Said

PIG

"Is the relinquishment of the trial by jury and the liberty of the press necessary for your liberty? Will the abandonment of your most sacred rights tend to the security of your liberty? Liberty, the greatest of all earthly blessings—give us that precious jewel, and you may take every thing else!... Guard with jealous attention the public liberty. Suspect every one who approaches that jewel."

Patrick Henry, speech to the Virginia Convention, Richmond, Virginia, June 5, 1788

The most influential argument in favor of ratification was made by Pennsylvania's James Wilson in a speech at the Pennsylvania State House on October 6, 1787. Wilson, a prominent Philadelphia Convention delegate and future Supreme Court justice, had been a nationalist at the Convention, but his version of the Constitution on that October day was thoroughly federal (or, in the language of the day, "foederal").

Wilson said opponents of the proposed constitution were not doing it justice, reminding the delegates that an important distinction needed to be made between state governments and the federal government. The people had invested their state representatives with "every right and authority" that the people themselves did not explicitly reserve. "But in delegating foederal powers," Wilson said, congressional authority comes "not from tacit implication, but from the positive grant." As a result, in the state systems, "everything which is not reserved, is given: but in the latter [the federal government], the reverse of the proposition prevails, and every thing which is not given, is reserved. The distinction being recognized, will furnish an answer to those who think the omission of a bill of rights, a defect in the proposed constitution: for it would have been superfluous and absurd, to have stipulated with a foederal body of our own creation, that we should enjoy those privileges, of which we are not divested either by the intention or the act that has brought that body into existence."

In other words, it was ridiculous for the Constitution to guarantee rights that Congress had no power to violate, and the federal government had *only* those limited and expressly stated powers granted it by the Constitution. Wilson went further and said that including a bill of rights might be dangerous, because if such a bill said that Congress could not infringe the freedom of the press, it would imply that Congress might have had implicit power to do so, and that it might have the power to restrict other unenumerated rights.

Turning to the claim that the Constitution was intended to "annihilate" the state governments, Wilson said this was impossible, given that *state* legislatures were to choose the senators, the people of the several *states* were to elect the representatives, and electors selected in a fashion chosen by each *state* legislature were to choose the president.

Other Federalists affirmed Wilson's analysis. In Massachusetts, William Cushing—another future Supreme Court justice—said much the same (that the federal government would have only the powers it was "expressly granted" through the Constitution) in a speech written for his state's ratification convention. In South Carolina, ratification opponents worried that the proposed constitution might threaten the institution of slavery. But General Charles Cotesworth Pinckney, a Philadelphia Convention delegate and future Federalist presidential nominee, assured his fellow Carolinians that "it is admitted, on all hands, that the general government has no powers but what are expressly granted by the constitution, and that all rights not expressed were reserved by the several states."

Pennsylvania and South Carolina Federalists achieved crushing victories in those states' ratification conventions. In Massachusetts,

Federalists and Anti-Federalists

The *Federalists* generally were not federalist, but nationalist.

Anti-Federalists (they were actually federalist, and they called themselves Republicans) were not opposed to strengthening the federal government; they merely wanted to amend the Constitution before ratifying it.

Federalists needed to persuade popular governor John Hancock to support ratification. To do so, they promised that they would ask the first federal Congress to amend the Constitution to include a bill of rights. (Even with that concession, Massachusetts approved the Constitution by only a narrow margin.)

The pivotal state, however, was the largest, most populous state: Virginia. Virginia had provided far more than its share of leaders to the Revolution, the Philadelphia Convention had been presided over by George Washington, and James Madison had provided the template for much of the Convention's discussion. Once the Convention finished its work, Virginians Edmund Randolph and George Mason became the initial leaders of the Anti-Federalist campaign.

If Virginia (which still included West Virginia and Kentucky) did not ratify the Constitution, the new Union would be cut in half. Perhaps more important, a Republican victory in Virginia would prevent George Washington from serving as the first president—and the Constitution's executive branch had been drafted with him in mind, as the one chief executive the states would trust. Such was Washington's prestige that it was assumed that once he had set the standard for proper republican presidential behavior, it would bind all his successors.

It all comes down to Virginia

The stakes in Virginia's summer 1788 Richmond Ratification Convention approached the stratosphere. A Republican victory would mean the defeat of the Constitution, as North Carolina and Rhode Island already had gone on record in opposition and New York stood poised to follow the Old Dominion's example.

Unlike those of other states, Virginia's political elite split right down the middle on ratification. George Mason, former congressional president Richard Henry Lee, future U.S. president James Monroe, and the dominant figure in the General Assembly, Patrick Henry, led the opponents; George Washington, James Madison, and veteran lawyer, judge, and politician Edmund Pendleton, along with Madison's lieutenant George Nicholas, favored ratification.

The Republicans, led by Mason, argued that the Constitution's grants of power to the new federal Congress and judiciary were too ill defined (and thus that the new institutions were apt to claim more authority than the people intended) and that any new constitution required a bill of rights. The Federalists argued the reverse.

Governor Edmund Randolph—who had supported the Virginia Plan and then opposed the Convention draft—announced early in the Richmond debates that while he considered the Constitution imperfect, and that it needed to be amended before it was approved, he no longer believed that option to be available. Eight of the nine states whose assent was needed to put the Constitution into effect had already ratified. The issue now, he insisted, was whether Virginia would be part of the Union. He, for one, said yes.

Patrick Henry mocked Randolph's newfound support of ratification and implied at one point that Randolph's motives were impure (and it seems that Randolph sent a second to Henry's camp to sound him out regarding a duel).

What a Patriot Said

"We have laid our new Government upon a broad Foundation, and have endeavoured to provide the most effectual Securities for the essential Rights of human nature."

George Mason on the Virginia Constitution and Declaration of Rights of 1776, in a personal letter, October 2, 1778

Federalists Who Lived Up to Their Name

Leading Federalists in several states (New York, Pennsylvania, Massachusetts, South Carolina, and Virginia) insisted that the new government would have only the powers "expressly delegated" to it—even though they might have preferred otherwise.

Surprisingly, Randolph (whom George Mason now called "Young Arnold" after Revolutionary War traitor Benedict Arnold) became the chief spokesman for ratification. He was chosen for the same reason he had been selected to present the Virginia Plan in Philadelphia: he was tall, handsome, and articulate, the very picture of a Virginia blue blood. The Randolphs were Virginia's leading family, including in their numbers Thomas Jefferson and John Marshall, while the brains behind the ratification operation, James Madison, was short, sickly, and—in debate—often inaudible. Randolph's explication of the text carried great weight.

The other delegates listened intently, then, when Governor Randolph explained that the new federal government need not be feared so much as Henry wanted it to be. No powers were being granted to the new Congress by implication, Randolph held. The new government would have only the powers it was "expressly delegated."

Federalists realized, however, that they had not persuaded a clear majority of delegates. Like their fellows in the Massachusetts Convention, they sought to persuade the unpersuaded with expedients they would not otherwise have adopted. They suggested, for instance, that Virginia could expressly state that it was approving the Constitution with the understanding that the rights of conscience and of the press were reserved free of federal interference. Moreover, they said, Virginia could reserve a right to reclaim its delegated authority if the federal government exceeded that which was given it through the Constitution. These positions would be included in Virginia's instrument of ratification, which established the terms by which the state approved the Constitution.

As the Federalists explained matters, the Constitution amounted to a compact, and Virginia was a party to it. In George Nicholas's words, "If thirteen individuals are about to make a contract, and one agrees to it, but at the same time declares that he understands its meaning, signification and intent to be, what the words of the contract plainly and obviously denote; that it is not to be construed so as to impose any supplementary condition upon him, and that *he is to be exonerated from it, whensoever any such imposition shall be attempted*—I ask whether in this case, these conditions on which he assented to it, would not be binding on the other twelve? In like manner these conditions will be binding on Congress. They can exercise no power that is not expressly granted them." (Emphasis added)

James Madison, too clever by half, wrote to a friend to say that this was all verbiage, that it would not really change anything. To Madison's mind, it was, in modern language, a lie: "The plan meditated by the friends [of] the Constitution," Madison said, "is to preface the ratification with some plain & general truths that can not affect the validity of the Act," along with proposed subsequent amendments. Were the rubes persuaded? Randolph privately said that five votes had been added to the Federalist column by his and Nicholas's explanation of the Constitution. In the end, the Richmond Convention ratified by a ten-vote margin—precisely the one Randolph counted. Madison conceded later that the Randolph-Nicholas explanation had been decisive.

Very soon, Virginia's instrument of ratification would be elevated by Virginia's moderate Federalists and Republicans into the first article of the Jeffersonian faith.

But what about *The Federalist*?

So you might well ask, if you learned about the Constitution in college, or by reading the opinions of Supreme Court justices (Chief Justice John

Marshall and Associate Justice Joseph Story were early proponents), or if you read some self-styled conservatives (who should know better) whose journalism or books treat *The Federalist* as political scripture.

The short answer is that *The Federalist* did not have much to do with the ratification of the Constitution in New York or anywhere else. Far from shaping the ratification debate throughout the United States, the arguments outlined in the Publius essays were unknown to virtually everyone outside the range of the New York papers. Virginia was the tenth state to ratify the Constitution, and its ratification convention was already meeting when the final *Federalist* essay first appeared in a New York newspaper. And the essays were not instantly reprinted in other states.

Did *The Federalist* at least provide the necessary boost for New York to ratify the Constitution?

Actually, no. When New York's convention met in Poughkeepsie in late 1788, ten states had already ratified. The question facing the Empire State, then, was whether it wanted to join Rhode Island and North Carolina in remaining outside the newly reconstituted Union. Besides that grim prospect, Republicans, led by Governor George Clinton, had to consider the possibility—bruited by Alexander Hamilton and others—that New York City would secede from New York State and ratify the Constitution on its own. It was on that basis, not out of love for the vision of the country presented by Alexander Hamilton, John Jay, and *The Federalist*, that New York held its collective nose and ratified the Constitution by a vote of thirty to twenty-seven.

The Federalist does merit consideration, however, because the monarchist-nationalist authorial coalition that produced it—Hamilton, Madison, and Jay—would play a central role in implementing the new Constitution once it was ratified. And what one finds in their collaboration is great confusion about the document produced by the Philadelphia Convention. At times, the three august revolutionaries describe the contemplated new government as federal, but at others, they make it "national." In some places they concede that the states would retain their central role in American politics under the new Constitution, but at others they read the grants of power to the new government very broadly.

A Book You're Not Supposed to Read

The Authority of Publius by Albert Furtwangler; Ithaca, NY: Cornell University Press, 1984.

As we have already seen, Hamilton frankly avowed his monarchism in the Philadelphia Convention, while Madison was just as clear in his desire to see the Confederation replaced by a national government. John Jay, let us add, found this company perfectly comfortable. Hamilton, in fact, wanted Jay as a New York delegate to the Convention, but Governor Clinton and the majority of the New York legislature regarded Hamilton, Jay, and the Federalist project with suspicion. Clinton and his supporters guessed, rightly, that the Hamiltonian Federalists had more in mind than modestly augmenting the power of the Confederation Congress.

Reading *The Federalist*, one can arrive at either of two conclusions regarding its authors: either they were very confused, or they were attempting to obfuscate. In Madison's case, in particular, there is just cause for arriving at either conclusion. For example, his justifications of the structure of the Senate in *Federalist* 62 and 63 directly contradict his more candid—and keenly negative—appraisal of that body in private correspondence with Jefferson, while his confusion about federalism in number 39 is consistent with his repeatedly self-contradictory musings on the same subject in "Notes on Nullification" and other anti-nullification writings forty years later.

Hamilton, on the other hand, did not have a reputation for tergiversation because he did not deserve one. His was the opposite failing: boundless loquacity, which often amounted to imprudent logorrhea. And if he was confused in some of his *Federalist* explications it was because he was honestly confused in his thinking. John Jay was always more diplomatic than Hamilton, but he also "never told a lie."

The question of sovereignty: Never really explained

Let us consider some of what *The Federalist* had to say about the nature of the proposed government. In number 9, Hamilton writes, "The proposed constitution, so far from implying an abolition of the state governments, makes them constituent parts of the *national* sovereignty, by allowing them a direct representation in the senate, and leaves in their possession certain exclusive and very important portions of sovereign power." Here we have a characteristic Hamiltonian muddle. Where had a "*national* sovereignty" come from? The states had been sovereign ever since establishing their independence (May 15, 1776, for Virginia; July 4, 1776, for the rest). Surely, then, their delegation of certain powers to a new federal government did not remake the states into components of a

Portrait of a Patriot

John Jay (1745–1829) played a leading role in the Revolution, both within New York and as a New York member (and sometime president) of the Confederation Congress. He and Alexander Hamilton led the Federalist Party in securing the Constitution's ratification in New York's ratification convention, partly through their series of newspaper essays, *The Federalist*. Jay served as the first chief justice of the United States, and during his tenure on the Supreme Court he negotiated Jay's Treaty with Britain. He next served as governor of New York under the state constitution of which he had been chief draftsman in 1777. His signal achievement as governor was signing into law New York's gradual emancipation act, which eventually brought slavery to an end in the Empire State.

nation, any more than the European Union's assumption of some powers formerly exercised by its sovereign members made Germany, France, Italy, and the rest parts of a sovereign European nation. Creating a federation made a federation, not a nation. The states would remain sovereign under the federal Constitution, just as George Nicholas and Edmund Randolph would soon explain to the Virginia Ratification Convention.

In *Federalist* 23, Hamilton admits that "the circumstances of our country are such, as to demand a compound instead of a simple; a *confederate* instead of a *sole* government." He thus admits the distinction between a federal and a national government. He goes on to say, however, "The government of the union must be empowered to pass all laws in relation to its powers. The local governments must possess all the authorities connected with the administration of justice between citizens of the same state." As Virginia philosopher-statesman John Taylor of Caroline noted, if sovereignty lies with the states (or with the people of those states), then the states (or their citizens) will have authority over the federal government, but if the federal government is sovereign, it will in the end have power over all the states (and the people of those states). (Taylor, it bears noting, made this point in 1823—long before its truth had been fulsomely verified by history.)

This point bears reiteration in regard to *Federalist* 28. There, Hamilton says, "In a confederacy the people, without exaggeration, may be said to be entirely the masters of their own fate. Power being almost always the rival of power; the General Government will at all times stand ready to check the usurpations of the state governments; and these will have the same disposition toward the General Government. The people, by throwing themselves into either scale, will infallibly make it preponderate. If their rights are invaded by either, they can make use of the other, as the instrument of redress."

In the same essay, Hamilton adds:

> The state governments will in all possible contingencies afford complete security against invasions of the public liberty by the *national* authority. Projects of usurpation cannot be masked under pretences so likely to escape the penetration of select bodies of men as of the people at large. The Legislatures will have better means of information. They can discover the danger at a distance; and possessing all the organs of civil power and the confidence of the people, they can at once adopt a regular plan of opposition, in which they can combine all the resources of the community. They can readily communicate with each other in the different states; and unite their common forces for the protection of their common liberty.

Hamilton concludes that essay by saying, "If the federal army should be able to quell the resistance in one state, the distant states would have it in their power to make head with fresh forces.... The people... are in a situation, through the medium of their state governments, to take measures for their own defence with all the celerity, regularity and system of independent nations." Here, Hamilton holds out the prospect of state resistance to dangerous federal policy as "the last ditch" of free people's resistance to a runaway federal government. He cannot resist, however, referring to the federal government as "national," which calls the reader's attention back to his earlier statements about sovereignty—and leaves the ground muddled. If the federal government possesses national sovereignty, on what basis can the non-sovereign states ever resist it? Clearly, Hamilton/Publius's teaching is self-contradictory: insofar as he says that the federal government is national and sovereign, it is inconsistent both with what he says about the states' role in the new Union and with what leading figures in the ratification debate, such as Charles Cotesworth Pinckney of South Carolina, Edmund Randolph of Virginia, George

Nicholas of Virginia, James Wilson of Pennsylvania, and William Cushing of Massachusetts, taught.

In *Federalist* 31, Hamilton says, "The State governments, by their original constitutions, are invested with complete sovereignty." In number 32, he concedes that the states, after the ratification of the Constitution, will "retain [the taxing] authority in the most *absolute* and *unqualified* sense; and that an attempt on the part of the *national* government to abridge them in the exercise of it, would be a violent assumption of power unwarranted by any article or clause of its Constitution." Under the new constitution, he adds, the state governments would retain "all the rights of sovereignty which they before had and which were not by that act *exclusively* delegated to the United States."

In number 33, interestingly, Hamilton wrote that the final paragraph of Article I, Section 8 of the Constitution— giving the government of the United States power to "make all Laws which shall be necessary and proper for carrying into Execution the . . . Powers vested by the constitution"—was merely a "tautology or redundancy." It did not imply that the federal government had any greater powers than those specifically stated.

A Book You're Not Supposed to Read

New Views of the Constitution of the United States by John Taylor of Caroline, edited and introduced by Kevin R. C. Gutzman; Leesburg, VA: Alethes Press, 2007.

How, then, did Hamilton imagine the Congress and the state legislatures cooperating in areas in which their jurisdiction overlapped—as it did in regard to taxation? In *Federalist* 34 he cites the Roman Republic, in which two separate legislative bodies each possessed the power to annul the acts of the other. Just as we have become accustomed, in other words, to the necessity of the federal House and Senate cooperating before either of them can enact its will, so Hamilton said that in the federal system, the state and federal legislatures would each be able to act in its own sphere irrespective of the acts of the other.

Hamilton hits upon this solution again in number 36: "As neither the federal nor state governments, in the objects of taxation, can control the other, each will have an obvious and sensible interest in reciprocal forbearance." The Congress and the state legislatures will each have a sphere, and within that sphere, each will act as it sees fit. John Taylor, on this point, agreed with Hamilton, writing that the federal and state legislatures "are co-ordinate, co-equal, and independent, neither being controllable by the other." One could deduce from this, then, that sovereignty did not lie in either the state governments or the federal government, but in the people of the several states—though Hamilton missed this logical implication.

The thinking behind Hamilton's statements that the federal government and the state governments were each to have some sovereignty can be explained by his preference for the British model of government. In

Portrait of a Patriot

Edmund Randolph (1753–1813) played leading roles in both the Philadelphia Convention and the Virginia Ratification Convention of 1788. Despite presenting the Virginia Plan (which was largely the work of James Madison) at the Philadelphia Convention's outset, Randolph came by the Convention's end to insist that a federal, not a national, constitution was what was needed, and he refused to sign the document. In Richmond, Randolph laid out a states-rights, federalist (not nationalist) version of the Constitution for his fellow delegates, insisting that Virginia would be as one of thirteen parties to a compact in the newly invigorated federal Union. His reassurances explain Virginia's narrow decision to ratify the Constitution. The first U.S. attorney general, Randolph sided with Jefferson in the cabinet's Bank Bill debate in 1791.

Britain, then as now, Parliament, not the people, was sovereign. As Sir William Blackstone had explained in 1765, final authority in all matters lay in Parliament. For Hamilton, final authority lay with the federal government in some issues and with the state governments in others. He never seems to have understood the theoretical change worked by the American Revolution,

A Book You're Not Supposed to Read

The Anti-Federalists: Selected Writings and Speeches, edited by Bruce Frohnen with foreword by Joseph Sobran; Washington, DC: Regnery, 1999.

which substituted popular sovereignty (authority in the people) for governmental sovereignty (authority in the government). This helps to account, also, for the divergence between what he said in *The Federalist* and what other Federalists more influential in the ratification contest were saying at the same time.

Who ratified the Constitution: "The American people" or the sovereign states?

On this issue of nationalism versus federalism, James Madison's contributions to *The Federalist* are similarly perplexing. In *Federalist* 39, in particular, he decides that the proposed government is to be neither national nor federal, but an amalgam. This is, alas, an impossibility—unless, like Hamilton, one assumes that "sovereignty" means "authority in a given area."

On the issue of most moment—the procedure by which the Constitution would be enacted—Madison says, "The constitution is to be founded on the assent and ratification of the people of America, given by deputies elected for the special purpose, not as individuals composing one entire nation; but as composing the distinct and independent States to which they respectively belong. It is to be the assent and ratification of the several States, derived from the supreme authority in each State, the authority of the people themselves. The act therefore establishing the Constitution, will not be a *national* but a *federal* act." (Madison's emphasis)

What does it mean that ratification was to be a federal, not a national, act—the act of "independent states," not of a nation? As Madison goes on to explain, "Were the people regarded in the transaction as forming one nation, the will of the majority of the whole people of the United States, would bind the minority; in the same manner as the majority in each State must bind the minority." So, "Each State in ratifying the Constitution, is considered as a sovereign body independent of all others, and only to be bound by its own voluntary act. In this relation then the new Constitution will, if established, be a *federal* and not a *national* Constitution."

Madison would have done well to leave off here. He goes on to state, however, that the Congress will have one house apportioned by state and another apportioned by population, which makes it, he says, partly national and partly federal. He then notes that presidential elections are to be through an electoral college whose apportionment is partly national and partly federal, and makes several other confused and confusing statements of the same kind.

There was nothing in the Declaration of Independence, in the Articles of Confederation, or in the ratification process of the federal Constitution to enable an American people to create a national government. If the states really were states, they would have had to cease to be so at some time to have made themselves into a nation. When did they do that? When did an "American people" ever assent to or ratify anything?

All of this talk about the Constitution making a "nation" must have been very distasteful to the population of New York, good Patriots who had vindicated their state's sovereignty in the Revolution. No wonder they did not flock to support Hamilton's vision. Instead, two-thirds of the delegates they elected to the state ratification convention opposed the Constitution. It was only New York City's threat of secession, coupled with the real prospect of independence from the other twelve states, that pushed an extremely hesitant New York into ratifying the unamended Constitution.

Chapter Four

JUDGES: POWER-HUNGRY FROM THE BEGINNING

What does the Constitution say about the courts? Not much. In describing the federal judiciary, Article III of the Constitution says, "The judicial Power of the United States shall be vested in one supreme Court, and in such inferior Courts as the Congress may from time to time ordain and establish." Article III also lists several types of jurisdiction that Congress may choose to grant to inferior federal courts and describes the Supreme Court's original jurisdiction. In addition, it grants federal judges "good behavior" tenure.

In the Judiciary Act of 1789, the first federal Congress established the three-tiered federal court system—with a supreme court at its apex, intermediate appellate courts, and federal district courts to conduct trials—with which Americans have had to contend ever since. This system violated James Madison's pledge during the ratification debates that the federal government would first try to get along without any federal trial courts (leaving trials of federal issues entirely to the state courts). But it proved uncontroversial in the first Congress, which was dominated by Federalists of various stripes. (Virginia's two senators were alone in that body in having opposed ratification of the unamended Constitution.)

Besides giving the federal judiciary a skeleton, the Judiciary Act included two other sections ultimately destined for great significance. In Section 25, the Act said that questions of federal law (including

Guess what?

- The concept of state sovereignty—so dear to the delegates at the Philadelphia Convention—was effectively dismissed by judges only six years later.

- The omnipotence of today's Supreme Court would have surprised and horrified the founders—even the Federalists.

- At least two states considered secession because of the Alien and Sedition Acts of 1798.

constitutional law) could be appealed from state supreme courts to the federal Supreme Court. The constitutionality of this provision, dubious then as now, would be hotly debated within a generation, and it would be controversial repeatedly in American history.

The Judiciary Act had another important provision. It concerned suits where federal courts were involved as neutral arbiters because the plaintiffs hailed from different states. Congress decided that the law of the state where the federal court sat would be the governing law. The congressmen wanted to prevent federal courts from devising a federal common law; the presumption was that state law should be applicable in everyday disputes. The creators of the federal government once again erred on the side of federalism, leaving matters to state governments rather than transferring decision-making authority to the federal government.

Judging the judges

President George Washington considered three criteria in appointing the first men to the Supreme Court: prospective appointees must be eminent in their states, they must have favored ratification of the Constitution, and they must, taken together, be of diverse geographic backgrounds. He had a chief justiceship and five associate justiceships to staff, and he made good on his intention to fill them with able Federalists.

The first chief justice, John Jay of New York, was a surprising choice for that post even to Washington himself. According to Jay family lore, Washington offered Jay any position he wanted in the new government. Washington wanted and expected Jay to take the senior cabinet position, secretary of state. Instead, Jay chose the top judicial appointment. As in New York during the Revolution, when he had opted for the top judicial post rather than the governorship, Jay believed that his judicial experience fitted that job uniquely well. As the chief negotiator of the Treaty of Paris, a former president of Congress (where he achieved such influence that a leading historian of the period, John Kaminski, recently called him a "prime minister" in that post), the chief author of his state's first republican constitution, and a coauthor of *The Federalist*, Jay was a fine choice for chief justice.

Jay's associates on the high court also brought outstanding qualifications as statesmen of a kind not seen in Supreme Court appointees today. Justices John Rutledge, James Iredell, William Cushing, and James Wilson had played eminent roles in writing the Constitution, ratifying it, or both. They were joined by John Blair of Virginia, who had experience in that state's high courts and in the Philadelphia Convention, and later replacements included William Paterson and Oliver Ellsworth, who had first been prominent in the Philadelphia Convention and then cooperated in writing the Judiciary Act of 1789.

What a Patriot Said

"A bill of rights is what the people are entitled to against every government."

Thomas Jefferson

The Court's first steps

The first significant constitutional case decided by the Supreme Court concerned the extent of federal power. In *Ware v. Hylton* (1796), the Court upheld the terms of the Treaty of Paris, which had ended the Revolutionary War. Thanks to John Jay's brilliant diplomacy, the Treaty of Paris had brought the Revolution to a spectacularly successful conclusion, with the United States gaining a western boundary not at the Appalachians—the boundary of American settlement at the time—but at the Mississippi. Borders, however, weren't at issue in the case; the issue was how to handle debts owed to the British. Specifically at issue was a Virginia law of 1777 intended to prevent British creditors from collecting on Virginia debtors.

As was his custom, the Virginians' attorney, John Marshall, had no compunction in taking a case even though he had a substantial personal interest in the outcome—in this case, an interest adverse to his clients': he was an investor in Virginia lands formerly owned by prominent Loyalists. Marshall argued that Virginia had acquired the status of an independent nation during the war, that independent nations had the right to confiscate enemies' property, and that Virginia had thus been perfectly within its rights to bar recovery of the debts in question. So far as the law was concerned, "the defendant owed nothing to the plaintiff" at the time of the Treaty of Paris in 1783. The Supreme Court disagreed. Justice Samuel Chase held that the Supremacy Clause of Article VI, which says that the federal government's treaties are the supreme law of the land, resuscitated the debt at issue.

Another 1796 case, *Hylton v. United States*, concerned the constitutionality of a federal carriage tax. The Constitution provided that direct taxes (taxes levied directly on the consumer or owner, in contrast to indirect taxes, like tariffs, which are imposed on the importer) must be apportioned equally among the states. Carriages were far more common in some states (notably Virginia, where many Tidewater planters owned carriages) than in others (particularly in Connecticut, where only two carriages fell under the tax). The Supreme Court held that the carriage tax was not a direct tax, that it therefore did not have to be apportioned equally among the states, and that it thus was constitutional.

Hamilton Splits the Difference

According to Alexander Hamilton, there is a difference between "necessary" and "absolutely necessary." (This is a very important point. Really.)

In *Ware v. Hylton* the Court had nullified a state statute. In *Hylton v. United States* it refrained from nullifying a federal statute, but in the process gave Congress greater discretion in levying taxes than the ratifiers had intended.

The limits on the Court's power to review statutes for constitutional-ity were at issue in the 1798 case of *Calder v. Bull*. The specifics of the case are not so important (it involved whether the Connecticut legisla-ture could grant a new hearing in a probate proceeding, enforcing a will). But the opinions written by Justices Samuel Chase and James Iredell are of great interest. In those early days of the Supreme Court, justices cus-tomarily delivered opinions *seriatim* (that is, each for himself) rather than joining in a common decision. Here, Chase's statements about natural law, and thus about the limitations on legislative power, drew a stinging rebuke from Iredell.

Chase began by saying that while the federal government's powers were strictly defined, the state governments retained all the power dele-gated to them by the people and not denied by the federal Constitution. A former Republican turned Federalist, he then went further. State legis-latures, he wrote, were not (as Parliament was under the British concep-tion of sovereignty) "absolute and without controul," even when the constitution of the state did not expressly limit their authority. Rather, he said, "There are certain vital principles in our free republican govern-ments which will determine and overrule an apparent and flagrant abuse of legislative power; as to authorize manifest injustice by positive law; or to take away that security for personal liberty, or private property, for the protection whereof government was established. An act of the legislature (for I cannot call it a law), contrary to the great first principles of the social compact, cannot be considered a rightful exercise of legislative authority."

In other words, according to Chase, state statutes that violated the "principles" of "free republican government" were not law at all. Such statutes, he wrote, were against "the general principles of law and rea-son." Chase's opinion thus set the stage for federal judges to substitute their individual understandings of the "principles" of "free republican government" for the judgments of state legislatures. The legislature might legislate, Chase said, but not all its statutes could qualify as "law."

This has become, over time, the majority opinion of the Supreme Court. But Justice Iredell leveled a blistering response to Chase's advocacy of judicial imperialism. The guard against untrammeled legislative power, Iredell insisted, was not natural law, but the system of written state and federal constitutions. "If any act of congress, or of the legislature of a state, violates . . . constitutional provisions, it is unquestionably void; though, I admit, that as the authority to declare it void is of a delicate and awful nature, the court will never resort to that authority, but in a clear and urgent case."

If Congress or a state legislature should pass a statute consistent with the power it had been granted, Iredell continued, no court may declare it void (that is, strike it down as "unconstitutional") "merely because it is, in their judgment, contrary to the principles of natural justice."

Iredell warned, "The ideas of natural justice are regulated by no fixed standard; the ablest and purest men have differed upon the subject." And if legislative power can be abused, "such is the tendency of every human institution," but the American system offers a constitutional corrective: legislative elections.

The Eleventh Amendment: Protecting the states from the Supreme Court

Surely the most controversial Supreme Court decision of the 1790s was in the 1793 case of *Chisholm v. Georgia*. In this case the Court claimed jurisdiction over a sovereign state, in apparent violation of Article III of the Constitution.

The case involved a claim that Georgia owed money to the estate of a dead South Carolinian for supplies provided during the Revolutionary

War. Georgia refused to submit to the federal court adjudicating the case, insisting through its counsel (who refused to say anything more) that it enjoyed sovereign immunity as a state; it could not be sued without consenting to be sued.

The Supreme Court issued a default judgment against Georgia because it had failed to appear. In their opinions, Chief Justice John Jay and Justice James Wilson denied that Georgia was sovereign in its relations with the Union. The United States Constitution, they held, was the creation of one American people. Justice Iredell, however, denied that the federal court had jurisdiction over the case at all. Georgia did not allow such suits in its own courts, and that meant that federal courts had no authority to hear such a case. Justice John Blair countered that when the states ratified the Constitution, they agreed to be amenable to such suits in federal courts. And Justice William Cushing affirmed that in giving the federal courts jurisdiction over suits between states, the Constitution assumed that states might be defendants in federal courts.

Justice Wilson went further. He mocked "the haughty notions of state independence, state sovereignty and state supremacy." The American people, he said, could subject the states to federal jurisdiction if they chose to do so. The language of the Constitution's preamble referred to the desires "to establish justice" and "to ensure domestic tranquility," which gave federal courts power to resolve such disputes.

Jay's opinion offered what one historian has called "a bit of hand-tailored history," which made Jay responsible for the "lamentable standards of American judicial historiography."[1] Jay said that when the Crown's authority ceased in America, thirteen sovereignties succeeded, but that the Americans thought of themselves "in a national point of view as one people." The preamble to the Constitution showed that it represented the sovereignty of a single people. If one citizen might sue all the shareholders of a corporation, and if one state might sue another, why would an individual's suit against a state be any different? The grant of jurisdiction under consideration, said Jay, should be construed liberally, because it was remedial. Such a reading, he concluded, would be both wise and useful.

It would not, however, be what the Federalists had argued when the Constitution was being debated. They had said then that federal courts could hear such suits only when they were initiated by the states. Alexander Hamilton, in fact, had said that suits against states would prove impractical because of the difficulty of executing judgments against them. Leading Federalist spokesmen like Edmund Randolph had said that the federal courts' jurisdiction would be read narrowly.

A Book You're Not Supposed to Read

Reclaiming the American Revolution: The Kentucky and Virginia Resolutions and Their Legacy by William J. Watkins, Jr.; New York: Palgrave Macmillan, 2004.

Virginia had refused to submit to a suit when summoned to do so in 1792 in the case of *Grayson, et al. v. Virginia*. Massachusetts soon joined Virginia and Georgia on the list of affected states. In response, Congress proposed, and the states instantly ratified, the Eleventh Amendment, which explicitly denies federal courts jurisdiction over lawsuits initiated "against one of the United States by citizens of another state, or by citizens or subjects of any foreign state."

Modern judges and legal academics often argue that the Eleventh Amendment is a narrow exception to Congress's broad power to create federal courts. But we know from the amendment's history that its purpose was exactly the opposite: to limit the federal courts' jurisdiction to the strict confines of Article III.

These early Supreme Court decisions, and the clamorous response to *Chisholm*, must be read in the context of the political disputes of the 1790s. At issue was just how much authority had been granted to the federal government through the Constitution.

Finally, a Bill of Rights!

Republican opponents of ratification had not been persuaded by the Federalists' promises that the powers of federal congresses and courts would extend only to areas expressly mentioned by the Constitution. In the end, following the lead of Massachusetts Federalists, those in several other states (notably New York and Virginia) vowed to seek amendments to the Constitution in the first federal Congress.

When Congress met, James Madison overcame his colleagues' hesitance to spend time on so "insignificant" a task, and Congress referred twelve proposed amendments (which ultimately became Amendments I–X and XXVII) to the states for ratification. The first ten of them, known as the Bill of Rights, were all about limiting the authority of the federal government.

Madison, still a nationalist, had described the proposed amendments as "safe, if not necessary, and politic, if not obligatory."[2] He had an amendment of his own—which would have given federal courts power to supervise state governments when it came to speech, the press, and religion—but it was so unpopular that it wasn't even sent to the states. Americans were looking to limit federal power, not expand it.

Of the first ten amendments actually adopted, by far the most important was the tenth. It made explicit what Edmund Randolph, James Wilson, Charles Cotesworth Pinckney, and other Federalists had promised was already implicit: "The powers not delegated to the United States by the Constitution, nor prohibited by it to the states, are reserved to the states respectively, or to the people." This could be understood only as a limitation on federal authority.

The same goes for what became the First Amendment, which says that "Congress shall make no law" impairing the freedom of speech, the press, or assembly; guarantees the right to petition; and establishes the right to the free exercise of one's religion. The entire thrust of Republican argument was about restricting the power of the federal government. And the Bill of Rights is framed, in the First and Tenth Amendments, with both specific and sweeping restrictions on the power of Congress.

The Washington factor

During the long, hot summer of 1787, as the Constitution was being written in Philadelphia, George Washington loomed large over the debates. He was the presiding officer at the Convention, but he did not often speak. Nevertheless, the understanding that he would serve as the first president of the United States guided the constitutional design of the executive branch. The delegates trusted him to behave—as he had during the Revolution and since—as a dedicated republican.

Partly at James Madison's recommendation, Washington made his former Continental Army aide-de-camp Alexander Hamilton the first secretary of the treasury. This brilliant admirer of the British constitution also admired the British financial system established earlier in the century by eminent Whig politician Robert Walpole. Hamilton proposed to replicate it, so far as was possible, in America.

Others, wary of Walpole's example and suspicious of Hamilton's republican bona fides, sniffed out monarchist plotting and determined to stop it. Some of these people, influenced by anti-Walpole British writers, resolved to oppose the new government in its early days, whatever it did. John Taylor of Caroline, for example, said that the course of a government is established at its beginnings, so the federal government's every move had to be eyed suspiciously. If it were allowed to set out on a career of exercising powers not expressly granted by the Constitution, it would eventually careen further and further from the pure republicanism of the Revolution.

Secretary Hamilton, like Washington, had suffered hardship, cold, and hunger at Valley Forge. Like his chief, he had seen the Continental Army constantly short of men and money. There must be a stronger federal government, he believed, so that in the event of future wars—and there would be future wars—government credit would be good. Then men and supplies would be plentiful. No American soldier would ever freeze to death in his winter quarters again. The United States would be able to defend themselves even in the absence of a French king willing to go bankrupt on their behalf.

As treasury secretary, then, Hamilton proposed a number of measures to solidify the financial structure. He had the first Congress assume responsibility for the debts incurred by the states in fighting the Revolution and persuaded Congress to fund a portion of the debt. The Virginia House of Delegates, under the leadership of Patrick Henry—the Old Dominion's foremost revolutionary figure and undisputed master of the all-powerful General Assembly—adopted a formal resolution decrying this assumption and funding of the states' debts as unconstitutional. Joining Henry was Henry Lee, who had helped lead the Federalists against him in the Richmond Ratification Convention. The federal government, they said, had not been expressly granted power to undertake any such measures, and so they were unconstitutional. Not only was the General Assembly suspicious of the federal government, but it was also prepared to resist it. (These were the same men, after all, who had made war on England less than a decade earlier on very similar grounds.) Hamilton, however, cut a deal with the Virginians, placing the federal capital between their state and Maryland in exchange for Virginia's accepting his debt assumption program.

Thomas Jefferson, as America's diplomat to France, had been absent during the writing and ratification of the Constitution, but he was a leading Republican voice on his return. In 1791, he joined James Madison (Virginia's leading Federalist, after Washington) in opposing another of Hamilton's financial measures. This one was intended to create an American version of the Bank of England to manage the government's debt.

But in the U.S. House of Representatives, to Hamilton's surprise, Madison classified the bill as unconstitutional. He noted that nothing in Article I, Section 8—where Congress's powers are enumerated—gave Congress power to create any kind of corporation, including a bank.

Congress nevertheless passed the bill incorporating a bank. President Washington then asked his cabinet—which included Edmund Randolph, Hamilton, and Jefferson—whether they thought Madison was right about the bill being unconstitutional. Jefferson responded with a classic affirmation of what the Constitution actually says and means.

The underlying principle of the Constitution, Jefferson wrote, is that "the powers not delegated to the United States by the Constitution, nor prohibited by it to the States, are reserved to the States respectively, or to the people." This is the language of the Tenth Amendment, which—although not yet ratified—had already been passed out of Congress.

How did one know if a power had been delegated to Congress by the Constitution? Jefferson looked at the list of Congress's powers in Article I, Section 8. There was nothing there about chartering corporations, let alone banks, so Congress had no such power. This meant, Jefferson said, that the power to charter banks remained in the state legislatures, where it had been before the Constitution was adopted.

Jefferson then turned to the so-called elastic clause, the Necessary and Proper Clause at the end of Article I, Section 8. It says that Congress has the power "to make all Laws which shall be necessary and proper for carrying into Execution the foregoing Powers [the previously enumerated powers of Congress], and all other Powers vested by this Constitution in the Government of the United States, or in any Department or Officer thereof." Supporters of the bank argued that under this clause Congress could charter a national bank. Jefferson countered that chartering a bank was not "necessary" to carry out any of Congress's enumerated powers, and thus was not permitted by the Necessary and Proper Clause. Attorney General Edmund Randolph concurred with Jefferson.

Hamilton, in rebuttal to Jefferson, made the classic argument for conceding to Congress nearly untrammeled discretion under the Constitution. Hamilton argued that clauses within Article I, Section 8 granted Congress powers related to the economy (such as the power to regulate trade with foreign countries, the power to regulate trade among the states, the power to regulate trade with the Indian tribes, the power to coin money, and so on). These clauses, taken together, reflected a mandate to Congress to supervise the national economy. Only it could decide how to do so. The Necessary and Proper Clause, according to Hamilton, granted Congress discretion in this regard. Contrary to Jefferson's argument, Hamilton stated that "necessary" did not really mean necessary, but that it might mean "helpful," "useful," or "convenient"—or, one supposes, "desired." There was nothing in the Constitution prohibiting Congress from chartering a corporation, Hamilton noted. Where the ends were constitutional and the means not prohibited, the means were constitutional.

Note the distinction between Jefferson's approach and Hamilton's. Jefferson started with the assumption that Congress has only those powers that are expressly delegated to it. (This was also what such leading Federalists as James Wilson, Edmund Randolph, and Charles Cotesworth Pinckney argued in 1787–1788.) Hamilton, on the other hand, started with the assumption that Congress was analogous to the British Parliament in having all powers the Constitution did not expressly deny it. This suited Hamilton's desire that the United States copy the British system (which he regarded as the most successful in the

What a Patriot Said

"I wish it were possible to obtain a single amendment to our constitution. I would be willing to depend on that alone for the reduction of the administration of our government to the genuine principles of its constitution; I mean an additional article, taking from the federal government the power of borrowing."

Thomas Jefferson, in a letter to John Taylor, November 26, 1798

world), but it was a model of congressional authority that the Philadelphia Convention had rejected when it rejected the nationalist Virginia Plan. Moreover, it was directly at odds not only with the Tenth Amendment (and later, the Eleventh Amendment), but with much of what Hamilton had written in his confused contributions to *The Federalist*. Washington, a nationalist, eventually followed Hamilton's advice by signing the bank bill.

The trouble with France

When the French Revolution began in 1789, Washington and many (but not all) Americans responded with cautious optimism. When Washington's friend the Marquis de La Fayette sent him the key to the Bastille, he put it on his mantle at Mt. Vernon—where it remains today.

In time, however, the Revolution took a most unsavory turn (as Gouverneur Morris, on site in Paris as American minister to the French court, had predicted from the start). The king was deposed, then killed, as was his queen. France eventually became involved in a series of first defensive, then aggressive wars, and the kingdom's traditional Catholicism was replaced by a new pagan religion of "Reason."

As France became embroiled in a world war against Britain (and other leading European powers), Hamilton, as treasury secretary, wanted to stay out of the mess entirely. America was far too weak to determine the outcome and could only hurt itself by becoming involved. Besides that, taking France's side would mean an interruption of trade with England—still America's chief trading partner. As federal tax revenue came mainly from tariffs (taxes on imports), interruption of foreign trade threatened the new government's financial future—and thus all Hamilton's plans for American credit.

Secretary of State Thomas Jefferson made two main points regarding America's stance: first, America had since 1778 been under treaty obligation to come to France's assistance if it were attacked. France had lived up to its side of the mutual defense treaty during the American Revolution, and if the United States did not reciprocate, France would have every moral and—under the law of nations—legal right to exact retribution militarily.

Hamilton said that the treaty in question had been between the United States and Louis XVI, who had been deposed in 1792. Thus, America was under no moral or legal obligation to assist France; in his view, the treaty had lapsed. Jefferson responded that it was for France to choose its form of government. True, we had entered into the treaty with the French monarch, but he had been the country's chief executive; if the French had chosen to replace their monarchy with a republic, how could the Americans criticize them for that?

Washington finally, in effect, opted for Hamilton's position. He issued a public proclamation that any American citizen who aided either side in the war would be prosecuted. For Jefferson, Madison, John Taylor of Caroline, and their Republican followers, the president's proclamation was an executive branch usurpation: the president was to execute policy, not make it. Madison wrote that this was only the latest attempt of the Federalists to assimilate the American constitution to the British one. In Britain, unlike in America, it was up to the king to declare war, to conclude treaties, and otherwise to make foreign policy. Madison went further and accused Hamilton (and pro-British Federalists) of being monarchist.

Republican clubs existed across the United States. Republicans celebrated partisan holidays—the Fourth of July was associated with Republican leader Jefferson—and they held dinners and parades in support of their party and of republican France. Partisan tension marked life within all the states and also among them.

With that in mind, in 1794 two northern U.S. senators, New York's Rufus King (later a Federalist presidential nominee) and Connecticut's

Oliver Ellsworth (later chief justice of the United States), buttonholed Virginia's John Taylor of Caroline and tried to convince him that the political divide between North and South was irreparable, and that they should broker a permanent scission of the Union. Taylor rejected the idea, saying that if Hamilton's financial program were repealed, inter-sectional grievances would end. But the idea of dividing the Union stayed in Taylor's mind, as we'll see.

Washington crusades for a whiskey tax

The year 1794 also witnessed the Whiskey Rebellion. In adopting Secretary Hamilton's financial proposals, the first Congress had imposed excise taxes on carriages and whiskey. It seems that the latter was a kind of "sin tax," but many Americans did not consider whiskey an optional component of their lives. Farmers in western districts who grew wheat could eat only so much of it, and transporting wheat to market on crude western roads was often impracticable. So they converted it to whiskey.

The excise, then, fell hardest on those least able to afford it: farmers in remote districts. Hamilton, however, saw the rebellion as a wonderful opportunity. By assuming the states' debts and paying the federal government's debt obligations on time, he hoped to convince foreigners that the United States government was a good credit risk. Using armed force to collect the whiskey excise could only improve America's credit rating.

Washington followed Hamilton's advice, called out the militia of four states, got on his horse, and became the only sitting president ever to lead an army in person when he rode out toward the rebels. The rebellion dissolved as the army approached, but the point had been made. Republicans now believed the Federalists would stop at nothing to impose their views. Hamilton had avowed his monarchist sympathies in Philadelphia in 1787. Republicans looked at the Federalist record—a "monarchist" financial system, sympathy for European monarchies against republican France, a monarchist reading of the federal Constitution, using the army to enforce federal law—and decided it all fit neatly together as a monarchist plot. (And as far as Hamilton goes they were right; in private conversation with Vice President John Adams and Secretary of State Thomas Jefferson, Hamilton had affirmed his belief in monarchy. And John Adams, for his part, had told Virginia's senators that the government must soon be replaced with a monarchy.)

As the political divisions deepened, Republicans saw themselves as defenders of the Constitution against Federalist usurpers.

Jay's Treaty sparks controversy

Republicans had another source of contention when, in 1795, Chief Justice John Jay brought home from England a treaty subsequently known by his name. Jay's Treaty purported to resolve some of America's outstanding issues with Great Britain—including the resolution of debt owed to Britain and settlement of the Canadian border—while increasing trade with the British Empire, even if at the price of restricting American cotton exports. The opposition took the treaty as a sell-out of American interests. The chief justice was a known Anglophile, a Federalist from New York, and a personal and political friend of Hamilton's. Jay, on the other hand, knew the treaty would be unpopular—it may have cost him the presidency—but believed it to be in America's interests, most especially because it voided the danger of war with Britain.

Opposition to the treaty centered in the House, where Madison had by this point come to the head of a unified Republican opposition. Although the Senate, at Washington's request, ultimately ratified the treaty, Madison held that the treaty could be effectively negated if the House refused to appropriate money to implement it.

Today, it's no surprise that many liberal professors take the Republicans' opposition to funding Jay's Treaty as proof that the Republicans weren't concerned with the "original understanding" of the Constitution. Why? Because the Constitution, they say, vests the Senate with the exclusive role in adopting treaties.

But, in fact, Madison's argument that the Jay Treaty could be defeated by the House's refusal to fund it was perfectly consistent with what Madison, the architect of the Constitution, had said during the ratification process. "It is true that this branch [of the Congress, referring to the House]," he said, "is not of necessity to be consulted in the forming of Treaties. But as its approbation and cooperation often may be necessary in carrying treaties into full effect; and as the support of the Government and of the plans of the President & Senate in general must be drawn from the purse which they hold, the sentiments of this body cannot fail to have very great weight, even when the body itself may have no constitutional authority."[3] Madison's Republicans suffered a narrow defeat, anyway, when the House voted to fund implementation of the treaty.

This ratcheted up the political fervor in the country. The treaty meant that the United States would have a closer trade relationship with Britain than it had since the Revolution. The Republicans were furious. What, they asked, about our mutual defense treaty with France? What about the fact that Britain impressed American sailors (albeit who might have been British-born) into the Royal Navy? From the Republicans' perspective, not to mention France's, the Federalists were

No Aliens Allowed

The Alien Enemies Act authorized the president to apprehend and deport resident aliens if their home countries were at war with the United States. Enacted July 6, 1798, with no expiration date, it remains in effect today.

ignoring America's moral and legal obligation to its fellow republic in favor of monarchical Britain.

Breaking the law is... against the law

Washington's retirement in 1796 and John Adams's election as the next president exacerbated the political rift in the country. Party divisions among Americans were fierce. Republican mobs threatened Federalists and even, according to Abigail Adams, the president himself.

Federalists (who fancied themselves "loyal Americans") worried about the large number of immigrants joining the Republicans. So they reformed the nation's immigration laws. Under the Naturalization Act, it would now take fourteen years of residency before an immigrant could become a citizen.

In 1798, an undeclared naval war with France began to protect American shipping from the French navy (which was trying to disrupt trade with Britain). Federalists in Congress levied new taxes to fund expansion of the army and navy. The Federalists also enacted the Alien Enemies Act, which authorized the president to apprehend and deport resident aliens if their home countries were at war with the United States. The Alien Friends Act authorized him to deport any resident alien considered "dangerous to the peace and safety of the United States." The Federalists also implemented the Sedition Act, signed into law by President Adams on July 14, 1798 (surely not by coincidence), which stifled dissent among Americans.

By this time James Madison had retired from Congress, and Jefferson remained in the government essentially as a figurehead. Jefferson and other leading Virginia Republicans, including John Taylor of Caroline, insisted that these Federalist laws were unconstitutional.

The Republicans had three objections to the Alien Friends Act: as "dangerous" aliens could be identified only through their associations, utterances, or publications, the act violated the First Amendment. Even aliens, they said, could claim the rights of free speech, freedom of the press, and free assembly—rights that Congress was prohibited from infringing.

Not so, said the Federalists. Foreigners had no claim to constitutional rights, and Congress was perfectly entitled to ask them to leave at any time. Republicans answered that the Constitution explicitly left it to the states to regulate immigration until 1808, so the statute was unconstitutional. They also insisted that the act violated the principle of the separation of powers by giving the president responsibilities properly confided to the judicial branch.

Of more concern to Republicans, however, was the Sedition Act. While the Alien Enemies Act applied to foreigners from hostile countries and the Alien Friends Act applied to foreigners from non-hostile countries, the Sedition Act was aimed at American citizens. Republicans said that the Sedition Act violated the Tenth Amendment, because no power to enact such a law was mentioned in the Constitution. Some portions of the Sedition Act were statements of the obvious: one section made it a crime to thwart federal law.

What was controversial, however, was the Sedition Act's ban on saying or publishing anything that portrayed the government—including all its agents except, in a hilarious exception, the vice president (Thomas Jefferson)—in a bad light. Among those punished by fine, imprisonment, or both for violating the Sedition Act were editors of major Republican newspapers and a Republican congressman.

Don't Trust Judges

Federal judges very happily sought out people to prosecute for their political opinions under the Sedition Act of 1798 (signed into law by monarchist—bet you didn't know that either—President John Adams).

Republicans insisted that these four acts were unconstitutional, but Federalists disagreed. The First Amendment, Federalists noted, did not say that Congress must allow people to say or print whatever they wanted to, but that their freedoms of speech and press could not be "abridged" by Congress. That meant that the preexisting limits on the freedom of speech—such as that one could not defraud a purchaser or commit perjury in court—continued to be in effect. In English common law, they said, sedition was illegal, so a federal statute banning sedition did not "abridge" freedom of speech. And because the Sedition Act made truth a defense, as common-law sedition prohibitions had not done, far from abridging freedom of speech, Federalists argued, the Sedition Act broadened it.

The Federalists' secret weapon: Judges

Federal judges in the period 1798–1801 were all Federalists. From the beginning, they had been chosen for their eminence—and because they were Federalists. Washington had enunciated those tests at the beginning of his administration, and while he later appointed former Republican opponents of ratification (and would have appointed more, had they accepted the jobs), he left office having filled the federal courts entirely with members of his party. All fell somewhere along the monarchist-nationalist continuum, which, ironically, had been repudiated at the Constitutional Convention in favor of a republican, state-centered model. So the Constitution was, arguably, in the hands of its enemies.

What a Patriot Said

"On every question of construction let us carry ourselves back to the time when the Constitution was adopted, recollect the spirit manifested in the debates, and instead of trying what meaning can be squeezed out of the text, or invented against it, conform to the probable one which was passed."

Thomas Jefferson

These men, then, enthusiastically supported the Sedition Act. And far from worrying about "checks and balances," federal judges believed—as John Jay once told Washington—that their chief obligation was to secure the success of Washington's and then Adams's administration.

Given that Congress had passed the Sedition Act, the president had signed it, and federal judges had enforced it, where could Republicans look for succor? From Monticello, Thomas Jefferson answered, "To the states." (He had been persuaded of this by John Taylor of Caroline.) In Jefferson's words, the states represented "the last ditch" of Republican resistance to the "reign of witches."

In early June 1798, Jefferson wrote Taylor a letter. Taylor, apparently, was now flirting with secession. Jefferson told him that the political problems of the 1790s would not be solved by Virginia and North Carolina leaving the United States to form a separate confederation. It was part of man's nature, Jefferson said, to be fractious, and so a union of Carolinians and Virginians must soon be divided between a Carolina party and a Virginia party; in the end, he said, each state would be left to itself.

Besides, Jefferson argued, the American people had been deluded into supporting the Federalists. Once the tax bills for the recent military buildup arrived, they would see the error of their ways and cast the Federalists out for good. Taylor was unpersuaded. He told Jefferson that a mere change of parties would not solve the problem, because the problem was human nature: men always wanted more power. A southern aristocracy ruling the country would be as bad as a northern one. Instead, Taylor's answer was to amend the Constitution extensively to prohibit federal overreaching.

Jefferson and Madison argue for states' rights

Virginia Republican leaders, meanwhile, met at Monticello and decided that Virginia and Kentucky, two Republican-controlled states, would adopt resolutions in their state legislatures spelling out their objections to the Alien and Sedition Acts.

Kentucky's Resolutions of 1798, drafted secretly by Jefferson to avoid prosecution under the Sedition Act, argued for state-centered constitutionalism. The Constitution had been ratified—and thus the federal government had been created—by the states for their own purposes. They had retained all powers not delegated by them to the federal government through the Constitution. When the federal government undertook to exceed the bounds of its authority, its acts were "unauthoritative, void, and of no force."

The states were sovereign and "to this compact [of the Constitution] each state acceded as a state, and is an integral party." Who, then, was to decide when the federal government adopted unconstitutional policies? Surely not the federal government, "since that would have made its discretion, and not the Constitution, the measure of its powers; but...as in all other cases of compact among parties having no common judge,

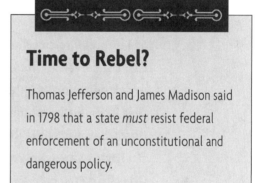

Time to Rebel?

Thomas Jefferson and James Madison said in 1798 that a state *must* resist federal enforcement of an unconstitutional and dangerous policy.

each party has an equal right to judge for itself, as well of infractions as of the mode and measure of redress." When it came right down to it, the states, which had created the federal government, still bore ultimate responsibility for ensuring that their monster did not oppress their people.

The Sedition Act, Jefferson said, was objectionable on two constitutional grounds. First, and most important, it violated the Tenth Amendment principle: that powers not expressly delegated to the federal government through the Constitution were reserved to the states or to the people. Second, it violated the First Amendment's prohibition on congressional infringement of the rights of free speech and press. It was, therefore, null and void.

In Virginia, James Madison drafted the resolutions adopted by the House of Delegates. He argued that when the federal government persisted in an unconstitutional and dangerous policy, as with the Alien and Sedition Acts, the states "have the right, and are in duty bound, to interpose" to prevent their enforcement within their "respective" territories.

The two Republican legislatures asked other states to join them in propounding the principles laid out in the Virginia and Kentucky Resolutions. No other southern state did so (though North Carolina considered it). But ten states north of Virginia issued their own refutations of the Resolutions.

On what grounds? In general, they argued that the Sedition Act was a good law that should have been adopted sooner, and that interpreting the federal Constitution was a task for the federal courts, not for the states.

Kentucky responded in 1799 with a second set of resolutions, these two conceived by Jefferson. Kentucky's legislature said that Kentucky loved the Union "for the purposes for which it was created," and insisted that it would be among the last states to secede. (This was an implied threat, because while Republican leaders had privately discussed the possibility of secession, only one, Virginia congressman William Branch Giles, had advocated it in public. So this was the first official mention of secession in the context of the Alien and Sedition Acts.) But when the federal government propounded unconstitutional and dangerous laws, it was the duty of the states to nullify those laws.

James Madison, too, wrote a sequel to his Resolutions. His *Report of 1800* did far more than simply defend the Virginia Resolutions of 1798. It objected to the entire direction of Federalist policy in the 1790s. Madison's most significant argument concerned the use of the word *state*. Federalists had objected to the idea that the states had created the federal government. The Philadelphia Convention, Federalist legislatures rightly noted, was not a state organ, nor were the ratification conventions parts of the state governments. Clearly, then, the states had not created the federal government.

Madison noted that the word *state* had three common significations: it could be used to refer to the territory of a state (as in "I'd like to go to the state of North Carolina"); it could be used to refer to a state government (as in "The state of Georgia was a party to *Chisholm v. Georgia*"); or it could refer to the sovereign people of a state (as in "The state of Virginia ratified the Constitution"). Federalists were reading the word *state* purely as referring to state government. The Virginia Resolutions used the word *state* to refer to the sovereign people of Virginia. In saying that the Union was a union of states, Republicans understood that the Union was a union of sovereign peoples: the people of Delaware, the people of North Carolina, the people of Maryland, the people of Rhode Island, and so on.

Most history and legal textbooks say that Jefferson and Madison invented the idea of state sovereignty. But as we've seen, they only argued for what the founders had already understood to be true about the sovereign states from the beginning, even if some of the founders (the nationalist and monarchist wings) wanted to change that understanding.

In the end, what Thomas Jefferson had predicted to John Taylor of Caroline proved to be true, or at least partly true. The Republicans won the election of 1800, and the Federalists lost control of Congress and the executive branch forever. The Sedition Act expired at the end of John Adams's term. Jefferson hoped that this sweeping victory—Republican vindication—meant that constitutional squabbles would now come to an end.

Chapter Five

THE IMPERIAL JUDICIARY: IT STARTED WITH MARSHALL

Jefferson's victory was supposed to inaugurate a new era of strict constitutional interpretation, putting an end to presidential, congressional, and judicial usurpations of power. It certainly wrought a radical change in the programs and policies of the federal government. Shortly after his inauguration, Congress repealed all internal taxes, so that the only sources of federal revenue would be tariffs and sales of federally owned land. It also slashed the military budget dramatically. Unlike modern "budget-cutting" politicians who claim to "slash" government spending while merely reducing its rate of growth by a point or two, Jefferson's Republicans ultimately eliminated all seagoing vessels from the navy and cut the army's manpower by nearly 95 percent.

The loathed Sedition Act expired on the last day of John Adams's administration, and Jefferson not only pardoned everyone convicted under it, but also returned the fines they had paid. (No historian has ever thought to question whether Jefferson had constitutional authority to refund fines paid by felons.)

Republicans also acted to rein in the federal judiciary. The last Federalist Congress had passed the Judiciary Act of 1801, expanding and reorganizing the judicial branch. Republicans hooted that the act was a nakedly partisan attempt to pack the courts with Federalists just as the people were throwing them from elected office.

Guess what?

- Supreme Court chief justice John Marshall had the nerve to tell one of the framers of the Constitution that he had been flat-out wrong!

- Based on Marshall's flawed reasoning in *McCulloch v. Maryland*, President Andrew Jackson almost invaded South Carolina.

- The phrase "high crimes and misdemeanors" refers to the holders of *high offices*—a fact that Marshall's Federalist cronies conveniently ignored.

One myth about this act, popularized by Republican propagandists at the time and echoed by professional historians even now, is that John Adams filled all the new posts established by the Judiciary Act with dedicated Federalists. In fact, Adams did not; some were not Federalists at all. But the run of professional historians and legal scholars, as this book should make apparent, rarely do their homework.

In any event, the Jeffersonian Republican Congress not only repealed the Judiciary Act of 1801, but, on April 23, 1802, it also passed a law proroguing the Supreme Court for fourteen months to ensure that before it returned to session, the Judiciary Act would be fully repealed.

A Book You're Not Supposed to Read

Impeachment: The Constitutional Problems by Raoul Berger; Cambridge, MA: Harvard University Press, 1973.

Federalists responded by talking among themselves about New England secession. But they were let down by the Supreme Court, which, when it returned, accepted the repeal's constitutionality.

Still, the reckoning between the Republican Congress and the Federalist judiciary had only just begun. The main battle centered on Congress's attempt to impeach and remove two federal judges.

High crimes and misdemeanors abound

United States district court judge John Pickering of New Hampshire appeared to be conducting his duties while severely intoxicated. Under the Judiciary Act of 1801, circuit judges could step in when a district judge was incapacitated (or, in this case, inebriated). As it had been repealed, however, Pickering had to do his duty himself.

Some of Pickering's friends tried to defend him by saying he was insane—not drunk. Other Federalists counseled him not to resign his office, and so he didn't. Jefferson referred the matter to the House in early 1803, but the Senate trial did not begin until March 1804.

The Constitution provides in Article II, Section 4 that "the President, Vice President and all civil Officers of the United States, shall be removed from Office on Impeachment for, and Conviction of, Treason, Bribery, or other high Crimes and Misdemeanors."

The phrase "high crimes and misdemeanors" was borrowed, like much else in the Constitution, from English precedents. It had a precise legal meaning when the Constitution was ratified: it covered not only "high crimes" and petty corruption, but also disability, including physical, mental, or psychological impairment. No one has ever claimed, however, that politicians were legal scholars, and most of the senators accepted Pickering's lawyer's argument that insanity was neither a high crime nor a high misdemeanor. Still, they removed Pickering from office anyway.

While the Pickering matter was pending before Congress, the Federalist Supreme Court under Chief Justice John Marshall rebuked the Jefferson administration in the landmark decision of *Marbury v. Madison*. This case affirmed that federal courts could review congressional legislation (and gratuitously lecture elected officials).

William Marbury had been nominated by John Adams for a very minor judicial post in the District of Columbia. The Senate had confirmed his appointment. President Adams had signed his commission. Then secretary of state and soon to be chief justice John Marshall had failed to deliver it to him. Thus, Marbury could not enter into his office.

Because the case focused on Marshall's own incompetence as secretary of state, presumably he should have recused himself, but he did not.

Marshall's Republican successor as secretary of state was none other than James Madison, and he had no intention of delivering Marbury's commission. Marbury responded by suing Madison in the Supreme Court.

Despite what most legal scholars will tell you, "judicial review" was uncontroversial before *Marbury v. Madison*. During the ratification of the Constitution, Federalists had said federal courts would have the power of judicial review, and Republicans (specifically Patrick Henry) said they hoped they would use it. Besides, both lower-level federal courts and the Supreme Court had at least implicitly exercised this power before. The repute granted *Marbury* rests more on Marshall's ringing claim on behalf of the powers of the Supreme Court—which he took directly from Alexander Hamilton's *Federalist* 78—than on judicial review's novelty.

Of more importance was the political element of Marshall's decision. In the federal system, we have two kinds of courts: courts of general jurisdiction (state courts) and courts of limited jurisdiction (federal courts). Before a federal court involves itself in a case, it must decide whether that case falls under its constitutional jurisdiction.

Marshall, however, did not begin with this question (or with the question of whether there was a federal law requiring Madison to give Marbury his commission). Instead, he asked, "Does Mr. Marbury have a right to his commission?" To ask the question, Marshall knew, was to affirm it. And Marshall duly argued that to deny Marbury his commission was to wrong him gravely. Nevertheless, the Court's authority to issue a writ of mandamus (forcing Madison to deliver the commission) rested in the Judiciary Act of 1789, which, Marshall said, was itself unconstitutional because it granted the Court jurisdiction beyond what the Constitution permitted. Therefore, the relevant portion of the Judiciary Act was null and void.

This was the first time the Court had declared a congressional act unconstitutional, and some have argued that Marshall's motivation was more political than anything else: he wanted to say that Marbury was right, but was fearful of a direct confrontation with Jefferson and Madison (because how, if it came down to it, could he force them to give the commission to Marbury?).

Chief Justice Marshall Touts *The Federalist*

Marshall never referred directly to the ratification debates in his opinions. He preferred to rely on *The Federalist*. But *The Federalist*'s nationalist explanations of the Constitution were rejected at the Philadelphia Convention and during the ratification debates.

The real precedent established by *Marbury v. Madison* was not for judicial review, but for the presumed right of the Court to lecture elected officials even when the Court had no jurisdiction over the question at hand.

Impeaching Justice Chase

Next on the congressional docket was Justice Samuel Chase. Republicans accused Chase, an ardent Federalist, of abusing his office in the interest of partisan politics. One notorious and illustrative case was the Sedition Act prosecution of James Callender, a journalist who had written scurrilous attacks on President John Adams. As one of the articles of impeachment against him put it, Chase, the presiding judge, showed "an indecent solicitude . . . for the conviction of the accused . . . highly disgraceful to the character of a judge, *as it was subversive.*" (Emphasis added) As Raoul Berger, the greatest of American legal historians, put it, Chase's behavior in the Callender trial went against his judicial oath—which said, in part, "I will faithfully and impartially discharge and perform all the duties incumbent on me."

Chase was far from impartial. He had "selected the victim, announced his intention to punish him for his 'atrocious and profligate' libel, procured his presentment by the grand jury, refused to excuse jurors who confessed their bias against the accused, at every step identified himself with the prosecution, and [taken] every means to disconcert, discredit, and disable counsel for the defense."

Chase's behavior in this and other cases had made him notorious in Republican circles. The House of Representatives believed that Chase's behavior warranted his removal from office and impeached him (making Chase the only Supreme Court justice ever impeached). It was proven beyond any doubt that Chase had conducted himself in a prejudiced, partisan way that made him unfit to serve as a judge, trial or appellate. But, in one of the great, reverberating mistakes in the history of American law, the Senate acquitted him.

Why?

His counsel argued that Chase had never committed "treason, bribery, or other high crimes and misdemeanors." Without an indictable criminal offense by Chase, his counsel argued, the Senate could not remove him from office. The Senate accepted this argument. But the argument is wrong.

In the English law tradition that shaped the Constitution, a "high crime" or "high misdemeanor" was different from an indictable "crime" or "misdemeanor." "High" was a category of misbehavior associated with high *office* and with *political* misbehavior.

Thus, in 1757, Sir William Blackstone—whose *Commentaries on the Laws of England* formed the bedrock of American legal education in the late eighteenth century—wrote that "the first and principal [high misdemeanor] is the *mal-administration* of such high officers, as are in the public trust and employment. This is usually punished by the method of parliamentary impeachment." As Berger notes, maladministration did not

Legal Latinisms

Mandamus: Latin for "we command." A type of writ that a court can issue to compel performance of a mandatory duty when the right, the duty, and the absence of an alternative remedy are all clear.

imply an indictable offense. In fact, among "high crimes and misdemeanors," as a historian of English law has pointed out, were cases in which "judges mislead their sovereign by unconstitutional opinions" as well as "attempts to subvert the fundamental laws, and introduce arbitrary power"—purely political offenses that would not be tried before an ordinary court.

Chase had certainly committed high crimes and misdemeanors, if not indictable offenses, by these standards. The Chase verdict forced Jefferson to conclude that impeachment was a farce and was no check at all on judicial misbehavior. At the end of his life, Jefferson wrote that "they [federal judges] consider themselves secure for life; they sculk from responsibility to public opinion, the only remaining hold on them .... A judiciary independent of a king or executive alone, is a good thing; but independence of the will of the nation is a solecism, at least in a republican government."

The Chase acquittal set the precedent that a federal judge may disobey his oath (because it is not an indictable criminal offense) by ignoring or effectively rewriting a statute or the Constitution, and nothing will come of it.

The Marshall Court soon took advantage of the Chase verdict.

The Supreme Court's march through Georgia (and Virginia)

In Article I, Section 10 the Constitution protects contracts from any state tampering: "No State shall pass any ... Law impairing the Obligation of Contracts." This is the so-called Contracts Clause. The original motivation behind the clause was to prevent states from adopting "stay laws" (as they sometimes had during the Revolutionary period) that prohibited lenders from collecting debts for stated periods of time. A provision similar to the Contracts Clause was included in the Northwest Ordinance of

1787, stating that "in the just preservation of rights and property, it is understood and declared, that no law ought ever to be made or have force in the said territory, that shall, in any manner whatever, interfere with or affect private contracts, or engagements, bona fide, and without fraud previously formed."

The first time the Supreme Court considered a case under the Contracts Clause was in *Fletcher v. Peck* (1810). This case arose out of the notorious Yazoo Scandal, one of the great public swindles in the history of the world. In that case, a group of land investors had bribed all but one member of the Georgia legislature to sell them an enormous area of public land—most of what is now the states of Alabama and Mississippi— virtually for nothing. The sale was completed in 1795 as a grant of land to a private company, but then repealed—and the bribed legislators cast out—in 1796. John Peck bought his title to some of that land in 1800, then sold it in 1803 to Robert Fletcher. Fletcher next sued Peck for the purchase price, saying that his supposed title had been negated by the legislative repeal of the original sale, and thus was worthless.

Chief Justice Marshall, for the Court, decided that the nub of the issue was whether a legislature's grant of public land qualified as a contract under the Contracts Clause. He and his fellow justices decided that it did. So the Supreme Court ruled the state law—Georgia's repeal of the 1795 land grant—unconstitutional and void, which in practical terms meant that, according to the Supreme Court, the people had no democratic remedy to correct the bribed action of a corrupt legislature!

Not only was Marshall's equivalence of grants and contracts dubious, but he also skipped over a crucial point, which was whether Georgia ever had a contractual "obligation," given that the land grant was the result of bribery, in the first place. As the Northwest Ordinance's contracts clause illustrates, the obligation of contracts was understood to be dependent on the absence of fraud (as well as coercion). This legal understanding was universal. But Marshall ignored it, with dire results.

The revolutionary—one might say anti-constitutional—nature of the *Fletcher* decision should not be overlooked. The Constitutional Convention had denied Congress the power to veto the acts of state legislatures. The Convention certainly did not mean such power to be assumed by the Court instead. During the entire debate on ratification in Virginia, where extremely able men teased out the meanings—and potential dangers— lurking unsuspected in each clause of the proposed Constitution, no one ever said, "And the least responsible institution of the federal government is to have a veto power over the everyday enactments of each of the state legislatures." Had anyone suspected that it did, he certainly would have pointed it out. No one intended to grant federal courts such authority.

Marshall had two incentives to rule as he did in the *Fletcher* case, one personal and one institutional. From a personal point of view, he was himself a substantial investor in unsettled lands, and so he might be expected to favor people who claimed to have received state grants. Institutionally, Marshall saw in the Georgia lands case an opportunity to buttress the position of the judicial branch in the federal system—and to help make national what had been intended as a federal constitution.

In *Marbury v. Madison*, Marshall had staked out the Supreme Court's authoritative claim to the power to review congressional enactments for constitutionality. In *Fletcher v. Peck*, he grabbed at the chance to claim

The Supreme Court vs. the Constitution

James Madison protested that if Marshall's nationalist decision in *McCulloch v. Maryland* (1819) (which said that Congress's powers were *not* limited to those "expressly delegated") had been foreseen, the Constitution would never have been ratified.

what ultimately would prove to be a far more significant right: that of federal courts to supervise enactments of state legislatures. If in *Marbury* he had exceeded the limits of his authority by lecturing the president on the merits of a case that he admitted the Supreme Court had no constitutional power to decide, in *Fletcher* he and his colleagues, in deciding the case incorrectly, forced Georgians to accept the validity of an enormous fraud.

There remained one more element of the triad of federal judicial power yet to be established: the federal courts' power to supervise the performance of state judiciaries. An opportunity presented itself in the 1816 case of *Martin v. Hunter's Lessee.* The case centered on whether Virginia laws that had allowed for the confiscation of Loyalist property during the Revolutionary War were rendered obsolete by treaties negotiated between the United States and Britain that protected Loyalist property. The Virginia Court of Appeals, Virginia's highest court, had ruled that these treaties did not conflict with or overrule the Virginia laws.

In *Fletcher v. Peck*, Marshall had written an outlandish opinion in order to protect the interests of land speculators generally. In *Martin*, most of the land titles at issue belonged to a company whose major shareholders included Marshall himself and his brother. (Marshall had a history of looking out for his brother's interests. After the Republican Congress's 1801 Judiciary Act, Marshall had tried and failed to get his fellow justices to join him in saving his brother's federal judicial post.)

The Supreme Court took the case from the Virginia Court of Appeals under Section 25 of the Judiciary Act of 1789, which said that the federal Supreme Court could hear appeals of federal questions from the states' top courts. The Supreme Court, in asking the Virginia court to send the record of the case for review, used peremptory language of a type a superior uses with an inferior, and Virginia's high court responded by saying, "The court is unanimously of opinion that the appellate power of the Supreme Court of the United States does not extend to this court, under a sound construction of the Constitution of the United States." In short, it would not forward the record of the case, so the Supreme Court would have nothing to review.

Marshall recused himself, so the Supreme Court's opinion came from Justice Joseph Story, a Marshall ally. Justice Story wrote that there must be one superintending authority to ensure that the law was applied in the same way throughout the Union. He reasoned that Article III of the Constitution established that states could be brought before federal courts in some cases, so there could be no valid objection to Section 25 of the Judiciary Act on that ground.

This argument had been made by the justices in *Chisholm v. Georgia*, and the people had instantly corrected it by adopting the Eleventh Amendment. The federal courts were thus limited to the types of jurisdiction listed in Article III, which did not include appeals from state supreme courts. The Virginians argued that while the Constitution provided that it was "the supreme law of the land," it also required that state judges take an oath to uphold it. In other words, state judges were to enforce the Constitution themselves without the supervision of a federal court.

It would have been odd, indeed, to come to any other conclusion. At the Philadelphia Convention, remember, the Virginia delegation first proposed, in its nationalist Virginia Plan, that Congress have a power to veto state laws it judged unconstitutional. This was one of the numerous nationalist features of the Virginia Plan that the Convention ultimately omitted from the finished Constitution. The Convention opted for a federal government with limited powers instead of a national government with unlimited powers. It rejected Hamilton's idea that the president should appoint state governors and U.S. senators. It rejected Madison's idea that the Congress should have a general legislative power. It rejected the idea that the federal courts should have a general jurisdiction. And it rejected the congressional veto.

How strange, then, that anyone should read the federal Constitution, with its list of powers of Congress and list of types of jurisdiction federal courts could be given, as giving federal courts a veto over state judiciaries. The same logic applies to this case as applied to *Fletcher v. Peck*'s claim that federal courts were supposed to superintend the behavior of state legislatures. In short, the Marshall Court, not the Virginia judiciary, was violating the Constitution. The result was not only that the Virginia courts were overruled, and the relevant Virginia laws were voided, but that the Supreme Court seized the power to supervise state courts, an entirely unconstitutional usurpation of power.

The Constitution created a federal system in which state governments, through elections, were held responsible by the people of the states. The constitutional model is a decentralized one of the type envisioned by Thomas Jefferson when he wrote *A Summary View of the Rights of British America*.

What judicial usurpation did to this model was to replace the authority of elected state governments with the authority of a few lawyers, appointed by a president to positions of lifetime tenure without any check on their power. Does that sound like the model of government approved by the ratifiers of the Constitution?

Supreme Logic: Fraud Is a Contract

According to John Marshall in *Fletcher v. Peck* (1810), a fraudulent land purchase was a "contract"—and was thus subject to the protection of the Contracts Clause. "Coincidentally," Marshall was a substantial land investor.

But if you studied constitutional law in school, you'll know that the Marshall Court is treated with veneration, based on the idea that the "law" is the body of Supreme Court decisions, rather than the Constitution itself (as understood by the ratification conventions). *Fletcher* and *Martin*—and our acceptance of those decisions—have given federal judges ultimate authority over wide swaths of our political life that the men who adopted the Constitution on our behalf never intended them to have.

Madison's banking flip-flops

By the end of the War of 1812, the United States government had run up a substantial amount of debt. To help manage it, President James Madison asked Congress in 1816 to charter the second Bank of the United States—which was ironic, as he had been the leading opponent of the constitutionality of the first Bank of the United States in 1791. He had then regarded congressional legislation to charter a bank as an unconstitutional threat to American liberties and a telltale sign that Hamilton and Washington wanted to overthrow the federal government. Only a politician could perform so breathtaking an about-face without feeling even slightly inconsistent, and Madison was up to the task.

The second bank charter echoed the first in giving the federal government a 20 percent share in the bank. With that in mind, House Republicans, led by Kentucky's Henry Clay and South Carolina's John C. Calhoun, sponsored the Bonus Bill. They would take the "bonus"—their name for the federal government's profit as a bank shareholder—and spend it on "internal improvements." These were what we now call "infrastructure": a network of roads, bridges, and fortifications, as well as the clearing of some major harbors and rivers. Madison and Jefferson had each asked Congress in their State of the Union messages to appropriate money for these purposes. When the Bonus Bill reached his desk, however, Madison—in his last major act as president—vetoed it.

In his Bonus Bill Veto Message in 1817, Madison explained his veto in terms virtually identical to those he had used in opposing Hamilton's bank charter bill in 1791: the Constitution's list of powers of Congress was exhaustive, the Bonus Bill's appropriations were for purposes not enumerated in the Constitution, and therefore the Bonus Bill was unconstitutional. He had to veto it.

It was true that he had called on Congress to adopt measures like this, but he had been careful, Madison pointed out, to note that Congress could make up for any deficiency in its authority by initiating the process of amending the Constitution. If it wanted to adopt measures such as the Bonus Bill, that avenue still lay open. Madison said that, as written, the Bonus Bill violated the basic tenets of Republican constitutionalism, as had Hamilton's bank bill. The second bank bill, though nearly identical in content to the first, did not raise similar constitutional concerns, he said, because of the precedent established by Hamilton's bank.

Madison said that he had made a good-faith argument against the first bank bill's constitutionality in 1791, but he had lost. Not only had Congress and President Washington considered the bill constitutional, but so had a succession of other Congresses and presidents—else they would have acted to repeal it. In Madison's estimation, the constitutionality of congressional legislation chartering banks had become a dead issue.

Madison's argument boiled down to this: If Congress undertook to exercise authority reserved to the states (the Bonus Bill), that was unconstitutional. If, however, the president signed Congress's bill exercising state powers (Hamilton's bank bill) and a string of Congresses and presidents joined in the exercise of those powers, what had been powers reserved to the states became powers delegated to the federal government. What Jefferson had called, in the context of King George III and the Declaration of Independence, "a long train of abuses and usurpations, pursuing invariably the same Object" now operated to transfer power from the states, where the people had intended to leave the power, to the federal government, to which they had meant to deny it! Small wonder, then, that John C. Calhoun and Henry Clay did not understand the constitutionalism of James Madison.

To some Virginia Republicans, Madison's odd constitutional course as president came as no surprise. In 1808, John Taylor of Caroline, John Randolph of Roanoke, and other disaffected Republicans who thought Jefferson had strayed from Republican principles—and that Madison was worse—lit upon James Monroe as their standard-bearer. We need a man of principle to oppose the Machiavellians in power, they said. To contrast themselves to the seemingly nationalist Madison and his supporters, these men called themselves "Old Republicans." It was a group that former president Thomas Jefferson himself sometimes supported. For example, as historians rarely note, Jefferson opposed Madison's bank bill.

Most Old Republicans were in the South. But Republicans in other parts of the country sometimes joined forces with the Old Republicans to oppose Madison. Many of them, in fact, opposed Madison's bank, and as soon as it was adopted, some states passed measures intended to exclude it from their territory. Ohio was a notorious example. A more prominent one, by the vagaries of fate, was Maryland.

Maryland decided that it would keep the Bank of the United States from opening a branch in its territory by imposing a stiff fee on it. The

Portrait of a Justice

John Marshall (1755–1835), the Great Chief Justice, was the fourth chief justice of the United States. Before accepting that post, he had been a Federalist delegate to the Richmond Ratification Convention, a congressman, a diplomat, and secretary of state. His handiwork as chief justice included writing the defeated (and, by the end of his tenure, defunct) Federalist Party's constitutional views into American constitutional law in cases such as *Fletcher v. Peck*, *McCulloch v. Maryland*, and *Gibbons v. Ogden*. More than any other man, Marshall was responsible for converting the nationalists' defeat in the Philadelphia Convention into a long-run total victory.

1818 Maryland banking law said that any bank established "without authority from the state" must issue only notes of certain denominations, and then only printed on stamped paper, unless the bank chose to pay an annual fee of $15,000. The Baltimore branch of the Bank of the United States failed to comply with these requirements, and so Maryland sued its cashier (branch manager), James William McCulloch.

The main issue presented to the Supreme Court in the case of *McCulloch v. Maryland* was the constitutionality of the Maryland law. Lurking behind that was the question of whether the Bank of the United States had been constitutionally chartered by Congress.

Everyone recognized the import of the case: according to Justice Joseph Story, when oral arguments were held, "the hall was full almost to suffocation, and many went away for want of room." Spectators got their money's worth, as the issues were debated with great skill by Daniel Webster—the nineteenth century's leading Supreme Court advocate—and William Pinkney on behalf of the Bank of the United States and by Maryland attorney general Luther Martin, who had been a prominent Philadelphia Convention delegate thirty-two years earlier, for his state.

Webster reiterated Alexander Hamilton's 1791 constitutional justification of the first bank bill: Article I, Section 8 of the Constitution does not provide an exhaustive list of congressional powers, but only a suggestive one. As several of the powers listed in Section 8 relate to the economy, Congress can be understood to have a general supervisory power over the economy. Congress might well decide that chartering a bank was useful in superintending the economy. Because the Constitution does not expressly prohibit Congress from chartering a bank, Congress is free to do so. Webster reasoned that nearly thirty years' unbroken acceptance of the constitutionality of such legislation had settled the question.

Marshall, in his opinion for a unanimous Supreme Court, wrote that Maryland had argued that the Constitution had been ratified by the states for express, limited purposes, and not only had Congress's chartering a bank not been among those purposes, but the Tenth Amendment had been added to the Constitution to underscore that the "powers not delegated to the United States by the Constitution, nor prohibited by it to the states, are reserved to the states respectively, or to the people."

However, Marshall rejected this notion. He wrote that while the Articles of Confederation had specified that Congress had only the powers it was "expressly delegated," the Constitution included no such language, so no such principle applied to it. This was an extraordinary argument, given that Marshall himself and other Federalists like Charles Pinckney, James Wilson, William Cushing, Edmund Randolph, and George Nicholas had assured their ratification convention colleagues that this very principle of limited federal power—in Randolph's words, that the federal government would have only the powers it was "expressly delegated"—was implicit in the unamended Constitution even before the Tenth Amendment was adopted.

Being right, however, does not guarantee a victory in court, as anyone who has been so unfortunate as to find himself before a judge can attest. In his opinion for the Court, Marshall "corrected" Martin's interpretation of the Constitution. It had not been created by the states, he insisted, but by one American people. Martin, said Marshall, simply did not understand the framers' intent!

The American people who created the Constitution, Marshall went on, had given the federal government certain powers, and the federal government must be supreme within its sphere—both as a logical matter and as the Supremacy Clause of Article VI expressly states. Thus, when Congress exercised one of its constitutional powers, a state could not interfere with it.

Was chartering a bank among Congress's constitutional powers? At this point, Marshall, like Webster, borrowed from Hamilton: the proper ends of congressional legislation are hinted at by the enumerated powers in Article I, Section 8; the means Congress adopts to achieve those ends (including management of the "national" economy) must be those that are "necessary" in the Webster/Hamilton sense of being "useful"; and the limitations on congressional discretion listed in the Constitution (for example, that Congress may not adopt an ex post facto law) are the only binding ones there are.

From the grave, the practically defunct Federalist Party and its late chieftain, Alexander Hamilton, had had their way. Despite its defeat in 1787, the Philadelphia Convention's monarchist-nationalist coalition had been handed an epochal victory in 1819.

Little did it matter that Marshall's "interpretation," if it may be called that, set the Tenth Amendment at naught, still less that it contradicted what the Federalists of 1787–1791, including (at least by implication) young John Marshall, had promised. As the Supreme Court had the final word in the matter, the clear contradiction between the process used to ratify the Constitution—its consideration by each of the sovereign states and ratification by each of them separately, on behalf of itself and only itself—and Marshall's assertion that "one American people" had adopted the Constitution also was not susceptible to correction. The Constitution was going to be read by the Supreme Court as the product of one American people, and the powers it gave the Congress were going to be the discretionary powers of a national legislature, not the enumerated powers of a federal legislature. In short, the Philadelphia Convention, the ratification process, the Tenth Amendment, and the political defeat of the Federalist Party (so thorough that the party ceased to exist) were all undone by the Marshall Court.

Almost as an afterthought, Marshall wrote in *McCulloch* that Maryland could not tax the Bank of the United States. In creating a

Legal Latinisms

Ex post facto law: A law passed after the commission of an act to change the act's legal consequences. Generally, the term refers to retroactive criminalization or heightening of a criminal penalty.

federal government, surely the American people had not intended that its powers could be overridden by an individual state government. "The power to tax is the power to destroy," and so the state of Maryland—which could not thwart federal measures—had no power to tax the bank.

Critics soon pointed out that Marshall's argument proved too much. If the people had created the federal government, whose instrumentalities a state therefore could not destroy, they had also created the state governments, so could the federal government interfere with them? The argument applied either way, logically—but not in the mind of John Marshall. Like Thomas Hutchinson, the last royal governor of Massachusetts, Marshall insisted that there must be an indi-

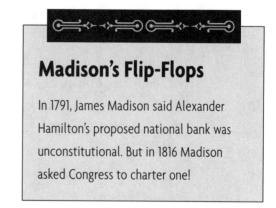

Madison's Flip-Flops

In 1791, James Madison said Alexander Hamilton's proposed national bank was unconstitutional. But in 1816 Madison asked Congress to charter one!

visible sovereign in every community, and that meant that all conflicts between states and the federal government must be decided in favor of the federal government. The Revolution had substituted the federal government for the Crown, as Marshall read things, and the states were still subordinate.

Marshall lamented in his correspondence that the bank decision drew down a powerful storm of criticism. When the *Richmond Enquirer* ran series of anti-*McCulloch* editorials, first by a Virginia appellate court judge, then by the Court of Appeals' chief judge himself, Marshall—like historians since him—accused his critics of preferring the Articles of Confederation to the Constitution, the same (disingenuous) argument he had used against Luther Martin.

Seemingly everyone had something to say about the decision. James Madison, for one, who had justified the second Bank of the United States on far different—though equally pernicious—constitutional grounds, wrote of *McCulloch* that if people had known in 1788 that the Constitution would be read as giving Congress such extensive discretionary powers, Virginia would never have ratified it. He was, as we have seen, absolutely right about that: George Nicholas and Edmund Randolph had assured the Richmond Convention that Virginia was to be one of thirteen parties to the Constitution, not somehow an organic part of "one American people."

Thomas Jefferson, for his part, found Marshall's decision highly vexing. Jefferson had long regarded Marshall as the greatest threat to federal republicanism, and he said that despite Federalism's decisive defeats at the polls, "we find the judiciary on every occasion, still driving us into consolidation." To Jefferson's mind, the branches of the federal government were coordinate and independent; the judiciary was not the final arbiter. That status belonged to the sovereign people of each state.

The year after *McCulloch* was decided, Jefferson wrote, "The judiciary of the United States is the subtle corps of sappers and miners constantly working under ground to undermine the foundations of our confederated republic. They are construing our constitution from a co-ordination of a general and special government to a general and supreme one alone." Jefferson's guiding principle was to favor local government. But it was an argument he was losing: the failure of the Chase impeachment had demonstrated to the judges that they could do as they liked, and they were.

"The wolf by the ear"

Marshall's opinion in *McCulloch v. Maryland* granting Congress powers limited only by its own will provoked a fiery response in part because it came as Congress was wracked by a dispute over slavery in the territory of Missouri. Missouri, a section of the Louisiana Purchase, applied for admission to the Union in 1819. The application included a draft state constitution, which provided that slavery should continue in the territory.

To the surprise of the political class generally, a New York Republican congressman named James Tallmadge, Jr. proposed that Congress amend the Missouri bill to phase slavery out of existence in the new state. His proposal would have stopped importation of slaves into Missouri, and it would have freed all slaves born after Missouri's admission to the Union as soon as they reached age twenty-five. The Missouri Crisis, which would divide Congress for two years, had begun.

To a Republican congressman of his acquaintance, former president Jefferson wrote that the Missouri dispute had struck him "like a firebell in the night," filling him with terror. "I considered it at once as the knell of the Union." He lamented that a geographical line had been established, with proponents of one principle on one side and advocates of a contrary one on the other. Could anything be done to end this division? Taking a metaphor from an ancient Greek proverb, he said, "We have the wolf by the ear, and we can neither hold him, nor safely let him go. Justice is in one scale, and self-preservation in the other."

To understand Jefferson's metaphor, we need to know two things: first, that so far as late eighteenth-century philosophers of whom Jefferson was enamored were concerned, self-preservation was the highest goal of society. Only it could outweigh justice. Second, Jefferson's notion that ending slavery would mean loosing a ravenous wolf reflected his fear that emancipation would lead to race war. He had expressed this fear as early as the 1780s. It gained added strength from the memory of the Haitian Revolution of 1791–1804, which had resulted in the death or exile of every white person from Haiti. Jefferson expected American emancipation to have similar results in the South.

Jefferson opposed Tallmadge's Missouri proposals on several grounds. First, he, like James Madison and others, believed that the slaves—and certainly the slaveholders in his own state of Virginia—would be better off if slavery were diffused across the whole continent instead of confined to the Southeast.

Second, he disliked Tallmadge's plan because it contradicted his conception of the Union. Perhaps Congress could exclude slavery from the territory of Missouri, but it could not impose conditions on the territory that would remain binding once it became a state. At that point, Missouri would have attained equal footing with the other states—just as the Northwest Ordinance had provided regarding the former trans-Ohio Virginia territory we now call the Midwest—and would be free, as other states were free, to make its own policy regarding slavery. If a northern majority in Congress could impose its will on a state despite that state's clear rights, what was to prevent the Yankees in Congress from doing the same to the older southern states?

The Dartmouth review

The year 1819 also saw Marshall's Supreme Court issue another momentous decision. This one, in the case of *Dartmouth College v. Woodward*, calls to mind his legerdemain in *Fletcher v. Peck* nearly a decade before. Dartmouth College, like Harvard, Princeton, Columbia, and other colonial colleges, operated under a royal charter as a charitable institution. It had been given its charter in order to perform the public service of educating New Hampshire youth, mainly—like Yale, William and Mary, and other colleges—for the ministry, and to educate Indians.

With the Revolution of 1776, Dartmouth found itself insulated from virtually any outside influence. When the Jeffersonian Revolution of 1800 finally worked itself out in the state politics of New Hampshire, Republicans saw Dartmouth College as ripe for reorganization. No longer, said the Jeffersonian Republicans ascendant in that state, should their state college be a bastion of privilege—a Federalist Party enclave untouchable by the new legislative majority. Therefore, the state legislature adopted legislation reorganizing Dartmouth.

Dartmouth College, in response, claimed the protection of the Contracts Clause of Article I, Section 10 of the Constitution for the terms of its original charter. The case went to the Supreme Court, and Chief Justice Marshall blithely accepted the college's argument that its charter amounted to a contract, the "obligation" of which could not be "impaired" by state legislation.

The Contacts Clause, however, had never been meant to cover college charters, and presumably a college chartered for the public's purposes could have its charter amended by the public. As so often before, Marshall might have been wrong, but his decision had lasting significance. It explains why Harvard, Yale, Penn, Dartmouth, Columbia, and Princeton—colleges established during colonial times and supported during that era with public money—came to be "private" in the early nineteenth century. Just as *Fletcher* was calculated to protect the interests of land speculators (such as Chief Justice Marshall), so *Dartmouth College* benefited the old Federalist elites who wanted to shield their colleges from Republican legislatures. Jefferson and the Republicans were, naturally, outraged, and the decision was unpopular, but there was no appeal from the Supreme Court.

The "great Lama of the mountains" vs. Marshall

In 1821, the Supreme Court decided the case of *Cohens v. Virginia*. The issue at hand was the effect of the Eleventh Amendment. The Supreme Court, predictably, ruled that the Eleventh Amendment banned only the *initiation* of suits against states in federal court, and as this suit was only being *appealed* to federal court against a state, the Eleventh Amendment did not apply.

Here, once again, we see that Marshall consistently read limitations on federal power as narrowly as possible. The Eleventh Amendment plainly does not have the limitations Marshall put upon it; it was meant to limit the federal courts to the role specified for them in Article III. If Marshall had read the amendment that way, he would have found Section 25 of the Judiciary Act of 1789—which gave the Supreme Court jurisdiction over certain appeals from state supreme courts—unconstitutional.

Interestingly, in an 1824 case, *Osborn v. Bank of the United States*, Marshall held that while the Eleventh Amendment banned the initiation of suits against states in federal courts, it did not protect employees of states from being sued in federal court for implementing state policies! With *Cohens* and *Osborn*, he had given the Eleventh Amendment as narrow a reading as possible; this was consistent with his general pattern of hostility toward limitations on federal power.

Marshall derisively called Jefferson "the great Lama of the mountains," but Jefferson recognized that the Supreme Court had become a threat to America's constitutional government. He worried that the Court had eliminated all checks on its power by misreading the clear meanings of Article III and the Eleventh Amendment. Even an unbroken string of Republican electoral victories had not changed the direction of the Court; in fact, these victories seemed to make Marshall more determined to write Hamiltonian principles into legal precedent.

Jefferson and Marshall were separated by differences over the very nature of law. For Jefferson, law was the framework of rules by which the people agreed to be governed; a judge's role was simply to apply the clear meaning and original understanding of the Constitution (or other legal document). But Marshall and his allies, like Justice Joseph Story, believed that law required judges who could see beyond the written law to the "natural law" that was superior to it. Jefferson's vision was republican; Marshall's was aristocratic or clerical. As Justice Iredell pointed out in *Calder v. Bull*, no two men agreed about the particulars of the "natural law"; instead, they tended to use "natural law" as a justification for legislating their own policy preferences. It is unsurprising, then, that Marshall and Story's "natural law" always led to a pro-Federalist outcome. Perhaps surprisingly, Marshall's vision of judging—the Federalist vision—continues to dominate lawyers' and judges' thinking about the judicial role even today.

Marshall finds the elastic in the Commerce Clause

One of the next great cases to come before the Court was *Gibbons v. Ogden* (1824). *Gibbons* concerned the most famous inventor of the age, Robert Fulton, who was widely credited with inventing the steamship. It would be hard to exaggerate the significance of his invention, which revolutionized trade within the United States. The question was: what reward should the inventor receive?

The New York legislature had granted Fulton and his business partner, prominent Republican politician and diplomat Robert Livingston, a thirty-year monopoly of "navigation of all the waters within the jurisdiction of that State, with boats moved by fire and steam." The issue, Marshall decided, was whether Congress's Commerce Clause power—"The Congress shall have power . . . to regulate Commerce with foreign Nations, and among the several States, and with the Indian Tribes"—belonged only to it, or whether states could also regulate "commerce," as in excluding certain ships from state waters.

Before he turned to that, however, Marshall had to define "commerce." Neutral readers of his opinion would have found much in his *Gibbons* definition of "commerce" to remind them of his *Dartmouth College* definition of "contract" and his *McCulloch* definition of "necessary." It turned out that the interstate "commerce" that Congress was empowered by the Commerce Clause to regulate included not only what my dictionary defines as commercial (that is, large-scale exchange or buying and selling involving transportation), but also transportation undertaken for transportation's sake. In support of his definition, Marshall pointed to the long-standing habit of Congress to adopt laws affecting interstate navigation; the fact that Congress had done so over a long period of time proved that it had a constitutional power to do so, he said. (Recall that he had made a similar argument about the constitutionality of the second Bank of the United States in *McCulloch v. Maryland*—and contrast Thomas Jefferson's statement at the outset of the Revolution that no matter how long the British oppressed the colonists, they would never acquire a right to oppress them by having done it repeatedly.) Thus, the transportation monopoly at issue in *Gibbons* was "commerce," said the Court, and therefore Congress could regulate it.

This odd definition, like those in *McCulloch* and *Dartmouth College*, would have enormous ramifications down the road. In time, Congress would claim, and the Supreme Court would agree, that it could regulate virtually anything on the ground that it even remotely affected interstate commerce. Marshall almost certainly would have welcomed that development.

But back to the steamboat monopoly. Having defined "commerce" in such a way as to include mere interstate transportation, Marshall had to decide whether Congress's power to regulate it was infringed by a New York statute affecting it. He decided that it was—that is, that New York's grant of a monopoly of steamboat transportation to Livingston and Fulton ran afoul of the Commerce Clause.

How could that be? Surely New York's legislation did not annul the congressional power to regulate interstate commerce, or even limit it. Marshall avoided saying that Congress's power to regulate interstate commerce was exclusive—that the Article I, Section 8 grant negated state power to act in that area. But Marshall did assert that Thomas Gibbons—

operating a competing ferry service licensed by Congress in 1793—could not be barred from New York waters under the terms of the Commerce Clause.

Marshall nullifies the Declaration of Independence

In 1831 and 1832, Marshall issued a pair of opinions—in the cases of *Cherokee Nation v. Georgia* and *Worcester v. Georgia*—that had even deeper ramifications. Marshall famously sided with the Cherokee against the state of Georgia by saying that the Indians' treaty rights must be respected by the state. (In response, President Andrew Jackson is supposed to have said, "John Marshall has made his decision, now let him enforce it.") Marshall's decisions in these cases are famous, but what is never noted is the significance of his reasoning.

Marshall went on at great length about the Indians' society in North America before the white man's arrival. The colonists had conquered them and taken their land, he said; their moral right had given way before the colonists' martial might. Sadly, they possessed only a slight remnant of their original empire.

Marshall, in this analysis, denied the entire Jeffersonian theory of American colonial history that underlay *A Summary View of the Rights of British America* and, through it, the Declaration of Independence. If the Indians in North America were not isolated bands of migratory Stone Age people, but settled civilizations, then—as Sir William Blackstone wrote in his *Commentaries on the Laws of England*—their law remained in effect until the king replaced it, and so the colonists did not have all the rights of Englishmen when they first arrived here. This meant that the Declaration of Independence was based on an inaccurate account of the colonies' relationship to the king, who had not had to concede any of the rights of Englishmen to the colonists. From Marshall's point of view, a rejection of the Jeffersonian version of the past buttressed opinions like the one in *Dartmouth College*—in which a royal charter took precedence (as the rights of the Indians took precedence) over state legislation. It also might be said to have justified Marshall in reasoning from general legal theories instead of directly from the Constitution and the constitutional understanding of the state ratification conventions.

State sovereignty? Never heard of it

The logic of Marshall's legal thinking nearly led to war in the early 1830s, when it was applied to the issue of tariffs.

In 1828, Congress had passed and President John Quincy Adams had signed into law the Tariff of Abominations, which raised the standard tariff rate to 50 percent. At a time when much of America was agricultural and many goods were only available from abroad, a 50 percent tax on all imports struck many as outrageous. The South Carolina legislature responded by issuing its Exposition and Protest, in which it went on record saying that each state had the right to interpose to prevent the enforcement of federal policy within its borders if the federal government adopted a policy that was unconstitutional and dangerous.

Matters worsened during the Nullification Crisis of 1832–1833. South Carolina responded to the Tariff of 1832 by electing a popular convention, which nullified the tariff.

President Andrew Jackson prepared to invade South Carolina. South Carolina's government and private citizens throughout the state prepared the militia to resist. Virginia's governor secretly planned to take South Carolina's side in case Jackson tried to march through Virginia to get at the Palmetto State. And Jackson issued a Nullification Proclamation denying the constitutionality of both nullification and secession. Nullification, he insisted, was treason. Repeating Marshall's arguments from *McCulloch v. Maryland*, Jackson argued that the United States had been created by one American people, not by separate states. Just as Jefferson had expected, the one thing that the Supreme Court and the executive could agree on was that federal power was supreme.

Senator Henry Clay stepped in to arrange a compromise. Tariffs were reduced—slowly. Senator John C. Calhoun of South Carolina would not be hanged for treason (for supporting his state). Jackson would not repent. The South Carolina Convention met again, repealed the nullification ordinance, nullified the statute empowering Jackson to put down nullification by force, and declared victory.

Marshall finally gets one right

This was the context of Marshall's last significant constitutional decision, *Barron v. Baltimore* (1833). The city of Baltimore, Maryland, had, in the course of making city improvements, altered the flow of water into the Chesapeake Bay, which in turn led to a buildup of silt around the wharf of John Barron. Barron said the value of his wharf had been so damaged that it amounted to a government seizure of his property for which he ought to be compensated by the city under the Takings Clause of the Fifth Amendment ("... nor shall private property be taken for public use without just compensation").

Marshall described the issue as one of "great importance, but not of much difficulty." The Fifth Amendment, like the rest of the Bill of Rights, had been adopted as a limitation on the federal government alone. The movement to affix amendments to the Constitution arose out of fears that the new government was too powerful, and the amendments' purpose was to

A Bill of Rights to Protect the Sovereign States

Even John Marshall conceded, in *Barron v. Baltimore* (1833), that the Bill of Rights did not affect the powers of the states, but only those of the federal government.

hedge that power. Thus, if Barron wanted Baltimore to be forced to compensate him for its injury to his property, he would have to seek his remedy in a state, not a federal, court.

In the end, then, Marshall decided a constitutional case correctly. This outcome calls to mind the old saying about the stopped clock.

Chapter Six

UNDOING MARSHALL— AND UNDOING THE UNION

E ven before John Marshall left office feet first in 1835, the winds of change were already buffeting the Supreme Court. First, a succession of Republican presidencies undercut his sway within the Court itself. Finally, Andrew Jackson's election in 1829 brought to power a man with a completely novel understanding of the federal system.

In 1832 Jackson vetoed a bill to recharter the second Bank of the United States. In his Bank Bill Veto Message, Jackson said that the *McCulloch v. Maryland* decision had not decided the issue of the 1816 bank charter's constitutionality. It might be that the Supreme Court thought so, he said, but he was sworn to uphold the Constitution as he understood it, not as the Supreme Court told him it was. As he adhered to the Jeffersonian view of congressional authority, he based his veto in part on the recharter bill's unconstitutionality.

Jackson also decried what he called the tendency of government to rain its blessings solely on the rich. In the manner of Jeffersonians before him and the Democrats he led, Jackson viewed banking as little more than a mechanism by which bankers could print money for their own benefit. The congressional requirement that federal tax revenues be deposited solely in the Bank of the United States ensured that the bank would make a profit. This profit would be realized as a transfer of money from the

Guess what?

- Chief Justice Roger B. Taney was one of the ablest in the history of the Court—and also one of the most disastrously political.

- Anti-slavery had been divisive from the beginning— and it was only the constitutional protections for slavery that brought and kept some Southern states into the Union.

populace at large to a few wealthy, well-connected shareholders, some of whom (gasp!) were British.

In the early nineteenth century, corporate charters were special privileges. Businessmen could not simply pay a nominal fee and fill out a short form to incorporate their companies, as they can today. Instead, they had to secure special legislation granting them the privileges of the corporate form: limited liability of shareholders and immortality of the corporation. Jackson was right, then, to see incorporation as a special privilege to which average men had virtually no access.

Not only did Jackson veto the bank recharter, but he also ordered his secretary of the treasury, Louis McLane, to remove the federal deposits from the Bank of the United States. McLane, mindful of the law requiring him to deposit the funds in the Bank, refused. Jackson fired him. It took Jackson a while and another short-lived secretary to come upon someone willing to ignore plain statutory requirements at the president's behest, but he finally lit upon the person of Roger B. Taney.

Jackson would reward Taney for his subservience by appointing him to replace John Marshall as chief justice of the United States. Serving in the post from 1836 to 1864, Taney would ultimately become the most controversial chief justice in American history. He also is generally regarded as among the ablest. Among his accomplishments was the elimination, at least by implication, of some of the Marshall Court's more absurd pronouncements.

"The object and end of all government"

The difference between Taney and Marshall is most clearly to be found in the 1837 case of *Charles River Bridge v. Warren Bridge*. That case involved the Massachusetts legislature's powers and the Constitution's Contracts Clause. Under a 1785 grant, the legislature had given the Charles River Bridge Company a charter to build a bridge connecting

Boston to towns to its north, along with the power to collect tolls. In 1828, it authorized the Warren Bridge Company to build a new bridge nearby and collect the tolls necessary to pay for the construction; once the construction costs had been covered, the bridge was to revert to the Commonwealth and tolls would cease to be collected.

Daniel Webster, who had represented Dartmouth College in the Marshall Court's signal Contracts Clause/charters case, argued that the Contracts Clause forbade the Massachusetts legislature's 1828 action. He said that this amounted to a repeal of the Charles River Bridge Company's charter, as it would become impossible for the Charles River Bridge Company to collect any tolls once a free bridge stood close by.

For the majority, Taney ruled against Webster and the Charles River Bridge Company. Writing in dissent, Justice Joseph Story argued that the 1785 grant to the Charles River Bridge Company should be construed "liberally"—inferring an implicit promise that nothing would be done to eliminate the value of the charter, such as chartering another company to build a free bridge nearby. In private correspondence, Story lamented the passing of the old Federalist order on the Court, saying that he was certain his old friend Chief Justice Marshall would have ruled differently from Taney.

But in his opinion for the Court, Taney said that disputes about grants by the public, when their implications were unclear, must be decided in favor of the public. "The object and end of all government is to promote the happiness and prosperity of the community by which it is established," he wrote, "and it can never be assumed, that the government intended to diminish its power of accomplishing the end for which it was created."

Technology had advanced rapidly since 1785, and Taney's opinion reflected that fact. The country was "continually advancing in numbers and wealth," he wrote, so that "new channels of communication are daily found necessary, both for travel and trade, and are essential to the comfort, convenience and prosperity of the people. . . . And when a corporation alleges, that a State has surrendered for seventy years its power of improvement and public accommodation, in a great and important line of travel . . . the community have a right to insist that its abandonment ought not to be presumed, in a case in which the deliberate purpose of the state to abandon it does not appear." State power, he concluded in language evocative of Jackson's Bank Bill Veto Message, should never be presumed to have been transferred "to the hands of privileged corporations."

Clearly much had changed since *Dartmouth College v. Woodward*. Note what had not changed, however: Taney and his colleagues did not undo the Marshall Court's egregious holding that a charter is a contract under the Contracts Clause. They merely read the charter in the Charles River Bridge case as not binding the state beyond its bare terms, construed narrowly. Where doubt was found, in other words, they would err in favor of the public, but without undoing the Marshall Court holding at root. This pattern of non-correction has come to characterize Supreme Court decisions revisiting dubious earlier decisions. Very seldom does the Supreme Court reverse an earlier holding when it first notices that it was simply wrong.

Taney tackles the Commerce and Contracts Clauses

This tendency of the Taney Court to respect state legislation the Marshall Court would have struck down was also clear in the 1837 case of *Briscoe v. Bank of Kentucky*. Article I, Section 10 of the Constitution prohibits the states from, among other things, issuing bills of credit. The question in this case was whether that prohibition applied to the Bank of Kentucky, a corporation owned by the state of Kentucky. The Court ruled that the prohibition did not apply, because the bank was not the state itself and the bills of credit were redeemable by the bank, not by the state. This decision allowed state banks to step into the breach left by Jackson's elimination of the Bank of the United States; they could issue notes that were the equivalent of paper money.

Also in 1837, in an opinion by Justice Philip P. Barbour (a Virginian neighbor of James Madison and staunch devotee of Jeffersonian principles), the Court decided in *New York v. Miln* to rein in Marshall's absurdly nationalistic Commerce Clause opinion in the 1824 steamboat case *Gibbons v. Ogden*. As in *Charles River Bridge*, however, the correction was merely implicit.

Miln involved state regulation of the port of New York. That state required ship captains to provide authorities with lists of the passengers on their ships, post bond for indigent passengers, and remove certain indigent aliens. The defendants protested that this violated the Commerce Clause. Justice Barbour, however, for the Court said that the New York law was merely a police law, and insisted that a state could as well protect itself against "the moral pestilence of paupers, vagabonds, and possibly convicts" as against "the physical pestilence" of sick people. A concurring justice pointed out that state commercial regulations had

Portrait of a Justice

Roger Taney (1777–1864) reined in the Marshall Court's constitutional nationalism in a series of decisions from the 1830s through the 1860s. He also braved the arbitrary government of Abraham Lincoln in cases such as *Ex parte Merryman*. His name is most associated, however, with the invention of "substantive due process" (the last refuge of judicial scoundrels) in *Dred Scott v. Sandford*—a blatantly partisan, rigged decision by the Court's Democratic majority. It should not surprise that Taney sank to such partisanship, because his appointment to the Court had been owing to his willingness as treasury secretary to follow Andrew Jackson's order illegally to remove the federal deposits from the second Bank of the United States.

previously been ruled unconstitutional (in the *Gibbons* steamboat case) only when they conflicted with federal ones. Justice Story dissented, citing *Gibbons* to argue that Congress had exclusive power over regulating commerce. No one joined Story's dissent.

The premier Taney-era Commerce Clause case was 1851's *Cooley v. Board of Wardens*. At issue was a Pennsylvania statute requiring every ship entering or leaving the port of Philadelphia to hire a local pilot. Aaron Cooley, who owned two ships named in the case, claimed that the law violated the Commerce Clause.

The Court ruled in favor of the state, noting that Congress had explicitly recognized state pilot regulations in one of its own statutes. Striking down this regulation as unconstitutional, the Court said, would mean striking down an untold number of other state regulations. And it noted that Congress had rarely intervened in this area. The Taney Court's moderate approach to the Commerce Clause's meaning for state legislative power has been retained, essentially, ever since.

Lest one conclude that Taney and his associates always favored states' rights, however, consider the 1843 case of *Bronson v. Kinzie*. Arthur Bronson attempted to foreclose on a property owned by his debtor, John Kinzie. He ran afoul of two 1841 Illinois statutes restricting the coercive power of creditors.

Bronson claimed that as the Illinois laws were retroactive, and as his contract with Kinzie had been entered into before 1841, the laws violated the Contracts Clause. Taney sided with Bronson, as he clearly should have, as these were exactly the kinds of circumstances to which the Contracts Clause had been intended to apply. (Remember those stay laws adopted by state legislatures during the American Revolution?)

States' rights did not mean to Taney—as they did not mean to Jefferson, Madison, or Taylor—that states were free under the Constitution to do whatever they wanted to do. In fact, the Constitution does prohibit certain kinds of state behavior, and judges were obliged to enforce these prohibitions, as Taney and his mainly Democratic colleagues did in *Bronson v. Kinzie*. Illinois had adopted legislation reducing creditors' rights (that is, impairing the obligation of a contract), and the Supreme Court held it to be unconstitutional. As we shall see, faced with similar legislation a century later, Taney's successors would not be so quick to live up to their oath to uphold the Constitution and to do equal justice to rich and poor.

The War for Southern Independence

Taney's term as chief justice is dominated in historical memory by the legal disputes leading up to and arising out of the war of 1861–1865. Before we can discuss those issues, we must first deal with the question of what to call the war.

Nearly as soon as shots were fired, people in the Union began calling it the "Civil War." This term is clearly misleading. A civil war is a war for control of a single government, like the civil wars of seventeenth-century England, twentieth-century Russia, and twentieth-century Spain. The English Civil War, between monarchists and supporters of the legal claims of Parliament, was for control of the English government, and whichever side lost would necessarily be ruled by the other. The same goes for the Russian Civil War between the Reds and the Whites and for the Spanish Civil War between Francisco Franco's forces and the Republicans.

In the American war of 1861–1865, the Confederate states had no desire to rule New York or Indiana. They wanted to separate from them, to achieve independence. The Union, for its part, wanted to subjugate the Confederacy, to force the seceded states to accept northern rule. In that sense, the war was analogous to the war of 1775–1783, in which the Americans had no desire to rule people in Yorkshire or Glasgow, while the British wanted to subjugate the Americans. No one, I think, would call the American Revolution a civil war.

What of "War of the Rebellion," which in some senses became the official Union name for the war? This title assumes the validity of the northern constitutional position of the day, which was that the Union of 1788 was not really a union of states but an amalgamation, a consolidation, and so the southern war effort was a rebellion—a war against legitimate authority. Yet, as we have seen, there was no point at which Virginia, for example, agreed to join in a consolidation, to be amalgamated into one American mass. Rather, the delegates to the Richmond Ratification Convention of 1788 were told that their state would remain one of thirteen parties to a confederation, and that it could reclaim all its old powers if the federal government should pervert those powers to Virginia's injury. Doing so, then, was not a rebellion, but part of the constitutional system that the 1788 convention in Richmond had agreed to accept. So "War of the Rebellion" does not fit either.

On the other hand, many southerners, such as former Confederate vice president Alexander Stephens of Georgia, have called it the War Between the States. In some sense, it is true that the war was between the states, and yet the war effort was waged on each side mainly by a federal government: the Union in the North, the Confederacy in the South. Thus, that name, too, seems inaccurate. The most descriptive nonpartisan name of the war I have seen is the War for Southern Independence. That was the issue. (I suppose one might call it the War against Southern Independence with equal validity, but no one ever does.)

Taney's tenure on the Supreme Court is remembered mainly for its relationship to the crisis leading up to, and for the Court's behavior during, the War for Southern Independence.

All men are (not really) born free and equal

Slavery had been an issue of legal controversy from the very beginning of the country. For example, in his original draft of Virginia's May 1776

Declaration of Rights George Mason asserted that all men are born equally free and independent. But this was inadequate, because the Virginia draftsmen recognized that they had to confront the existence of slavery. So they amended that first American declaration of rights to say that all men are born *free and equal*, and, *when they enter into a state of society*, government has to protect their rights. Black slaves' exclusion from the process of making the new republican society left the new government without any responsibility to protect their rights. Thomas Jefferson and his Virginian peers viewed the blacks in their midst not as "African Americans," but as captive Africans, a foreign people.

Northern states felt freer to act against slavery because they faced fewer social and economic complications from it. Thus Massachusetts's 1780 constitution, which today is the world's oldest constitution, said that all men were born free and equal. Massachusetts courts in the 1780s declared slavery unconstitutional in the Bay State on that basis. Generally, the farther north a state was, the more at ease it felt in acting against slavery immediately.

It Wasn't a Civil War

The war of 1861–1865 was not a civil war, because the southern states did not want to rule the North.

When the Philadelphia Convention of 1787 got around to discussing slavery, opinion was divided. Delegates from northern states like Gouverneur Morris lamented the existence of slavery in the United States in the harshest terms and did not want it protected in the new constitution.

George Mason argued in favor of ending the importation of slaves immediately. He too argued that slavery was a moral blight, and said that nothing good could come from importing more slaves.

From the Deep South states of Georgia and South Carolina came a completely different kind of argument. The Palmetto State's leading revolutionary politician, future Supreme Court chief justice John Rutledge, insisted on protection for slavery. He wanted to leave individual states able to continue to import slaves at their discretion, and he wanted states into which slaves escaped to be required by the new constitution to return them to their masters. Without significant protection for slavery, he thundered, South Carolina would never ratify any new federal charter. His South Carolina colleagues, as well as all the Georgians, agreed.

The Deep South's delegates were a minority, yet they proved adept at political maneuver. Virginia's Mason, representing the export-producing southern states, held that Congress should not be given a power to levy tariffs—taxes on imports—by mere majority vote, and New Englanders, whose states were home to the great shipping companies that stood to benefit from differential duties on domestically and foreign-owned ships, disagreed.

Finally, Connecticut's Roger Sherman approached Rutledge with a deal: support the right of a bare congressional majority to levy tariffs, he said, and we will go with you on importing slaves for twenty more years. Rutledge happily agreed. To boot, the Constitution gave Rutledge the Fugitive Slave Clause on which he had insisted; it also counted each slave as three-fifths of a person for purposes of apportioning the House of Representatives, which also affected apportionment of the electoral college, which gave slaveholders more say in choosing all appointed officials. Thus the Constitution was full of pro-slavery provisions.

As the Philadelphia Convention met, the old Confederation Congress was adopting the Northwest Ordinance to establish how the Northwest Territory could enter the Union as several states. Among the provisions of the Northwest Ordinance was one "forever" prohibiting slavery from the Territory.

Opponents of slavery in Taney's day pointed to the Northwest Ordinance's geographic restriction of slavery as evidence that the men who guided the Revolution and the federation of 1788 opposed slavery in the abstract, on moral grounds. This idea is given the lie by the correspondence of Virginia congressman William Grayson (then president of Congress). The night Congress passed the Northwest Ordinance, Grayson wrote a letter boasting that it was a wonderful development for Virginia, because it guaranteed that the Northwest would never be able to compete with Virginia tobacco production. In other words, he saw the banning of slavery in the Northwest Ordinance as an economic benefit to the South, not a moral victory for slavery's opponents.

In 1789, in the first Congress under the new Constitution, a proposal was made in the House to tax the importation of slaves. South Carolina congressman Aedanus Burke countered that any such tax would mean the end of the Union, as South Carolina would sooner secede than see such a tax implemented. Moreover, as we have already seen, leaders of the 1790s Jeffersonian opposition like Virginia's John Taylor of Caroline warned that one implication of the Hamiltonian reading of congressional powers behind adoption of the carriage tax, one ground on which that tax must be opposed, was that a mere majority in Congress could tax property in slaves. Slavery was a touchy subject, then, from the beginning.

The Jeffersonian revolution of 1800 put an end to this fear until 1819. But fear that Congress might act against slavery, reawakened by the Missouri Controversy, underlay South Carolina's growing opposition to the tariffs favored by the New England states in the 1820s. In addition, because tariffs hit the agricultural South harder than the industrial North, South Carolinians could see tariffs as a partisan measure threatening their slave-based agricultural economy.

The matter reached a crescendo in the 1840s and 1850s over the issue of the United States' westward expansion. In 1836 Texas had declared and won its independence from Mexico. Texas wanted to be annexed by the United States, but Democrats in control of the federal government in Washington refused. The Democrats feared inflaming anti-slavery feeling by adding so enormous a slave territory to the Union. President John Tyler, however, finally did annex Texas in 1845, through some constitutional legerdemain: when the Senate refused to ratify an annexation treaty with the Lone Star Republic, he persuaded Congress to accept Texas into the Union by concurrent resolution—the mechanism long used to elevate American territories to statehood.

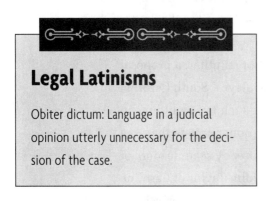

Legal Latinisms

Obiter dictum: Language in a judicial opinion utterly unnecessary for the decision of the case.

As the Mexicans had warned, the Mexican War (1846–1848) soon followed. Its importance for us here is that even before the war had been won, Pennsylvania congressman David Wilmot proposed legislation barring slavery from any territory wrested from Mexico. Congress could not decide whether to accept Wilmot's idea. South Carolinian John C. Calhoun had seen this coming and had opposed the Mexican War because he feared that disputes over slavery in the new territories would destroy the Union.

Henry Clay managed to paper over the differences for a moment. The Compromise of 1850 (the year Calhoun died) immediately admitted California to the Union as a free state, but also included a new fugitive slave law, which gave teeth to the Constitution's Fugitive Slave Clause.

Northern opposition to implementation of the Constitution's Fugitive Slave Clause had already been growing. In 1843 Vermont and Massachusetts had adopted laws nullifying the 1793 Fugitive Slave Act, and they adopted similar measures against the Fugitive Slave Act of 1850. In 1854, the Wisconsin Supreme Court followed suit in *In re Booth*. The same political interests that had opposed South Carolina's nullification of an arguably unconstitutional protective tariff now supported nullification of the Fugitive Slave Clause of the Constitution itself.

Throw into the mix the ongoing tension in Congress over settlement of the western territories and you have a powder keg of sectional hostility. Presidential ambition made it more likely that the powder keg would be lit.

In 1854, Illinois senator Stephen Douglas proposed the Kansas-Nebraska Act. It negated the Missouri Compromise's exclusion of slavery from most of the Louisiana Purchase territory and substituted what Douglas called "popular sovereignty." Douglas, a Democrat who needed Southern support, adopted the Jeffersonian principle of home rule: the people in Kansas and Nebraska should decide the slavery issue for themselves.

President Franklin Pierce (a great-uncle of Barbara Bush) signed the Kansas-Nebraska Act into law. Pierce was from New Hampshire, but the act was immediately unpopular in the North and was responsible for the founding in 1854 of today's Republican Party.

Originally, the Republican Party was a single-issue party opposed to slavery's expansion. In 1856 it nominated a virtual political unknown, John C. Frémont, for president. The Democrats countered with James Buchanan, who had been governor of Pennsylvania, a senator, a cabinet member, and a minister to Britain. Buchanan won—narrowly.

Dred Scott v. Sandford

This, then, was the political milieu in which the most significant of Chief Justice Taney's rulings, in political terms, would be made. From Buchanan's point of view, as from the intensely partisan Taney's, something had to be done about the slavery issue. Republicans had made no pretense of appealing to the entire country; they were frankly anti-Southern, they had nominated a nobody for president against an extremely qualified Democrat—and they had almost won. Buchanan and Taney feared the Republicans might destroy the Democratic Party and the Union.

President-elect Buchanan and Chief Justice Taney engaged in extensive correspondence about the issue. Taney thought he had a solution. If the pending case of *Dred Scott v. Sandford* were decided in the "right" way, it could resolve the issue once and for all. Besides agreeing that this must happen, Buchanan and Taney also lobbied the other Democrats on the Supreme Court extensively to secure this outcome. They succeeded, but the results were devastating.

Dred Scott was a slave. He had been taken into free territory by his master and then returned to his home state of Missouri. He sued in federal court to establish that he was a free man because of his sojourn in free territory. Under Missouri case law, Scott was entitled to his freedom. In the context of the growing turmoil over slavery, however, the top Missouri court reversed the lower court's ruling freeing Scott.

Scott brought his appeal under the federal courts' diversity of citizenship jurisdiction. That is, he claimed that he was a citizen of one state, his owner (by now living in New York) a citizen of another, and so the federal courts were empowered to hear the dispute between them. The Supreme Court ultimately denied that Scott's assertions about citizenship were true.

Why? Because Scott was black. According to Taney, there had been a consensus in the country at the time of the Constitution's adoption that black people had "no rights that a white man is bound to respect," and thus the makers of the Constitution had not intended to allow blacks to become citizens of the United States. They could be citizens of particular states, he said, but not of the United States. Thus, Scott was not entitled to bring a federal appeal under the federal courts' diversity jurisdiction.

Now, if Taney had simply, at the beginning, denied that the case fell under the federal courts' jurisdiction, that would have been that. Since they have only limited jurisdiction, federal courts typically begin by asking whether they have jurisdiction over a particular case, then close the books if they don't. But Taney's primary interest was to make a political point and help the Democratic Party, so although he had already concluded that the Court had no jurisdiction, he took up other issues surrounding the case.

Taney wrote that Scott remained a slave because Congress had no power to exclude slavery from federal territory. Slaves were property protected by the Constitution, and to prohibit citizens from taking them into federal territory was a violation of the Fifth Amendment's prohibition of deprivation of property without due process of law. The provision of the Missouri Compromise purporting to exclude slavery from the remaining portion of the Louisiana Purchase north of Missouri's southern border was therefore unconstitutional.

Taney also pointed out that the status of a person like Scott in Missouri was entirely a matter of Missouri law. If Missouri considered him to be a slave, a slave he was. This was not a federal issue.

For some reason, Buchanan and Taney expected this decision to quiet the roiling waters of American slavery politics. Among other things, *Dred Scott* had declared the Republicans' platform—"no slavery in the territories"—unconstitutional. So, they thought, there would be no further Frémont scares for hyper-qualified Democratic presidential nominees like Buchanan.

In dissent, however, Justice Benjamin Curtis had a field day with Taney's opinion (which, it should be noted, did not command a majority among his colleagues in all its particulars). Among other things, he said, "When a strict interpretation of the Constitution, according to the fixed rules which govern the interpretation of laws, is abandoned, and the theoretical opinions of individuals are allowed to control its meaning, we have no longer a Constitution; we are under the government of individual men, who for the time being have power to declare what the Constitution is, according to their own views of what it ought to mean."

Does Justice Curtis's lament in dissent that the Court is not relying on "a strict interpretation of the Constitution, according to the fixed rules which govern the interpretation of laws" sound familiar?

Before 1857 passed into the history books, *Dred Scott* was joined by two other notable events in sparking northern anti-Democratic outrage.

First, President Buchanan reneged on his pledge to give Douglas's popular sovereignty formula a fair trial in Kansas. Instead, he threw his weight behind the Lecompton Constitution, which pro-slavery forces had adopted through a transparently corrupt process. As a result, Douglas—the leading Democrat in the Senate—broke with Buchanan.

Second, South Carolina congressman Preston Brooks used a cane to beat Massachusetts senator Charles Sumner silly on the Senate floor, for the crime of viciously mocking South Carolina senator Andrew Butler. Northern newspapers, clergymen, and others responded with outrage, while Brooks received a supply of fresh canes from across the South—including one from students at the University of Virginia inscribed "Hit Him Again!"

One legacy of *Dred Scott v. Sandford* was that after 1857, virtually any Republican candidate was sure to beat Buchanan for president in 1860—which would almost certainly mean the dissolution of the Union. Republicans, despite their advantages, opted not to nominate one of their established statesmen, but chose instead someone nearly as obscure as their 1856 candidate had been: Abraham Lincoln.

Chapter Seven

〜✦〜✦〜

THE WAR FOR SOUTHERN INDEPENDENCE AS A CONSTITUTIONAL CRISIS

The Republican platform of 1860 was anathema to Southerners. It called for a high protective tariff, it opposed the *Dred Scott* decision, and it implicitly raised the question of how federalism could survive a federal administration hostile to the South.

As a politician in the 1850s, Lincoln had said excluding slavery from the United States' western territories was the first step to abolishing it everywhere. Further, he said that the deportation of all blacks from the United States would be a "glorious consummation."

Southerners feared that a Republican president would circulate anti-slavery literature among southern slaves, refuse to enforce the Fugitive Slave Law, bar slavery from the territories, and generally make their situation very dangerous. Not a single southern state had voted for Lincoln, and between his election in 1860 and his inauguration in 1861, the seven Deep South states seceded from the Union.

The seceding states justified their actions chiefly on the basis that the northern states were unwilling to comply with the Constitution—and thus were a threat to slavery in the South. South Carolina, following Calhoun's teaching and the example of 1832's Nullification Convention, seceded through exactly the same type of convention as had ratified the Constitution in the first place. In the spirit of the Declaration of Independence, the

Guess what?

🪶 Republicans argued that secession was impossible—but then set conditions (ratifying the Fourteenth Amendment) before allowing the Southern states back into a Union they allegedly had never left!

🪶 The Fourteenth Amendment was never constitutionally proposed to the states by Congress and never constitutionally ratified by the states, and yet today it stands as one of the most significant parts of the American legal system.

people had decided that the federal government was not protecting their rights, and so they were reclaiming their powers from it.

Other Deep South states seceded in different ways, including referendum and legislative enactment. Some, such as Virginia, convened secession conventions and decided, for the moment, not to secede.

Then, shortly after his inauguration, Lincoln declared a blockade of southern ports. Under the law of nations, only a country could be blockaded, which raises the question of whether Lincoln was implicitly recognizing the Confederacy's independence. He next called for volunteers to invade the states of the Deep South and force them back into the Union. At that point, Virginia's secession convention reconvened and opted to secede, as did Arkansas, Tennessee, and North Carolina.

Initially, many northerners conceded the validity of secession. In fact, some abolitionists had been calling for northern secession for years. In Congress, several congressmen from northern states proposed amendments to limit the right of secession, de facto conceding that the right of secession already existed. And, logically, it had to exist, because without such a right, the American colonies/states could not have seceded from the British Empire.

The Federalists always insisted during the ratification debates—knowing they had to in order to win approval for the Constitution—that the states were individual parties to a federal compact. Spelling out the logic of the compact, three states—Virginia, New York, and Rhode Island—explicitly reserved (in the act of ratifying the Constitution) their right to secede from the Union. And one can easily deduce a right to secession from the language of the Tenth Amendment: because the Constitution does not prohibit secession, that power, like all the other "powers not delegated to the United States by the Constitution, nor prohibited by it to the states," is "reserved to the states."

Yet, in his inaugural address, Abraham Lincoln called secession an impossibility. Representative Otis S. Ferry of Connecticut must have been surprised at this, as he had only weeks before proposed an amendment to the Constitution forbidding secession without the consent of Congress, the president, and the other states. Still, Lincoln said that states could not secede.

In response to opponents of his war measures, Lincoln suspended the writ of habeas corpus—the ancient English protection against arbitrary arrest and imprisonment. Article I of the Constitution empowers Congress to suspend access to the writ in times of emergency, but Lincoln acted as both legislator and executive (as he had when he called for volunteers for a war Congress had not yet agreed to fund). In *Federalist* 47 James Madison had written that "the accumulation of all powers, legislative, executive, and judiciary, in the same hands, whether of one, a few, or many, and whether hereditary, self-appointed, or elective, may justly be pronounced the very definition of tyranny."

Lincoln used the arbitrary power he had thus granted himself to muzzle opposition, whether in the form of critical newspapers, Democratic politicians, or potentially unfriendly state legislatures, in numerous ways. In Maryland, this took the form of imprisoning state legislators who disagreed with him. In one particularly notorious case, *Ex parte Vallandigham*, a prominent Ohio politician, Clement Vallandigham, was expelled from the United States—banished to the Confederacy—because of his criticism of Lincoln's conduct.

Vallandigham's precise words were that the "present war is a wicked, cruel, and unnecessary war, one not waged for the preservation of the Union, but for the purpose of crushing out liberty and to erect a despotism." He was arrested by a military commission despite the fact that he was not a member of the armed forces and not in a war zone, and he asked the nearest Supreme Court justice for a writ of habeas corpus. He was rebuffed, because to grant such a request would be to "embarrass or thwart" President Lincoln.

Taney examines "the very definition of tyranny"

Chief Justice Taney became involved in the habeas corpus controversy in *Ex parte Merryman* (1861). The case centered on Lieutenant John Merryman, who served in the Maryland cavalry and allegedly sympathized with secessionists in his home state. As part of the Lincoln administration's crackdown on dissent, he was arrested.

Chief Justice Taney issued a writ of habeas corpus and tried to have it served, but the generals involved in the case said that the public interest required that Merryman be kept under arrest. Taney tried to force the issue. He ruled that Merryman should be released and he denounced the president's exercise, through his generals, of arbitrary authority and unconstitutional power. Only Congress could suspend the writ of habeas corpus, he thundered, not the president. (Indeed, the power to suspend the writ is in Article I, the legislative article, of the Constitution. It would make no sense for the executive to be able to suspend the writ, which is a protection against arbitrariness in the executive branch.)

Lincoln's Doublespeak

Lincoln's blockade of southern ports introduced an interesting constitutional question: according to the law of nations, blockades were allowed only between warring countries. Lincoln insisted that the Confederacy was not a country, but a rebel region—so was he violating international law or recognizing Confederate independence? Neither outcome would have been very good for him, so the Supreme Court handily rescued him in 1862 by deciding that the Confederacy was a foreign country in regard to blockades, but a rebellious region in all other respects!

Taney noted of Lincoln that, in suspending the writ, he had exercised legislative power, and in arresting and punishing Merryman without due process, he had exercised judicial power. Merryman could as easily have been brought to trial before a federal court in Baltimore. As Taney saw things, "if the authority which the constitution has confided to the judicial department and judicial officers, may thus, upon any pretext or under any circumstances, be usurped by the military power, at its discretion, the people of the United States are no longer living under a government of laws but every citizen holds life, liberty and property at the will and pleasure of the army officer in whose military district he may happen to be found." But he could not enforce his ruling, he said, in the face of a military force "too strong for me to overcome."

The *Chicago Tribune* and the *New York Tribune* both criticized Taney as a foolish old man. The latter wrote that he "takes sides with traitors" and hoped that Taney would not have to be arrested. The *Washington Evening Star* opined that Taney had been correct as to the law, but had ignored the state of things. The law, it seems, was very inconvenient to the Republican administration. And no one, apparently, could enforce the law. When the House of Representatives asked for information on people who were being held without access to habeas corpus, Lincoln simply refused.

Taney, of course, was a Maryland Democrat, opposed to the Lincoln administration. Privately, the chief justice hoped that North and South would negotiate "a peaceful separation with free institutions in each section" instead of "the union of all the present states under a military government & a reign of terror." But whatever his personal opinions, no one has ever been able persuasively to argue that Taney was not upholding the Constitution or that Lincoln was not violating it.

Lincoln responded to Taney's order by explaining to Congress that he had empowered generals throughout the country to suspend the writ of habeas corpus as necessary. He asked, "Are all the laws, but one to go unexecuted, and the government itself go to pieces, lest that one be violated?" His implicit answer was "no," and so he would decide from time to time which particular laws to ignore and which constitutional provisions to violate in his quest to subjugate the Confederacy.

In taking this approach, Lincoln established what would become an enduring pattern of presidential behavior. What made Chief Justice Taney different from most of his wartime successors on the Supreme Court was his determination to enforce constitutional limitations on wartime executive power.

Lincoln also early proclaimed a blockade of southern ports. This step involved some difficulty, both constitutional and diplomatic. Diplomatically, the law of nations of the day allowed blockades only between warring countries, and yet Lincoln insisted that the southern Confederacy was not a country, but a rebel region. So was Lincoln violating international law, or was he recognizing Confederate independence? Not to worry: in the *Prize Cases* (1862), the Supreme Court held that the Confederacy was a foreign country when it came to blockades, but a rebellious region for all other purposes! Here the Supreme Court effectively abdicated its role of (as John Marshall put it) declaring "what the law is" in favor of John Jay's theory that the judges should work toward the success of the administration.

Constitutionally, Lincoln here once again was acting as Chief Legislator. No one argued that declaring blockades was not a legislative function. But then, no branch of the federal government was determined to hold Lincoln to the law (although a minority of four justices did say in the *Prize Cases* that the blockade had not been legal until Congress made it so).

Republicans, angry with Taney over *Dred Scott* and *Merryman* and not particularly interested in the rule of law, discussed abolishing the Supreme Court and establishing a new one. In 1862 they expanded the Court to ten members. Between 1860 and 1863, three Taney allies on the Court departed (one resigned and two died). When Taney died in 1864, the Supreme Court effectively became Lincoln's Court.

Before he died Taney had drafted memoranda showing that federal conscription and the federal government's issuance of paper money were both unconstitutional (neither power is listed in the Constitution). But he never had the opportunity to act on his memoranda.

The Emancipation Proclamation

Of course, the most astounding constitutional innovation Lincoln made was his Emancipation Proclamation of 1863. By that act, which he justified on the basis of his war powers as president, Lincoln abolished slavery—but only in those portions of the Confederacy not occupied by the Union.

Patrick Henry had predicted in the Richmond Ratification Convention of 1788 that a president would someday invade Virginia, burn down delegates' houses, declare it a military necessity, and free the slaves. Even now, more than 140 years since it actually came to pass as Henry predicted, this prognostication is treated as demagogic scare-mongering in most accounts of the Richmond Convention and most biographies of Henry and James Madison.

Indeed, it was an outlandish claim. Who would have thought that an American president would do such a thing? After all, Lincoln had no constitutional warrant for it whatsoever—only what he called his "inherent powers," a term broad enough to cover almost any wartime behavior. The Court never ruled on the constitutionality of the Emancipation Proclamation, and the issue became moot after the ratification of the Thirteenth Amendment, which the southern states (except Mississippi) were coerced into "ratifying" at the end of the war.

The sum of Lincoln's constitutionalism seems to have been "whatever I favor is constitutional." He waged a war to prove the impossibility of secession, yet he supported secession in 1863 when he recognized the western—pro-Union—counties of Virginia as the new state of West Virginia. He did the latter despite the Constitution, which requires a state's consent before a new state can be formed from its territory.

In an essay on the Confederacy, journalist H. L. Mencken noted that it was the South that was fighting for "government of the people, by the people, for the people." He could have added that the southern states had a higher regard for the Constitution than did the president who forcibly returned them to the Union.

The "reconstruction" of the Constitution

After the war, the North occupied the southern states with the intent of "reconstructing" them on a submissive line. Lincoln hoped to incorporate the southern states into his remade United States as quickly as possible. So as the Federal armies brought wide swaths of the Confederacy under Union control, he favored leniency in allowing former Confederate officers to vote and hold office. He tried to persuade southerners of his conciliatory intentions by running on a Union (not a Republican) ticket in 1864 with Tennessee Democrat Andrew Johnson as his running mate.

Lincoln's assassination at the end of the war made Johnson president. Johnson immediately antagonized the Republican Congress (which didn't like him anyway) by pardoning high-ranking and wealthy Confederates. He vetoed the Civil Rights Act of 1866 as a violation of states' rights (on the grounds that contracts, real estate transactions, and access to courts had always been within states' rights to regulate, and nothing had happened to change that).

Republicans in Congress responded with the Fourteenth Amendment. Here we have a budding revolution in American constitutional government—if indeed it can still be called that. The Fourteenth Amendment was ultimately "ratified" in 1868, according to the official version. In reality, as eminent constitutional historian Professor Forrest McDonald has demonstrated, the Fourteenth Amendment was never ratified at all.

Under Article V of the Constitution, three-fourths of the states must ratify any constitutional amendment. It is taken for granted, of course, that the states would be acting free from coercion. If Iran suddenly conquered the United States and compelled three-fourths of the states to adopt an amendment making Muslim sharia law the law of the land, that amendment would, of course, be invalid. But something very similar to this outlandish scenario happened with the Fourteenth Amendment.

Legal Latinisms

Habeas corpus: Latin for "you have the body." The primary function of a writ of habeas corpus is to release someone from unlawful imprisonment. It directs the person holding a prisoner to either justify the detention to a court or release him.

The northern Republicans who dominated Congress refused to seat southern congressmen on the grounds that the southern states had not been properly "reconstructed" yet (and had elected Democrats). By seceding from the Union, the Republicans argued, the southern states had ceased to exist as states. President Johnson countered that excluding southerners from Congress meant that there was no valid Congress at all. If Lincoln was right that secession was impossible, then the southern states did not secede because they could not secede; an amendment proposed by a Congress representing twenty-five states could therefore not constitutionally be ratified to bind the thirty-six-state Union. Besides that, Nevada and West Virginia, admitted to the Union during the war, had not been constitutionally admitted as states.

The Senate vote on the Fourteenth Amendment was thirty-three votes in favor to eleven opposed, with five abstentions (and one senator who voted nay didn't have his vote counted because he was ejected from the chamber on a majority vote of the Senate—an expulsion that should have required a two-thirds vote). The four senators from West Virginia and Nevada voted aye. If one subtracts these four dubious votes and adds twenty-two nay votes from the excluded southern states, the Fourteenth Amendment did not even have majority support in the Senate.

As the amendment wended its way toward "ratification," three northern states that had ratified it rescinded their ratifications. In the South, every state except Tennessee at first voted not to ratify, then changed their votes under congressional threat. Only Mississippi held out.

In Tennessee, when opponents of the Fourteenth Amendment absented themselves from the state house—in order to deny proponents a quorum—two absent members were arrested. They secured a court order that they be released pursuant to a writ of habeas corpus, but the House ignored the writ, held them in a cloakroom, overruled the House Speaker's decision that they were not present, and voted to ratify the amendment.

In Oregon, the Republicans had a clear majority in the Senate but only a narrow one in the state's House of Representatives. Two Republican representatives whose elections had been challenged were seated, and they accounted for the margin of ratification. Their seats were later awarded to Democrats, and ratification was rescinded.

By the time the first southern states took up the matter, five northern states had "ratified." Texas led the way among southern states: the Texas Senate voted no by twenty-seven to one, and the House joined in by seventy to five. Two weeks later, Georgia's Senate voted no unanimously; its House had only two aye votes. Florida, Arkansas, and the Carolinas joined in by similar—or even greater—margins. (In Florida, both houses were unanimous in rejecting the amendment.)

California's governor refused to call a special session to consider the matter. Virginia, Alabama, Mississippi, Louisiana, Kentucky, and Delaware all added their votes to the nay column. Maryland followed next. Ohio and New Jersey would soon rescind their ratifications.

In March 1867, Congress used the Reconstruction Act to extort ratification of the Fourteenth Amendment. State ratification of the Fourteenth Amendment, Congress declared, must precede readmission of the states to the Union; until that had been achieved, there were "no legal state governments" in the South. Oddly, this pronouncement applied even to the six former Confederate states whose votes had counted toward ratification of the Thirteenth Amendment. It also overturned Lincoln's entire rationale for the war—that the southern states had never actually seceded, because they could not do so. Congress now said that they had seceded, which meant that the "civil war" had really been a war of conquest against a foreign country (the Confederacy), and Congress could now set the terms by which the Confederacy's states could be forcibly returned to the Union.

Meanwhile, in *Ex parte Milligan* (1866), the Supreme Court greatly restricted the ability of the executive branch to enforce its will in wartime. Lambdin P. Milligan had been charged with conspiring to seize federal munitions and to free Confederate prisoners. Justice David Davis, for the unanimous Court, said that the Constitution was not suspended in wartime, but applied "equally in time of war and peace." Thus trials before military commissions such as Milligan had received in Indiana— well behind Union lines, well away from the war zone—fell afoul of the Constitution's requirements that suspects be indicted before trial and that they be tried publicly before juries so long as civilian courts were functioning.

The relevance of this decision to the ratification of the Fourteenth Amendment lies in its recognition that the chief executive is not empowered by the Constitution to extort whatever he wants from the citizenry or the states. Just calling a state a military district (as the southern states were designated by the federal government) did not give Republicans carte blanche to dub the Constitution "amended." President Johnson, for his part, called Congress's action—forcing southern approval of the

Fourteenth Amendment by putting congressional representation at risk—an unconstitutional bill of attainder (declaring someone guilty without a trial) against the nine million people living in the southern states. It was more than that. As Wisconsin senator James Doolittle put it, "The people of the South have rejected the constitutional amendment," so the North would "march upon them and force them to adopt it at the point of the bayonet." They would remain under military dictatorship, Doolittle said, "until they do adopt it."

The South Was Right

The southern states had every right to secede in 1860–1861. In fact, Virginia, Maryland, and Rhode Island had ratified the Constitution on the explicit understanding that they could withdraw from it.

Milligan asked the Supreme Court to block Congress's political blackmail, and the Court replied that before any court issued a ruling, "the rights in danger...must be rights of persons or property, not merely political rights, which do not belong to the jurisdiction of a court."

And so the Fourteenth Amendment was "ratified." As Forrest McDonald puts it, "Despairing of stopping the congressional juggernaut, ruled by military commanders who removed governors and judges at will, and swept by rumors that Congress intended to confiscate and redistribute their property (as some Radicals indeed did), the southern states began to capitulate."[1]

Arkansas voted to ratify the amendment by April 6, 1868—although it still had not been recognized by Congress as having a valid government under the 1867 act. Next came Florida, which decided, in its own words, "as dictated by the Acts of Congress as conditions precedent to admission," to ratify on June 9. Congress recognized that the Florida legislature had ratified the amendment with language different from the congressionally proposed version. But when it noticed that New York, Pennsylvania, Michigan, and Wisconsin had done the same, Congress decided to accept

Florida's ratification as valid and ignore the sometimes marked differences among the versions the states had approved!

Congress next decided, on June 25, 1868, that the remaining southern states would be entitled to statehood once they ratified the amendment. But, of course, only a state can ratify an amendment. Soon enough, North Carolina, South Carolina, Louisiana, and Alabama had "ratified." Secretary of State William H. Seward then proclaimed that the amendment had been ratified.

Thus, the Fourteenth Amendment was never constitutionally proposed to the states by Congress and never constitutionally ratified by the states, and yet today it stands (after the Constitution's structural provisions) as the most significant part of the American legal system. As we will see, when Americans think of, for example, their First Amendment rights, the supposed rights they have in mind are almost always actually their Fourteenth Amendment Due Process Clause rights—rights that come from an unratified amendment.

A case concerning the constitutionality of the Republican rump Congress's Reconstruction methods made its way to the Supreme Court in 1869. That case, *Ex parte McCardle*, arose from the military arrest of a Vicksburg, Mississippi, newspaper editor. William McCardle had dared criticize the Reconstruction Acts as unconstitutional, which was not allowed in occupied Mississippi. He requested a writ of habeas corpus of a federal court in Mississippi, which rejected his request, so he turned to the Supreme Court. Congress, fearing that its unconstitutional treatment of the South might well be struck down, at least in this particular, passed a law removing the Supreme Court's power to hear such appeals.

On the same day, in *Texas v. White*, the Court declared that the Constitution "looks to an indestructible Union, composed of indestructible states," and ruled that in fact Texas had never seceded, and that Texans had been wrong to think otherwise. The ruling was five to three, with the majority decision issued by Chief Justice Salmon P. Chase, a former

Lincoln cabinet member (who arguably should have recused himself) whose logic was less than convincing. Its constitutional basis was in Article IV's statement that "the United States shall guarantee to every State in this Union a Republican Form of Government." Allegedly this proved that the Constitution supposed "an indestructible Union." The Latin phrase for such decisions is *ipse dixit*: asserted but not proved. Chase's decision nevertheless had the force of law.

The following year, the states ratified the Fifteenth Amendment, which eliminated restrictions of the right to vote based on "race, color, or previous condition of servitude." One little-noticed but important aspect of the Fifteenth Amendment is that it effectively overturned Section 2 of the Fourteenth Amendment. That section penalized states by reducing their congressional representation if they denied people the right to vote. The Fourteenth Amendment, then, did not ban all discrimination, a distinction that will be important later.

Legal Latinisms

De facto: Latin for "in fact, indeed, actually." Used to characterize something or someone present in fact, but illegal or illegitimate.

The Court's first pass at interpreting the Fourteenth Amendment came in the *Slaughterhouse Cases* of 1873. The issue before the Court was the extent to which the Fourteenth Amendment had remade American federalism; its decision was "not much."

The appellants in the case were white butchers from the area around New Orleans, Louisiana. As Ronald M. Labbé and Jonathan Lurie make clear in *The Slaughterhouse Cases: Regulation, Reconstruction, and the Fourteenth Amendment*, the Court faced a stark choice: bring virtually every area of state lawmaking under the supervision of federal courts, or not. The justices decided not to.

The butchers claimed that a state law confining butchering to one location in the New Orleans region affected them in four negative ways:

1. It created an involuntary servitude in violation of the Thirteenth Amendment.

2. It deprived them of "privileges or immunities of citizens of the United States" in violation of Section 1 of the Fourteenth Amendment.

3. It denied them the equal protection of the laws in violation of Section 1 of the Fourteenth Amendment.

4. It deprived them of property without due process of law despite Section 1 of the Fourteenth Amendment.

The Court easily rejected the idea that the butchers' plight resembled slavery, so the state law itself did not violate the Thirteenth Amendment. But when it came to allegedly violating the butchers' "privileges or immunities of citizens of the United States," the Court noted that the Fourteenth Amendment retained a distinction between state and federal citizenship, and thus deduced that not all rights enjoyed by Americans were rights they had as citizens of the United States; some areas of law were still provinces of the several states. The Court recognized that to call a right "federal" would mean that the power of the federal courts over the states would expand. Surprisingly, the Court limited its supervisory power.

Here, the Court was helped by circuit court justice Bushrod Washington's decision in *Corfield v. Coryell* (1823). Washington had said (and here he did not innovate in any way) that the rights of state citizenship included "protection by the government, with the right to acquire and possess property of every kind, and to pursue and obtain happiness and safety, subject, nevertheless, to such restraints as the [state] government may prescribe for the general good."

In *Slaughterhouse*, the Court asked, "Was it the purpose of the Fourteenth Amendment, by the simple declaration that no State should make or enforce any law which shall abridge the privileges and immunities of *citizens of the United States* [emphasis in the original], to transfer the security and protection of all the civil rights which we have mentioned, from the States to the Federal government? Such a construction...would constitute this court a perpetual censor upon all legislation of the States."

In general, legal academics despise the *Slaughterhouse* decision because they *do* think the federal courts should be "a perpetual censor upon all legislation of the States." The Supreme Court of 1873, however, was more restrained. The specifically federal rights covered by the Fourteenth Amendment's category of "privileges or immunities of citizens of the United States," it decreed, were few. The Court identified the right to travel to the federal capital, the right to seek federal government protection, the right to work for the federal government, the right to use American ports, the right to federal protection when traveling on the high seas, and other rights of a similar nature as rights of federal citizenship.

It also rejected the idea that the Fourteenth Amendment's Due Process Clause (which gave federal courts the power to enforce due process requirements against the states) applied to the butchers' claim. The Court noted that the Due Process Clause was intended to protect the freedmen in former slave states against arbitrary action by state governments, adding, "We doubt very much whether any action of a State not directed by way of discrimination against the negroes as a class, or on account of their race, will ever be held to come within the purview of this provision. It is so clearly a provision for that race and that emergency, that a strong case would be necessary for its application to any other."

The justices who dissented from the Court's majority ruling said that the Privileges or Immunities Clause was supposed to apply to all the rights of citizens of free governments, and one dissenting justice said that the butchers had indeed been deprived of property without due process. Though the dissenters lost the day, their time would come, as future

Courts gladly used the Fourteenth Amendment to claim a capacious national judicial authority.

Three years later, in *Munn v. Illinois* (1876), the Court upheld an Illinois law establishing maximum storage rates in grain warehouses in Chicago and certain other places as consistent with the Fourteenth Amendment's Due Process Clause. The Court said that while the Due Process Clause protected private property, the warehouses in question ceased to be strictly private when they were "devote[d]...to a use in which the public has an interest."

Soon, however, the public's interest would be determined less often by elected state legislatures and more often by unelected federal judges.

Chapter Eight

THE PRO-SEGREGATION SUPREME COURT

The Supreme Court of the 1870s took a surprisingly Jacksonian view of the Constitution. It had announced in *Texas v. White* (1869) that the Union was permanent, as Jackson had insisted in nullification days, and it then refused in the *Slaughterhouse Cases* of 1873 to use the new Fourteenth Amendment to expand the Court's power radically.

But the Court did enforce the amendment. In *Strauder v. West Virginia* (1879), the Court confronted a case in which a black man had been found guilty by an all-white jury (only whites were allowed to sit on juries in West Virginia) of murdering his wife with a hatchet. The accused, Taylor Strauder, was clearly guilty, but he appealed the verdict under the Equal Protection Clause of the Fourteenth Amendment, claiming that the clause entitled him to a jury that included black jurors.

The Court said that the real question was not whether a defendant had a right to a jury that included members of his race, but whether members of his race could be excluded from the jury pool.

The Fourteenth Amendment's purpose, the Court said, was "securing to a race recently emancipated, a race that through many generations had been held in slavery, all the civil rights that the superior race enjoy." In other words, it said, blacks had under the Fourteenth Amendment "the right to exemption from unfriendly legislation against them distinctively

Guess what?

- The Fourteenth Amendment was meant to apply only to newly freed blacks, not to other categories of people, but the Supreme Court quickly expanded it to cover non-citizen residents and even corporations.

- The Supreme Court's first segregation decision held that Louisiana could not bar segregation.

- The Supreme Court ruled that the income tax was unconstitutional.

139

as colored—exemption from legal discriminations, implying inferiority in civil society, lessening the security of their enjoyment of the rights which others enjoy."

The West Virginia statute concerning all-white juries was therefore in violation of the Fourteenth Amendment and was struck down. The Fourteenth Amendment's purpose was to prevent "discrimination because of race or color"; it did not apply to qualifications based on sex, property, citizenship, age, or educational attainments, which might legitimately be applied to potential jurors.

"Instrumentalities of the state"? Sounds like socialism to me

The Court remained loyal to the view of the Fourteenth Amendment established in *Slaughterhouse* and *Strauder* in its most significant nineteenth-century decision about it: the *Civil Rights Cases* of 1883. The cases concerned the Civil Rights Act of 1875: "an Act to protect all citizens in their civil and legal rights."

The act would have taken many areas of public policy reserved by the Constitution's framers and ratifiers exclusively to the states and given supreme authority over them to the federal government. Among other things, the act extended to "all persons within the jurisdiction of the United States" protection of their purported right of access to "inns, public conveyances . . . , theaters, and other places of public amusement." And it was on these grounds that the act was contested: does Congress have constitutional authority to make laws about private decisions regarding access to hotels, theaters, and the women's car on a train? Congress claimed that its power to adopt the Civil Rights Act flowed from the Fourteenth Amendment.

But the Court held that the Fourteenth Amendment did not give Congress such sweeping powers. The Court ruled that the Fourteenth Amendment banned "State action of a particular character," not the private actions of hotel owners or theater operators. The Fourteenth Amendment did not give Congress the power to force individuals or businesses to allow equal access to their private property. ("The prohibitions of the amendment," the Court majority said, "are against State laws and acts done under State authority.") Nor could the act be justified under the Thirteenth Amendment, because private decisions denying people access to inns, railroad cars, or theaters did not amount to slavery.

As Section 1 of the Fourteenth Amendment says that "No State shall" deprive anyone of the privileges or immunities of U.S. citizens, "nor shall any State deprive anyone of life, liberty, or property, without due process of law; nor deny to any person within its jurisdiction the equal protection of the laws," there can be little doubt that the Court was right: the Fourteenth Amendment was designed to prevent state governments from discriminating against blacks, not empower Congress to open private facilities to them.

The Court did not stop with mere textual analysis, although that was convincing enough. Instead, as in the *Slaughterhouse Cases*, it asked what would happen to the federal system if it ruled the other way. Such a holding, it said, would grant enormous new powers to Congress and would be "repugnant to the Tenth Amendment of the Constitution."

This ruling seems self-evidently true, but the majority of history professors, law professors, and judges won't tell you that. They'll all refer you to the dissenting opinion entered by Justice John Marshall Harlan.

Harlan argued that the Court's majority opinion was merely "a subtle and ingenious verbal criticism." Private decisions denying people access to public accommodations were "badges of slavery and servitude," he said, and thus could be banned by Congress under the Thirteenth Amendment.

Turning to the Fourteenth Amendment, Harlan said that its extension of state citizenship to blacks guaranteed them "exemption from race discrimination in respect of any civil right belonging to citizens of the white race in the same State." Even if the Fourteenth Amendment did not extend to completely private acts, Harlan continued, all the private organizations—"railroad corporations, keepers of inns, and managers of places of public amusement"—amounted to "agents or instrumentalities of the State . . . because they [we]re amenable to governmental regulation."

Consider that claim again: Harlan reasoned that anyone "amenable to governmental regulation" was, because the government could regulate him, an "agent or instrumentality of" the state government. Is there any area of life in which twenty-first-century Americans are not subjected to "governmental regulation"? If not, they are all "instrumentalities of the State" in everything they do, by Harlan's reasoning.

Harlan's opinion was, thank goodness, a minority opinion at the time. But it would not remain so.

Segregation is in the eye of the beholder

The Court's evident interest in limiting the postwar amendments' effect on the federal system also manifested itself in a case not well known today. In *Hall v. DeCuir* (1877), its first segregation decision, the Court said that states could not bar segregation in passenger ships on the Mississippi River. Think about that: the Supreme Court's first segregation decision held that Louisiana *could not bar* segregation. As the ships in the case traveled between Mississippi and Louisiana, the commerce was interstate—thus, the Court said, under Congress's exclusive control. Therefore, a state could not require a ship to offer integrated facilities to any of its passengers, even those who traveled solely within one state. A concurring justice defended what later would be dubbed the "separate but equal" doctrine upholding local racial custom against state legislation.

The Supreme Court revisited the question of disparate treatment of the races in the famous 1896 case *Plessy v. Ferguson*. That case involved segregation in railroad cars, a practice that had come to be nearly universal in the former Confederate states.

Homer Plessy, a black man, entered a segregated railroad car with the intention of challenging the 1890 Louisiana state law requiring segregation of such cars. He claimed that exclusion on the basis of his race deprived him of the equal protection of the laws guaranteed by Section 1 of the Fourteenth Amendment. The Court disagreed.

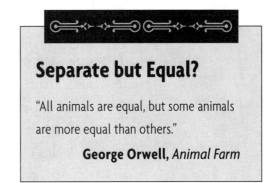

Separate but Equal?

"All animals are equal, but some animals are more equal than others."

George Orwell, *Animal Farm*

"The object of the amendment," the Court said, "was undoubtedly to enforce the absolute equality of the two races before the law, but in the nature of things it could not have been intended to abolish distinctions based upon color, or to enforce social, as distinguished from political equality, or a commingling of the two races upon terms unsatisfactory to either."

Note the distinction the Court here made: legal or "political" equality was not the same as "social" equality. It continued:

> Laws permitting, and even requiring, their separation . . . do not necessarily imply the inferiority of either race to the other, and have been generally . . . recognized as within the competency of the state legislatures in the exercise of their police power. The most common instance of this is connected with the establishment of separate schools for white and colored children, which has been held to be a valid exercise of the legislative power even by courts of States where the political rights of the colored race have been longest and most earnestly enforced.

In plain English, the Court was saying that equality before the law, which the Equal Protection Clause required states to respect, was not a generalized equality. It did not include social equality. Segregation of the races by legislation was permissible, as was demonstrated by the fact that even in Boston, Massachusetts—the most pro-black jurisdiction in the country—public schools were segregated. The Fourteenth Amendment must be understood as having a limited reach, in other words, because everyone knows that public schools can be segregated without violating it.

Having made this distinction, the Court then asserted its right to judge the Louisiana segregation statute by a "reasonableness" standard. You may wonder where in the Constitution the Court is given the power to judge state statutes on the basis of "reasonableness." The answer is "nowhere." But the Court claimed to find it in the Due Process Clause of the Fourteenth Amendment.

The Court proclaimed that if it deemed a state law "unreasonable," it would "strike it down." In other words, the Court was assuming a veto power over "unreasonable" state laws. One might have thought that the question of "reasonableness" belonged to elected state legislatures and the people who elected them. It was one of the ratifiers' fundamental principles that Americans should resolve disputes about what is reasonable through elections. They did not expect judges to take over the role of King George. But the Court assumed that government by judiciary is preferable to government by legislators, a breathtaking arrogation of power by an institution that owes its existence to a Constitution ratified by state ratification conventions.

In its "reasonableness" review in *Plessy v. Ferguson*, moreover, the Court delivered itself of one of the great "constitutional" howlers of all time. Louisiana's segregation law was reasonable, it concluded, because the Louisiana legislature was free to consider "established usages, cus-

Doesn't Sound Reasonable to Me

By the Court's "reasonableness" standard, segregation is reasonable—and so is the rule of judges rather than elected officials.

toms and traditions of the people, and . . . the promotion of their comfort . . . and the preservation of the public peace and good order." If blacks believed segregation was an insult and an attempt to enforce white superiority, "it is not by reason of anything found in the act, but solely because the coloured race chooses to put that construction upon it."

Elsewhere in its opinion, the majority noted that Congress had segregated the public schools in the District of Columbia without objection. This policy shed light on the proper understanding of the Equal Protection Clause.

Once again in dissent, Justice John Marshall Harlan issued a ringing objection. "The Constitution of the United States does not, I think, permit any public authority to know the race of those entitled to be protected in the enjoyment of [civil rights, common to all citizens]," he insisted. He decried the disjunction between the majority's statement that the stigma associated with segregation was only in black people's minds and the reality that laws like the Louisiana railroad segregation statute had been adopted "not so much to exclude white persons from railroad cars occupied by blacks, as to exclude colored people from coaches occupied by or assigned to white persons." He then asked, perhaps rhetorically, why a state entitled to segregate railroad cars might not as easily segregate various other areas of life.

Justice Harlan noted that everyone would agree that Chinese people might properly be segregated, but they were different from blacks. This offhand observation did not reflect a generalized Supreme Court hostility to Asians, however, as had been demonstrated by the Court's decision in *Yick Wo v. Hopkins* (1886). In that case, the Court—taking an approach very similar to the one it had taken in *Strauder*—vindicated the claim of a Chinese resident of California.

Yick Wo involved San Francisco city ordinances regulating the laundry business. San Francisco allowed city supervisors to determine (allegedly for reasons of safety) what wooden buildings could be used as laundries. By the time Yick Wo took the matter to court, the supervisors had denied all of the approximately two hundred applications by Chinese to run laundries, but had granted all but one of approximately eighty applications by non-Chinese. Yick Wo was already running a laundry business and refused to pay a fine for not abiding by the city supervisors' regulations. So he was thrown in jail, as were other Chinese laundry owners, and subsequently petitioned for a writ of habeas corpus.

In its opinion, the Court said that the protection of the Fourteenth Amendment was not confined to citizens of the United States (many of the Chinese in San Francisco, including Yick Wo, were not citizens), that enforcement of the ordinance was blatantly discriminatory, and that the Court had the right to strike down such abuses of power by local authorities. The Court then ordered Yick Wo and his fellow laundry men released from prison.

Supreme logic: A corporation is like a freed slave

In that same year of 1886 the Court also heard arguments in *Santa Clara County v. Southern Pacific Railroad Co.* The historic decision in this case actually happened before the ruling. The chief justice announced that the Court didn't need to hear an argument about whether a corporation was a "person" entitled to the protection of the Equal Protection Clause. The justices, he said, had already agreed that it was!

In reality, of course, the Fourteenth Amendment had nothing to do with corporations. It was directed particularly at freed slaves, but the late nineteenth-century Court favored corporations and used the Fourteenth Amendment to create the outcome it wanted.

This predilection received one of its classic expressions in *Allgeyer v. Louisiana* (1897). At issue in *Allgeyer* was a Louisiana statute that regulated insurance companies selling marine insurance in the state. In applying the Fourteenth Amendment's Due Process Clause ("nor shall any

State deprive any person of life, liberty, or property, without due process of law"), Justice Rufus W. Peckham announced:

> The liberty mentioned in [the Fourteenth Amendment] means not only the right of the citizen to be free from the mere physical restraint of his person, as by incarceration, but the term is deemed to embrace the right of the citizen to be free in the enjoyment of all his faculties; to be free to use them in all lawful ways; to live and work where he will; to earn his livelihood by any lawful calling; to pursue any livelihood or avocation, and for that purpose to enter into all contracts which may be proper, necessary and essential to his carrying out to a successful conclusion the purposes above mentioned.

As Supreme Court expert David P. Currie put it, "This, of course, is not what was provided in Magna Charta, from which the due process clause had been derived, but Peckham did not pause to justify his momentous and latitudinous interpretation; and thus liberty of contract found its way into the Constitution by bald fiat." Indeed, and apparently whatever "liberty" meant under the Fourteenth Amendment, it did not include the right of a freely elected legislature to enact laws for the public benefit under the terms of the state's constitution.

What practical effect did this "bald fiat" have in the case at hand? The Fourteenth Amendment's Due Process Clause was meant to ensure that defendants were guaranteed "due process of law." Now it was being misappropriated by the Court so the justices could sit in judgment on state statutes.

It depends on your definition of "is"

When President Bill Clinton said in his grand jury testimony, "It depends on what the meaning of the word 'is' is," he could have been trying out for a seat on the Supreme Court. The Court has always had its own artful way with words, defining travel as commerce, charters as contracts, "necessary" as not really necessary, and so on. When it comes to "due process," the Court created the idea of "types" of due process. There are "procedural due process" and "substantive due process," which really amounts to a distinction between due process as it is meant in the Fourteenth Amendment and due process as an excuse for judicial usurpation. (The Court used the Fifth Amendment's Due Process Clause the same way in *Dred Scott v. Sandford* when it ruled that the clause required Congress to allow slavery in federal territories.)

For four decades, the Supreme Court used "due process" to create a laissez-faire principle of "liberty of contract" in American "constitutional" law. One might contend that laissez-faire is a good principle, but the goodness of laissez-faire is not the issue. The question is whether Americans are to be governed by their elected officials or by unelected judges who enforce whatever "principles" happen to appeal to them at any given time.

Once the Court had undertaken to legislate in the name of "due process," it could not be expected to forever confine itself to policing the economy in the interests of laissez-faire. Power tends to corrupt, after all, and Supreme Court justices love power as much as anyone and have no lack of confidence in their own economic and moral insights.

Congress not only acquiesced in the Supreme Court's usurpation of power, but also actively encouraged its expansion (as part of the general campaign to expand the powers of the federal government). At the end of the nineteenth century, Congress began creating administrative agencies with legislative, executive, and judicial powers, and it practically begged the courts to assume legislative functions.

In 1887 Congress created the Interstate Commerce Commission. This agency, which would be responsible to no one, was to enforce an act requiring that railroad rates be "reasonable and just." Members of the five-man commission could hear complaints, audit railroads' accounts, and compel testimony. Its power to issue "cease and desist" orders to violators gave it what amounted to the power to set rates.

Did the Constitution give Congress the power to create such agencies? Certainly not. But respect for—even understanding of—such basic constitutional principles as the separation of powers had virtually vanished since the disputes over the Neutrality Proclamation of 1793 and the Alien Friends Act of 1798.

In 1890 Congress adopted the Sherman Antitrust Act. It hardly amounted to "law" at all; it was merely a license to federal courts to concoct anti–big business rules. In fact, the language of the act does not even provide clear rules for avoiding violation of it. As Professor Thomas J. DiLorenzo has pointed out, the act was pushed by farmers who didn't want to have to compete with "giant wheat farms" (what they called "land monopolies") and by other groups that wanted to regulate railroad rates. The interests behind the act help to explain its incoherent and even nonsensical nature. The real purpose of the act was to allow politicians to claim they were fighting for the average Joe while they doled out benefits to organizations with political clout—small farmers' associations, inefficient sugar producers, inefficient petroleum producers, and others— who were failing to compete with successful businesses that were growing rapidly and lowering prices.

TR and Taft Go Trust-Busting

The Sherman Antitrust Act was utilized most vigorously in the early 1900s by Presidents Theodore Roosevelt and William Taft, who crusaded against such "trusts" as the Northern Securities Company, Standard Oil, and the American Tobacco Company—often with deleterious results.

The Sherman Act banned attempted monopolies or combinations of companies "in restraint of trade." But in the course of a decade, the Court differed over how the act should be enforced. In *U.S. v. E.C. Knight Co.* (1895), the Court allowed a corporation to acquire 98 percent of the American sugar industry's manufacturing sector. According to the Court, the Sherman Act did not cover purely intrastate activities such as refining.

Justice John Marshall Harlan dissented, and just nine years later he won a majority to his dissenting approach. The 1904 case *Northern Securities Co. v. United States* turned on the question of whether a company's ownership of three railroads amounted to an "unreasonable restraint of trade." By a five to four vote, the Court said yes.

Not only is "reasonableness" an inconsistent non-standard for businesses trying to keep within the "law," but what exactly are the grounds for handing federal judges authority to define "reasonable" business practices? To win an appointment to a federal court takes three qualifications: first, a law degree; second, the favor of a president; and third, the consent of the Senate. None of these three qualifications is any guarantee of business expertise.

In fact, in the Sherman Act, Congress unconstitutionally delegated its legislative powers to the courts. It also gave the courts de facto power to violate the Fifth Amendment due process rights of business owners. They could now be penalized for "violating" vague and indefinite laws regarding "reasonable" business practices. Nevertheless, the Court accepted the delegation, and so the Sherman Act is still on the books.

The income tax was unconstitutional

In 1895, the Court considered whether the income tax statute of 1894 was constitutional. The law levied a tax of 2 percent on all annual incomes over $4,000. Like the Sherman Act, the income tax had been adopted in a spasm of class-based animus.

The Supreme Court, however, ruled in *Pollock v. Farmers' Loan and Trust Co.* (known as the *Income Tax Case*) (1895) that Congress had no constitutional authority to impose such a tax. The Court split violently over the *Income Tax Case.* In his concurring opinion, Justice Stephen J. Field warned, "The present assault upon capital is but the beginning. It will be but the stepping-stone to others, larger and more sweeping, till our political contests will become a war of the poor against the rich; a war constantly growing in intensity and bitterness." While the majority was right that the income tax was unconstitutional because it was a direct tax not apportioned equally among the states, Field's argument was more philosophical, even political, than legal. Soon enough, the Court would follow Field's lead in assuming the role of defender of capital against state-level legislative majorities. This itself was unconstitutional, given the Constitution's division of powers between the state and federal governments.

Block That Trust!

Since its inception in 1922, the National Football League has been exempt from the Sherman Antitrust Act. The NFL is allowed to operate its franchises (i.e., the teams) not as individual businesses but as a single entity, with each team getting an equal share of NFL-generated revenue.

In *Lochner v. New York* (1905), the Court went much further. In 1895, New York State had passed legislation to regulate working conditions in bakeries (among other things, bakery employees were limited to ten-hour work days and sixty-hour work weeks). Joseph Lochner, a baker who had been fined for overworking his employees, called the legislation unreasonable and invoked the Due Process Clause of the Fourteenth Amendment.

The Court perhaps predictably agreed with Lochner that the statute violated the Due Process Clause. Justice Rufus W. Peckham, author of the Court majority's opinion in *Allgeyer v. Louisiana*, believed that the Fourteenth Amendment established a generalized liberty of contract—including the right to labor unlimited hours per week in a hot, stuffy bakery. The issue, then, was, "Is this a fair, reasonable, and appropriate exercise of the police power of the state, or is it an unreasonable, unnecessary, and arbitrary interference with the right of the individual to his personal liberty, or to enter into those contracts in relation to labor which may seem to him appropriate or necessary for the support of himself and his family?"

Justice Peckham's answer to this question for the Court was, "The employee may desire to earn the extra money which would arise from his working more than the prescribed time, but this statute forbids the employer from permitting the employee to earn it."

We may (I do) believe the statute at issue in *Lochner*, and other legislation like it, to have been unwise. We also may consider it no coincidence that one of the majority justices in this case was the son of a bakery owner. Still, that does not change the fact that the Constitution left legislation in this area entirely to the states. The Fourteenth Amendment's Due Process Clause was not intended to give a majority of Supreme Court justices veto power over all laws they did not like. Peckham's insistence that "this is not a question of substituting the judgment of the court for that of the legislature" shows that he recognized the obvious objection to the Court's ruling, but he proceeded to substitute the Court's judgment for the legislature's anyway.

In 1908 (*Adair v. United States*) and 1915 (*Coppage v. Kansas*), the Court invoked "liberty of contract" so that employers could prohibit workers from joining labor unions, despite state laws to the contrary. The Court also pointed to "liberty of contract" to knock down minimum-wage legislation for women and children in *Adkins v. Children's Hospital* (1923). Congress had passed the legislation for the District of Columbia (for which Congress acts as a sort of state government). The Court held that because the Nineteenth Amendment now guaranteed women the vote, special legal protections for women were no longer necessary.

The Court even become involved in theater ticket prices in *Tyson & Bro.-United Theatre Ticket Offices v. Banton* (1927), in which it invoked "liberty of contract" to strike down a state statute on theater ticket pricing.

States had regulated economic activity since colonial days in ways that the Court now deemed "unconstitutional." Legislatures that ratified the Fourteenth Amendment did not intend for the Supreme Court to sit in judgment on theater ticket prices. Nor did they intend to surrender their Tenth Amendment rights to govern themselves. Yet here was the Supreme Court using its own "liberty of contract" doctrine to judge the economic regulations of the states.

In the twentieth century, the Court's appetite for such power would only grow.

Chapter Nine

THE COURT VS. FDR

Supreme Court justices soon found another way to justify imposing their personal preferences on "constitutional law": they reached for trendy sociological studies and gave them equal or greater weight than the actual words of the Constitution.

Perhaps the most famous example of this in the early twentieth century was in the case of *Muller v. Oregon* (1908). The question was whether Oregon could limit women's working hours (in order to protect their health). The counsel for Oregon was future Supreme Court justice Louis D. Brandeis, who presented a wide-ranging brief John Marshall would have loved. He argued that there was a correlation between the hours women worked and their health, which justified Oregon's legislation restricting the number of hours women could work. The remarkable thing about Brandeis's brief was that it was nearly devoid of citations to precedent, or of any legal argument at all; its argument was sociological, not constitutional or legal. And yet the Court was persuaded. Even though it had struck down New York's law restricting working hours for bakers, it upheld Oregon's law limiting working hours for women. Brandeis took advantage of the fact that the Court had lost all sense of the distinction between a court's function and a legislature's, and that it would rule in favor of whichever policy prescription it thought best.

Guess what?

- The Supreme Court used foreign law to decide that the federal government could conscript men into the military.

- America's constitutional traditions impeded the socialist doctrines that swept most other countries in the 1930s.

- Before FDR threatened the Supreme Court, it generally ruled against the state's economic legislation.

In 1917 the Court upheld legislation on maximum working hours for manufacturing employees in *Bunting v. Oregon*. Oregon's counsel presented another sociological brief, this one showing that employees' health was affected by the hours they worked. The Court, mesmerized by this data, upheld the legislation by a narrow majority.

The Court's holdings in *Muller* and *Bunting* did conflict with the general "liberty of contract" trend. They can be understood as representing an older and more significant tendency of the Supreme Court, however: the tendency to act as the nation's supreme legislative chamber, overruling state legislatures and Congress. What was new was the growing conviction among politicians, journalists, lawyers, and academics that the Court was right to impose its will because the Constitution itself was outmoded and in need of replacement.

This trend gained strength when Woodrow Wilson was elected president in 1912. Wilson, a political scientist, had long argued that America should move away from the Constitution's federal, three-branch system to something closer to the British model. The Constitution, Wilson said, was simply too inefficient; such cumbersome mechanisms as bicameralism and the presidential veto too often thwarted the popular will, to the detriment of the American public.

Wilson believed the president should be the tribune of the people, largely unrestrained by the Constitution's limits on presidential authority. And the manifest trend of the twentieth century, supported by intellectuals and populist nationalists, was the consolidation of the power of the federal government at the expense of state sover-

American Law, Anyone?

The Supreme Court's 1918 decision that federal conscription is constitutional was explicitly based on contemporary practice in the German Empire, Austrian Empire, Russian Empire, Turkish Empire, British Empire, Japanese Empire....Do you see a theme?

eignty. In 1913 the Constitution was amended so that U.S. senators were elected directly by the people (rather than by the state legislatures), and Congress was given the power to levy income taxes. The First World War exacerbated this centralizing trend.

Uncle Sam wants YOU!

The Court reflected the nationalistic, centralizing approach in the *Selective Draft Law Cases* (1918). When Lincoln enacted a military draft in 1863 it had led to riots, and Chief Justice Taney drafted an opinion (never delivered; there was no case before the Court) denying that such legislation was constitutional. Taney reasoned that the Constitution did not give Congress the authority to draft men into service. Instead, it said it could raise and regulate armies, and it gave the federal government authority over the states' militias in certain circumstances. As the Continental and Confederation Congresses had raised armies by requisitions on the states and through economic inducements, Taney reasoned, that was the extent of Congress's power to "raise" armies.

The defendants in 1918 made arguments similar to Taney's. They also made reference to the Thirteenth Amendment, which had been ratified since Taney's death and which said that only convicts could be subjected to involuntary servitude. The Court would have nothing of this.

Chief Justice Edward D. White's decision for the Court leaped over the Constitution to argue that because foreign governments conscripted soldiers, this power was obviously one of the attributes of a national government; in other words, the Court argued that anything the Kaiser could do to his subjects, or the Commissars to theirs, the United States government could do to Americans. So much for "interpreting" the Constitution, and so much for the Constitution as a compact of sovereign states with powers protected by the Tenth Amendment. White said that citizenship entailed the "supreme and noble duty of contributing to the defense of the rights and honor of the nation," which is language not found in the Constitution.

Can you put that protest on hold until *after* the war?

In another case related to the war, the Court supported the executive branch in *Schenck v. United States* (1919). *Schenck* involved the circulation by antiwar activists, including the general secretary of the Socialist Party, of pamphlets encouraging resistance to the draft. Here, Justice Oliver Wendell Holmes, the supposed avatar of freedom of speech, let forth the following enlightened blast: "When a nation is at war many things that might be said in time of peace are such a hindrance to its effort that their utterance will not be endured so long as men fight and . . . no Court could regard them as protected by constitutional right."

In other words, the Sedition Act of 1918, which banned saying anything to obstruct the war effort or bring the government into ill repute, was valid and constitutional. Apparently there is no constitutional right to protest against a war during a time of war, although you are free to protest the war once the war is over.

Holmes, writing for a unanimous Court, said that Charles Schenck should be punished because his behavior was analogous to "shouting 'fire' in a theatre and causing a panic." The First Amendment would have protected him "in many places and in ordinary times," but not just then.

The next year, in *Abrams v. United States*, the Court, using the precedent of *Schenck*, upheld the conviction of Jacob Abrams, who was prosecuted for passing out leaflets urging munitions workers to go on strike, a violation of the Espionage Act of 1917. But this time Holmes dissented.

A Book You're Not Supposed to Read

The Military Draft: Selected Readings on Conscription, Martin Anderson, ed.; Stanford: Hoover Institution Press, 1982.

He argued that there had been a clear and present danger in 1918, but not in 1919. "It is only the present danger of immediate evil or an intent to bring it about that warrants Congress in setting a limit to the expression of opinion where private rights are not concerned." But by what authority did Holmes set this standard? Surely not the First Amendment, which says that "Congress shall make no law... abridging the freedom of speech, or of the press."

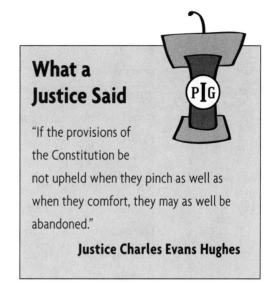

What a Justice Said

"If the provisions of the Constitution be not upheld when they pinch as well as when they comfort, they may as well be abandoned."

Justice Charles Evans Hughes

The political platform of the Supreme Court: Pro-war, pro-child labor

If the Court supported the war effort and the Wilson administration's efforts to squelch dissent, it also continued to support economic freedom—this time despite constitutional allocation of power to Congress. In *Hammer v. Dagenhart*, also known as the *Child Labor Case* (1918), the Court intervened when Congress attempted to restrict child labor. The legislation prohibited interstate commerce by businesses that employed children; Congress invoked the Commerce Clause to justify it. The law was protested by a father of two teenaged North Carolina mill hands. He and other opponents of the law argued that it hurt poor families, and that only states, not the federal government, had the right to regulate labor.

The Court struck down the law, saying that Congress could not prohibit interstate commerce in legitimate products. The Court majority conceded that in the past it had allowed Congress to use the commerce power to ban interstate travel for purposes of prostitution and to regulate the purity of food and drugs, but here it drew the line. Textiles were not human bodies or impure drugs. Note that the distinctions the Court made here had no basis whatsoever in the Constitution. Still, regulation of labor remained within the states' exclusive legislative ambit, and when Congress tried again to regulate child labor through its new powers of direct taxation, the Court again rejected the attempt in 1922's *Child Labor Tax Case.*

The Supreme Court's habitual elevation of its own legislative preferences over the Constitution was highlighted in *Pierce v. Society of Sisters of the Holy Names of Jesus and Mary* (1925). The case involved a 1922 Oregon initiative that required nearly all children between the ages of eight and sixteen to attend public schools. The district court held the law invalid on the basis of the Due Process Clause of the Fourteenth Amendment, and, on appeal, the Supreme Court agreed. The Court announced that the "liberty" recognized by the Due Process Clause extended to the right to send one's children to a non-public school, and so the Oregon enactment was invalid. But what this "right" had to do with "due process" (the Due Process Clause bars states from depriving anyone of life, liberty, or property without due process of law) remained a mystery. The Supreme Court's ruling in this case is still regarded as a binding precedent.

The Supreme Court vs. the Roosevelt Democrats

While federal judges adhered to the doctrine of freedom of contract, alas, the other two branches of the federal government did not. Instead, by first constricting the money supply, then adopting enormously counterproductive tariffs, the Federal Reserve and the Republican Congress of the 1920s launched the country into the Great Depression.

By the time President Herbert Hoover came up for reelection in 1932, he was just as doomed to defeat as James Buchanan had been in 1860. His Democratic opponent, New York's Franklin Roosevelt, ran on a traditional free-trade, limited-government, Democratic platform. And he defeated Hoover overwhelmingly.

Almost immediately upon taking office, however, Roosevelt performed the greatest about-face in American political history: he instigated an enormous assertion of federal authority over the economy. The problem, as he and his lieutenants saw things, was that the American economy was *too free*. What were needed were some political geniuses in Washington to determine prices, quantities of output, working conditions, wages, bank schedules, and any other factors of economic life that came to mind, just as in the Soviet Union and Mussolini's fascist Italy. American intellectuals trumpeted the great accomplishments of fascists and communists abroad. Walter Duranty of the *New York Times* even won a Pulitzer Prize for laudatory reporting from the Soviet Union—while intentionally concealing Communist mass murder. Why shouldn't the United States share the pleasures of a centrally planned economy?

The Supreme Court had its first notable confrontation with the rapid growth of government (which was occurring at both the state and federal levels) in 1934. In *Home Building & Loan Association v. Blaisdell*, the Court, perhaps for the only time in history, considered the validity of a state law that actually violated the federal Constitution. The law granted

What a Justice Said

"Emergency does not create power. Emergency does not increase granted power or remove or diminish the restrictions imposed upon power granted or reserved. The Constitution was adopted in a period of grave emergency. Its grants of power to the federal government and its limitations of the power of the States were determined in the light of emergency, and they are not altered by emergency."

Justice Charles Evans Hughes

Minnesota courts the power to exempt property from foreclosure for a temporary "emergency" period of time, "and in no event beyond May 1, 1935." The Home Building and Loan Association called this law a violation of the Contracts Clause in Article I, Section 10 of the Constitution.

The Contracts Clause had been written with a case precisely like this in mind. It was meant to protect creditors and their ability to collect debts by prohibiting states from interfering with the obligation of contracts. And yet the Supreme Court upheld the law! Why? Because, in the words of Chief Justice Charles Evans Hughes, the law was "of a character appropriate to the emergency and allowed upon what are said to be reasonable conditions." Although the Constitution has no "emergency" clause attached to the Contracts Clause and no definition of "reasonable conditions," the Court felt fully justified in amending the Constitution, because, after all, what the Court said was "law."

A Book You're Not Supposed to Read

The Politically Incorrect Guide™ to American History by Thomas Woods; Washington, DC: Regnery, 2004.

The Court began to move away from its liberty of contract ideology in *Nebbia v. New York* (1934) when it said that states could regulate milk prices. The Constitution does not actually prohibit such regulation, but the Court had to invent a justification for its ruling because it had previously struck down state economic regulations under the Due Process Clause of the Fourteenth Amendment. So the Court now took an expansive view of businesses that were "affected with a public interest" and thus could be regulated by the state.

Yet surely the Supreme Court, so long a friend of "liberty of contract," would stand against the New Deal's litany of economic regulations? For a moment, and in part, it did.

In *Schechter Poultry Corp. v. United States* (1935), the Court ruled the New Deal's National Industrial Recovery Act (NIRA) unconstitutional. The case came to the Court as an appeal. Schechter Poultry had been convicted of violating the "code of fair competition" under the act, because the corporation had hired people at lower wages and set them to work for longer hours than the president had decreed to be legal. Moreover, the corporation was accused of selling "an unfit chicken." The corporation's defenders argued that, with the unemployment rate hovering around 25 percent, the corporation was providing people with work at fair market wages.

But the New Deal planners believed not only in raising wages and prices, but also in other elements of centralized economic planning. The NIRA regulations had come straight from the White House, not from Congress (which had delegated the president this power because of the economic "emergency").

The Court found the NIRA void because it delegated excessive power to the president. The full extent of the president's powers under this act, the Court said, was "virtually unfettered." It was as broad as Congress's power under the Commerce Clause. "This," wrote Justice Benjamin Cardozo, "is delegation run riot." If the United States was swept somewhat less by the rising tide of socialism that appeared in the Soviet Union, Germany, and Italy, besides Britain, France, and elsewhere to varying degrees in the 1930s, it was because America's constitutional traditions impeded it. These traditions did not, however, avert it completely. Indeed, in the end, *Schechter* proved to be an aberration—but not before the old guard on the Supreme Court struck down some additional New Deal legislation.

In *U.S. v. Butler* (1936), the Court ruled that the New Deal's Agricultural Adjustment Act was unconstitutional, with Justices Benjamin Cardozo, Louis Brandeis, and Harlan Fiske Stone dissenting. The Court ruled that the price- and production-setting powers claimed by the federal government were reserved to the states, as shown in the Constitution's ratification debates and the Tenth Amendment. One would be hard-pressed to name another Supreme Court decision of the twentieth century that so

Bet Your Law Professor Never Told You

FDR, and most presidents ever after, essentially tried to read the Tenth Amendment out of the Constitution.

accurately interpreted the Constitution. Legal scholars, however, generally sympathize with the New Deal, and so you won't find much praise for the Court's decision in *U.S. v. Butler*. To these scholars, it's not the Constitution but their own policy preferences that matter.

In *Carter v. Carter Coal Company* (1936), the Court struck down similar legislation regulating the coal industry, though this time using its faulty "liberty of contract" theory.

That same year the Democrats scored overwhelming electoral victories, and FDR called on Congress to help him fight the Supreme Court. His strategy was to appoint blatantly partisan justices who would rubber-stamp his policies. Purportedly because many of his measures' opponents on the Court were more than seventy years old, he asked Congress to expand the Court by adding one justice for every sitting justice over seventy.

Most historians and legal scholars criticize Roosevelt for his "court-packing" scheme because they think it violates the Constitution's separation of powers. In other words, they criticize FDR not for trying to pack the Court, but for asking Congress to assert authority over it, diminishing the Court's significance. But Roosevelt was exactly right to demand congressional oversight of the Court, even if he did so for the wrong reason (which was essentially to read the Tenth Amendment out of the Constitution completely).

For many, however, this was too radical. There was serious division, then, among Democrats over the desirability of the court-packing plan. Roosevelt's plan drew united opposition from southern Democrats and from Republicans. To borrow a phrase, it withered on the vine.

Meanwhile, a change of heart occurred on the Court. Justices Charles Evans Hughes and Owen J. Roberts joined in "the switch in time that saved nine" by voting with the three-justice pro–New Deal minority in upholding New Deal legislation. The Court's new attitude made its first appearance in *West Coast Hotel Co. v. Parrish* (1937).

The case involved a Washington state minimum wage law covering women and minors. Elsie Parrish, a maid at the West Coast Hotel, sued for the difference between the wages she had been paid and the wages she should have been paid under the law, which had been on the books since 1932. The hotel argued that the law was unconstitutional. But the Supreme Court, overturning its own "liberty of contract" precedents, ruled in favor of Parrish.

Writing for the majority, Charles Evans Hughes exploded the doctrine of liberty of contract. "In each case the violation alleged by those attacking minimum wage regulation for women is deprivation of freedom of contract," Hughes wrote. "What is this freedom? The Constitution does not speak of freedom of contract. It speaks of liberty and prohibits the deprivation of liberty without due process of law."

"In prohibiting that deprivation," Hughes said, "the Constitution does not recognize an absolute and uncontrolled liberty. . . . Regulation which is reasonable in relation to its subject and is adapted to the interests of the community is due process."

The Court's decision was correct as a matter of constitutional law—the Fourteenth Amendment was not intended to make the Supreme Court into a protector of "freedom of contract" against state social legislation. Hughes did cloud the Court's opinion with superfluous economic pontifications about the "exploitation of a class of workers." But should anyone be surprised? Supreme Court justices have rarely spared us their uninformed opinions.

Chapter Ten

THE GRAND WIZARD'S IMPERIAL COURT

Having given up its brief opposition to the New Deal, the Supreme Court now became FDR's rubber stamp. Seeing the Court reverse itself and (correctly) uphold the right of states to adopt minimum wage laws in *West Coast Hotel Co. v. Parrish*, Congress unconstitutionally adopted similar legislation—with no judicial opposition. (Where the Court formerly had prevented both the states and Congress from doing what the states alone had the right to do, it now allowed both the states and Congress to do what the states alone had the right to do.)

Then, in *National Labor Relations Board v. Jones & Laughlin Steel Corporation* (1937), the Court again eliminated its own precedents. Jones and Laughlin Steel had tried to prevent its workers from unionizing and fired those who did. The federal government intervened on the side of the fired workers, invoking the New Deal's pro-union National Labor Relations Act (commonly known as the Wagner Act). The steel corporation protested that the Wagner Act was unconstitutional—and lower courts agreed. But the Supreme Court backtracked from its own precedents and ruled that Congress, under the Commerce Clause, could regulate the economy in ways previously thought beyond its reach.

Helvering v. Davis (1937) was the third case (after *Jones & Laughlin* and *Parrish*) that represented the Court's "switch in time" that staved off

Guess what?

- The states have the right to establish religions.

- In 1942 the Supreme Court ruled that a farmer couldn't grow "surplus" wheat to feed his family and his livestock.

- Justice Robert H. Jackson wrote in 1953 of himself and his fellow justices, "We are not final because we are infallible, but we are infallible only because we are final."

FDR's threat to pack it with his supporters. *Helvering* concerned the Social Security Act of 1935. Businesses, now subject to the Social Security tax, charged that the Social Security Act was unconstitutional, and certainly there is no provision in the Constitution for the federal government to run a pension program.

The Court's opinion was again larded with the sort of sociological data that might have been appropriate for a legislature considering legislation but not for a court interpreting the Constitution. What did ruminations about an aging population, a decline in charitable donations, declining state revenues, and other alleged effects of the Great Depression have to do with the Constitution? Precisely nothing, but the Court tried to make something out of nothing by ruling that the General Welfare Clause of Article I, Section 8 of the Constitution—which restricts Congress's taxation powers to promoting the "general" (as opposed to special interest) welfare—was actually a grant of power to Congress. Congress, the Court said, could itself determine what taxes (and what spending) promoted the "general welfare," thus once again ignoring the Tenth Amendment and shifting power from the states to the federal government.

"Updating" the framers

Professor Bernard Schwartz speaks for most academic analysts of the pro-FDR Supreme Court when he says, in his book *A History of the Supreme Court*, that the Court was simply "adjust[ing] the intent of the Framers to contemporary needs." Thus, the pre-1937 Court's defense of the Constitution against the New Deal's massive expansion of federal power had been, he says, "government by judiciary."

The Court continued to "adjust [one might say "ignore"] the intent of the Framers." In 1941's *United States v. Darby*, it upheld federal minimum wage legislation and overruled *Hammer v. Dagenhart*—the *Child Labor Case*—so that poor families could no longer send their children to work (except on family farms and in other family businesses).

In the 1942 case of *Wickard v. Filburn*, the Court produced a decision so absurd as to be beyond parody. The case concerned enforcement of the Agricultural Adjustment Act of 1938, which restricted the acreage on which individual farmers could grow wheat. (Congress's stated goal was to prop up Depression farm incomes, not to starve the legions of already malnourished unemployed.) Roscoe Filburn, a wheat farmer in Ohio, exceeded his allotment by growing wheat to feed his family and his livestock. Filburn insisted that as his extra wheat was not intended for interstate commerce, Congress had no power to regulate it and could not punish him for growing his own food.

A Book You're Not Supposed to Read

Government by Judiciary: The Transformation of the Fourteenth Amendment by Raoul Berger (second edition); Indianapolis: Liberty Fund, 1997.

The Supreme Court conceded that Filburn's actions had not been "commerce," but nevertheless ruled that this was immaterial. According to the Court, Congress could regulate any activity that "exerts a substantial economic effect on interstate commerce." "That [his] own contribution to the demand for wheat may be trivial by itself is not enough to remove him from the scope of federal regulation where, as here, his contribution, taken together with that of many others similarly situated, is far from trivial."

As professor Richard Epstein of the University of Chicago has noted, by this measure the Commerce Clause gives Congress power to regulate "just about anything." It also makes an absolutely dead letter of the Tenth Amendment's reservation of undelegated powers to the states.

How the Constitution got "incorporated" rather than interpreted

In *Darby*, the Court had offered up the sage claim that the Tenth Amendment "states but a truism that all is retained which has not been surrendered. There is nothing in the history of its adoption to suggest that it was more than declaratory of the relationship between the national and state governments as it had been established by the Constitution before the Amendment."

As we have seen, the second sentence of this statement is true: Edmund Randolph and other leading Federalists had vowed during the ratification process that Congress would have only the powers it was "expressly delegated," and the Tenth Amendment was only a restatement of this principle already said to be implicit in the unamended Constitution. But that does not answer the objection that nowhere in the Constitution was Congress "expressly delegated" power to undertake the extensive regulation of the economy—and, ultimately, of virtually every other conceivable area of human endeavor—that the Supreme Court allowed it to undertake after 1937. In other words, just because the Tenth Amendment principle that virtually all power was reserved to the states was understood before the Tenth Amendment was adopted does not mean that the Tenth Amendment principle should never be applied!

A typical law school casebook, Donald Kommers, John Finn, and Gary Jacobsohn's *American Constitutional Law* (second edition), follows its excerpt from *Wickard* with the Tenth Amendment snippet from *Darby*, and then asks, "Do you agree?" Of course, without more, an aspiring lawyer can only weigh his political preferences; he cannot understand that what was under way in *Darby*, *Wickard*, and contemporary cases was a radically anti-constitutional transformation of the American federal system—a virtual judicial coup d'état.

If the Court was going to get out of the business of limiting state and congressional initiative in the economic realm, what was it going to do instead? A hint came in the most famous (though, as we shall see, not the most revealing) footnote in the Court's history: *U.S. v. Carolene Products Co.* (1938), footnote four. There, in the midst of a majority opinion announcing that regulatory statutes would be presumed to be rational (thus blunting the old rational-basis test for statutes' constitutionality), the Court said that it was not necessary to consider whether such a "presumption of constitutionality" was appropriate in cases involving application of Bill of Rights provisions against the states, cases related to the political process, or cases involving "discrete and insular minorities."

In other words, having left the business of enforcing authentically constitutional limitations on Congress's economic and social powers and having overturned its own unconstitutional (although largely socially desirable) limitations on state economic regulation, the Court had found a new role for itself: enforcer of Bill of Rights provisions and protector of "discrete and insular" (meaning, at first, mainly racial) minorities.

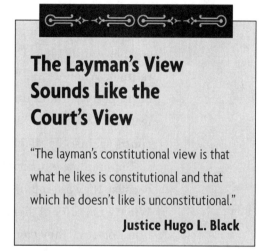

The Layman's View Sounds Like the Court's View

"The layman's constitutional view is that what he likes is constitutional and that which he doesn't like is unconstitutional."

Justice Hugo L. Black

Ironically, the Court's new use of the Bill of Rights was akin to the old laissez-faire majority's use of the Due Process Clause of the Fourteenth Amendment. In the old cases that the Court disavowed beginning in 1937, it had created a doctrine—"freedom of contract"—found nowhere in the Constitution, and it had used that doctrine as justification for invalidating a plethora of state policies the justices disliked.

In the new Bill of Rights cases, the Court would invent a concept—"incorporation"—unrelated to the Constitution's language and history and would use that concept as a justification for invalidating myriad types of state social policy.

So what is "incorporation"? "Incorporation" was (and is) the Court's subterfuge to get around the plain historical fact that the Bill of Rights was ratified to limit the powers of the federal government alone. This fact had been affirmed by the unanimous Marshall Court decision in *Barron v. Baltimore* (1833).

According to proponents of the Incorporation Doctrine, *Barron* was good law until 1868. Then the Fourteenth Amendment was (supposedly) ratified. When it said that no state could deprive anyone of life, liberty, or property without due process of law, it made the Bill of Rights (or at least the Court's favorite Bill of Rights provisions) enforceable by federal courts against the states.

To paraphrase Justice Robert H. Jackson, the justices are not supreme because they are infallible; they are infallible because they are supreme. When a majority of them set their minds to enforcement of an Incorporation Doctrine, they can have their way.

You might think that if a majority of justices set out to enforce a doctrine, like the Incorporation Doctrine, that is plainly at variance with historical truth, they would be hooted down in legal academia and the legal profession generally, and that eventually their mistake would be corrected through the appointment process. Three factors combined to allow the Incorporation Doctrine bacillus to work its way through the legal system:

1. The nature of contemporary legal education

2. The long-lasting ascendancy of the New Deal congressional (and intellectual) majority

3. The appeal to the intellectual class of the model of government that the Incorporation Doctrine decisions represent

Legal education today is much different from what it was in John Marshall's day, or even early in the twentieth century. When Thomas Jefferson and Edmund Randolph, John Marshall and Patrick Henry studied law, they did so by reading treatises in what was called the science of law. Common-law study was in its nature historical and theoretical, and familiarity with the history of England was essential to it.

Now, however, American law students are almost universally subjected to the case method. Their texts are collections of judicial opinions, or in a few cases of statutes, with absolutely no historical context. One prominent legal academic at a leading law school responded to my friend's query why he had not assigned readings from *The Federalist* to his introductory class in constitutional law by saying that *The Federalist* was "irrelevant" to the subject of "constitutional law"—and he was right.

In short, if the judges make a particular false assertion about the Constitution in numerous cases, students reading those opinions have no way of recognizing that assertion's falsity. They are provided no tools for analyzing judges' claims—only with scads of the opinions incorporating those claims. This is one reason why legal training should not be confused with an education.

When the pro–New Deal position began its long (one might argue permanent) ascendancy on the Supreme Court, academia and the legal profession generally remained stocked with opponents. Non-liberals were in a decided minority among academics, then as now, but adherents to the old view on federalism remained numerous. Over time, however, Democrats' reign over Congress—nearly uninterrupted from 1933 to 1994—meant that the federal courts came to be stocked with, stacked with, New Dealers—in fact if not in name. Even today's "conservatives" like Justice

Antonin Scalia give little thought to overturning the Incorporation Doctrine, for example, or the three 1937 precedents marking the Court's capitulation to the new political reality.

The centralized model of government that the New Deal embodied appeals to the socialist leanings of most intellectuals. Something in the typical intellectual finds the idea of the philosopher king—or the philosopher court—appealing. Who needs all those dirty elections, all that demeaning electioneering, anyway, when you can get the right result by following the Rule of Five: he who has five votes, rules? (The term "Rule of Five" comes from the late Justice William Brennan, the outstanding example of an American judge who promiscuously used his power to substitute his preferences for the preferences of the Constitution's ratifiers and the electorate.)

With the thin reed of the Fourteenth Amendment's Due Process Clause as its support, the Court undertook to redefine American church-state

Portrait of a Justice

Hugo Black (1886–1971) was the leading proponent of the Incorporation Doctrine by which the Supreme Court in the twentieth century applied various provisions of the federal Bill of Rights against the states—and thus inverted the federal system created by the ratifiers of the Constitution and Bill of Rights. Black, a former Ku Klux Klansman, also took the lead in writing the twentieth-century Klan's views on church-state relations into "constitutional law" in cases such as *Everson v. Board of Education* and *Engel v. Vitale*. It is to Black that we owe the prominence of Thomas Jefferson's inapt "wall of separation" metaphor in the Court's twentieth-century church-state jurisprudence. Black's first purpose on the Court, however, was to support Franklin Roosevelt's New Deal, and he joined a new majority that eschewed the Supreme Court's traditional (intended) role of checking congressional efforts to legislate beyond its enumerated powers.

relations, race relations, federal-state relations, the rights of accused criminals, the freedoms of speech and the press, and, in the end, sexual mores—even normality. The jumping-off point was a determined (and ongoing) attempt to secularize American society, thus bringing more of it under the Court's own purview and that of the federal government.

How the Ku Klux Klan separated church from state

In deciding the 1940 case of *Cantwell v. Connecticut* the Court took the Free Exercise Clause of the First Amendment ("Congress shall make no law...prohibiting the free exercise [of religion]") and turned it upside down. The case involved the prosecution of Newton Cantwell, a Jehovah's Witness, for disturbing the peace: he had gone door-to-door on behalf of his religion and played an anti-Catholic record in a Catholic neighborhood.

The purpose of the Free Exercise Clause was to keep the federal government from interfering in religious matters (and laws) in the states. But using the Court's handy Incorporation Doctrine and the Fourteenth Amendment, the Court ruled that by arresting Cantwell, Connecticut had violated his First Amendment rights. The Free Exercise Clause had become a vehicle for federal judges' oversight of state policies affecting religion!

The Court performed a similar feat with the Establishment Clause in *Everson v. Board of Education of Ewing Township* (1947). Writing for the majority was Justice Hugo Black, once a stridently pro–New Deal senator from Alabama who in winning election to the Senate had had the active support of his fellow members of the Ku Klux Klan. To its nineteenth-century racism, the Klan in the twentieth century had added anti-Catholicism as well as anti-Semitism. And the most important issue of the time for anti-Catholics was opposing any sort of government support for parochial (meaning, in most cases, Catholic) schools.

Black claimed that not only did the First Amendment Establishment Clause apply to state and local governments (which it decidedly did not, in its original understanding, as some states at the time of ratification had established state churches), but that it also erected, in language not found in the Constitution, "a wall of separation between church and state."

Black reasoned thus:

> A large proportion of the early settlers of this country came here from Europe to escape the bondage of laws which compelled them to support and attend government favored churches. The centuries immediately before and contemporaneous with the colonization of America had been filled with turmoil, civil strife, and persecutions, generated in large part by established sects.
>
> These practices of the old world were transplanted to and began to thrive in the soil of the new.

"These practices," Black continued, "became so commonplace as to shock the freedom-loving colonials into a feeling of abhorrence." Such feelings "found expression in the First Amendment."

In support of this claim, Black pointed to the history of revolutionary Virginia, which suspended collection of taxes to support the Anglican establishment in June 1776 and, at James Madison's instigation, adopted Thomas Jefferson's Virginia Statute for Religious Freedom, with its free-thinking first section, ten years later. "This Court has previously recognized that the provisions of the First Amendment, in the drafting and adoption of which Madison and Jefferson played such leading roles, had the same objective and were intended to provide the same protection against governmental intrusion on religious liberty as the Virginia statute."

"In the words of Thomas Jefferson," he concluded, "the clause against establishment of religion by law was intended to erect 'a wall of separation between Church and State.'"

As an essay in history, Black's opinion was remarkable for its ignorance—which has not stopped it, and especially Jefferson's phrase, from being invoked ad nauseum. The First Amendment does not say that there shall be no establishments of religion in the states. And in fact, the first federal Congress pointedly rejected Madison's proposal to address the question of state establishment of religion.

The purpose of the First Amendment was to ensure that Congress would neither establish a religion for the United States nor interfere in the religious policy of individual states—including Massachusetts, Connecticut, and New Hampshire—that retained their colonial religious establishments.

But what about the "leading role" Justice Black assigned to Thomas Jefferson, author of the "wall of separation" metaphor? As every student who passes my History 101 course knows, it is a myth. Thomas Jefferson played no role in drafting or adopting the Establishment Clause. He was neither a member of the first Congress that drafted the First Amendment and sent it to the states for ratification nor a member of the Virginia General Assembly that voted to ratify it. And the metaphor of a "wall of separation" between church and state was coined by President Jefferson in a letter written a decade after the First Amendment's ratification. Moreover, the letter concerned not the issue of state establishments, but an explanation of why Jefferson did not issue presidential declarations of Thanksgiving and fasting, as Presidents Washington and Adams had done.

If Only...

"The public welfare demands that constitutional cases must be decided according to the terms of the Constitution itself, and not according to judges' views of fairness, reasonableness, or justice."

Justice Hugo L. Black

And even the broadest reading of the Due Process Clause of the Fourteenth Amendment cannot be seen as inviting the Supreme Court to supervise the religious policies of states, counties, cities, and school boards. Yet the Supreme Court has done this—and done it with the approval of dominant liberal opinion.

Surely the most notorious Court decision building on *Everson* came in the 1962 case of *Engel v. Vitale*—the *School Prayer Case*. In this case, the Court considered the constitutionality under *Everson* of a New York policy requiring school districts to have children recite a supposedly innocuous prayer each morning. The prayer said, "Almighty God, we acknowledge our dependence upon Thee, and we beg Thy blessings upon us, our parents, our teachers, and our country." Jewish, Unitarian, and nonbeliever parents of ten students in the New Hyde Park, New York, school district challenged this practice as violating the Establishment Clause.

The Court's resident expert in early American history, former Klansman Hugo Black, wrote for a seven-justice majority. "There can be no doubt," he solemnly scribbled, "that New York's state prayer program officially establishes the religious beliefs embodied in the Regents' prayer." This, apparently, was an Establishment Clause-as-applied-to-the-states-by-the-Incorporation-Doctrine no-no.

How could that be? What, exactly, were the "religious beliefs" reflected by this anodyne prayer? Apparently that there was a god and that the students were dependent upon it.

A traditional Christian might have objected to the prayer on the grounds that it did not invoke the name of the Trinity. Black's objection was rooted in his peculiar understanding of the First Amendment's history. But even if one assumed (as Black incorrectly did) that Thomas Jefferson's personal views somehow informed the Establishment Clause, shouldn't we remember that Jefferson had written, with editorial help from John Adams and Benjamin Franklin, that all men were "endowed by their creator with certain unalienable rights"? If that reference to God—and President Jefferson's references to God in his annual messages to Congress—did not offend his sensibilities, why would he have been offended by the New Hyde Park prayer?

Engel v. Vitale's ban on prayer in public schools provoked widespread outrage. As well it should. It was essentially a judicial coup de main that amended the Constitution without troubling to go through the arduous process of amending it the constitutional way (as specified by Article V). The amendment process was made difficult in order to protect the states from federal innovation. Back then, however, no one assumed that Supreme Court justices would simply ignore the Constitution—or that Congress would let them get away with it. But the justices do, and Congress does, and thus Justice Black's handiwork continues to shape our public schools, which now bear the imprint of an anti-Catholic Klansman who advanced the cause of left-liberal secularists.

The Supreme Court vs. Christianity

Having spat the constitutional bit out of its mouth, the Court raced further and further from the Constitution on issues of church and state. In 1971, the Court announced the "*Lemon* test" for judging state laws regarding religion (from *Lemon v. Kurtzman*, a 1971 case that barred Pennsylvania from reimbursing non-public schools—mostly Catholic parochial schools—for some of their educational expenses). In order to pass constitutional muster, the Court said, the challenged state law must have a secular purpose, it must have a primary effect that neither advances nor inhibits religion, and it must not foster excessive church-state entanglement.

How the Supreme Court found the *Lemon* test within the language of the Establishment Clause barring Congress from making laws "respecting an establishment of religion" is not a mystery: it didn't. And the same holds true for finding some alleged justification in the Fourteenth Amendment's Due Process Clause for enforcing this test against the states.

The Supreme Court was not only unconstitutionally making law, but was also making law that the ratifiers of the Bill of Rights and the Fourteenth Amendment would have rejected.

Chief Justice Warren Burger said that America needed the *Lemon* test because

> To have States or communities divide on the issues presented by state aid to parochial schools would tend to confuse and obscure other issues of great urgency. We have an expanding array of vexing issues, local and national, domestic and international, to debate and divide on. It conflicts with our whole history and tradition to permit questions of the Religion Clauses to assume such importance in our legislatures and in our elections that they could divert attention from the myriad issues and problems that confront every level of government.

With this in mind, "the Constitution's authors sought to protect religious worship from the pervasive power of government."

To paraphrase: "Common citizens, as represented in state legislatures, are not bright enough to walk and chew gum simultaneously. Fortunately, I, Warren Burger, lead a committee of well-connected lawyers established for the purpose of determining which issues should be plucked from the state legislatures and decided in the way the intellectual elite prefers. Whenever anyone points out that the Constitution does not actually address such matters, except insofar as the Tenth Amendment says that powers not delegated to the federal government are reserved to the states, we tell them that the Constitution is actually extremely complicated, and that only three years of law school and appointment to a judicial post can prepare one to interpret it."

As we shall see, Chief Justice Burger applied a mixture of condescension and historical ignorance to a huge array of questions. Like his immediate predecessor, Earl Warren, he understood the Court as a permanent

What Part of This Didn't Justice Black and the Court Understand?

"I believe the Court has no power to add to or subtract from the procedures set forth by the founders.... I shall not at any time surrender my belief that the document itself should be our guide, not our own concept of what is fair, decent, and right."

Justice Hugo L. Black

constitutional convention, a nine-man committee to decide issues purposely left to the states.

One response to *Engel v. Vitale* was Alabama's 1981 statute authorizing a period of silence "for meditation or voluntary prayer." The legislature hoped to make the law palatable to the Court by leaving out the state-mandated prayer decreed unconstitutional in *Engel*.

At trial in the federal district court, Judge Brevard Hand correctly pointed out that "the Establishment Clause of the First Amendment to the United States Constitution does not prohibit the state from establishing a religion." He then dismissed the plaintiffs' claims against Alabama's statute. The Circuit Court of Appeals reversed him, and the case found itself in the Supreme Court.

Justice John Paul Stevens called it unsurprising that Hand had been reversed. Turning to the *Lemon* test rather than to the Constitution, Stevens found no difficulty in declaring the Alabama law "unconstitutional"—meaning "inconsistent with Supreme Court precedent." No surprise there. The interesting element of the Court's performance in this case, *Wallace v. Jaffree* (1985), lay in the dissent filed by Justice William Rehnquist.

Rehnquist had been appointed to the Supreme Court by President Richard Nixon, whose 1968 presidential campaign took aim at the Supreme Court. And Rehnquist took dead aim at Hugo Black's *Everson* decision: "It is impossible," Rehnquist wrote, "to build sound constitutional doctrine upon a mistaken understanding of constitutional history, but unfortunately the Establishment Clause has been expressly freighted with Jefferson's misleading ['wall of separation'] metaphor for nearly forty years." After noting that Jefferson had had no role in writing or ratifying the Bill of Rights, including the Establishment Clause, Rehnquist concluded that Jefferson "would seem to any detached observer as a less than ideal source of contemporary history as to the meaning of the Religion Clauses of the First Amendment."

Rehnquist went on to describe the First Amendment's course through the first federal Congress, noting, among other facts, that James Madison's original draft had said, "The civil rights of none shall be abridged on account of religious belief or worship, nor shall any national religion be established, nor shall the full and equal rights of conscience be in any manner, or on any pretext, infringed." When another congressman pro-

There Are "Absolutes"—and There Is the Court's Absolute Power

"It is my belief that there are 'absolutes' in our Bill of Rights, and that they were put there on purpose by men who knew what the words meant and meant their prohibitions to be 'absolutes.'"

Justice Hugo L. Black

posed changing this to "[N]o religion shall be established by law, nor shall the equal rights of conscience be infringed," he was met with the objection that this might tend "to abolish religion altogether" in the public sphere, and his proposal was rejected.

Madison then said that his intention was to provide "that Congress should not establish a religion, and enforce the legal observation of it by law, nor compel men to worship God in any manner contrary to their conscience." His proposal, he further explained, responded to ratification opponents' claims that the new government would establish a national church.

When a congressman from Connecticut, which still had an established church (and would for nearly thirty more years), objected that the proposal might interfere with his state's religion policy, Madison answered that it would not. In the wake of this discussion, the House passed the current language. It also rejected Madison's proposed amendment giving federal courts power to enforce certain individual rights against state governments—which is why the Incorporation Doctrine had to be invented by twentieth-century federal judges bent on overturning perfectly constitutional state laws in this area.

Note that, as Rehnquist pointed out, James Madison did not advocate making the Virginia Statute for Religious Freedom the federal government's policy. Had he made such a proposal, congressmen desiring to protect their states' established churches against federal intervention would have defeated him. His role, rather, was to seek a compromise provision preventing Congress from establishing a federal church. So Judge Hand was entirely correct in opining that the Establishment Clause did not bar Alabama from establishing a religion: it had been crafted partly to prevent Congress from interfering with states' establishments.

The issue, of course, in *Wallace v. Jaffree* was not whether Alabama should establish a state church. It was whether the people of Alabama should decide their state's religious policies (as per the Constitution) or whether federal judges should decide and dictate their own policy preferences to the people of Alabama, despite the Constitution.

The Court's excesses have never been reversed. *Everson, Engel, Lemon,* and *Wallace* remain what lawyers call "good law"—the precedents courts follow in lieu of the Constitution. They cannot plead ignorance in doing so, for Rehnquist's dissent is right there in the casebooks law students study in law school.

On the basis of this line of cases, the Court has struck down science curricula the justices disliked [*Edwards v. Aguillard* (1987)]; banned the centuries-old tradition of having invocations at school commencement ceremonies [*Lee v. Weisman* (1992)]; held a city's display of a nativity scene unconstitutional, but its display of a menorah constitutional [*County of Allegheny v. ACLU* (1989)]; negated a Texas statute exempting religious publications from taxation [*Texas Monthly, Inc. v. Bullock* (1989)]; and struck down a Massachusetts law banning the sale of alcoholic beverages within five hundred feet of a church or school if the church or school objected [*Larkin v. Grendel's Den* (1982)].

Need it be said that none of the statutes had anything to do with establishing a national church? The joined decisions about menorahs and nativity scenes seem to demonstrate that the Court majority really just dislikes Christianity—any religion is okay, so long as it is not Christianity.

The Court also found that the Nebraska legislature's practice of having a chaplain say prayers was somehow permissible under *Lemon.* There was, the pompous Chief Justice Warren Burger counseled in *Marsh v. Chambers* (1983), "no real threat," posed by the chaplain, "while this Court sits."

The arrogance of that line—that the Supreme Court exists to protect Nebraskans from decisions their elected officials make about religious observances—says all that needs to be said.

Chapter Eleven

THE COURT ON PORNOGRAPHY, CRIME, AND RACE

The First Amendment guarantees that "Congress shall make no law...abridging the freedom of speech, or of the press." But legal academics have used this perfectly clear language as an excuse to concoct "freedom of expression," another of those elastic judicial concepts that swallow the clear intent of the Constitution.

In 1943, at the height of American involvement in World War II, the Court said in *West Virginia State Board of Education v. Barnette* that children could not be compelled to salute the flag and say the Pledge of Allegiance because that would violate their freedom of thought. "If there is any fixed star in our constitutional constellation," wrote Justice Robert H. Jackson, "it is that no official, high or petty, can prescribe what shall be orthodox in politics, nationalism, religion, or other matters of opinion or force citizens to confess by word or act their faith therein."

What historical evidence did he cite in support of his claim, which, incidentally, reversed the Court's decision in a virtually identical case, *Minersville School District v. Gobitis* (1940), handed down only three years earlier? To ask the question is to answer it: none at all. Nor did he feel the lack: Jackson pointed to no specific clause of the First Amendment to justify his ruling and did not even bother with the pretense of dragging in the Incorporation Doctrine.

Guess what?

- The First Amendment protects freedom of speech and press—not freedom of armbands, freedom of flag burning, or freedom of Internet pornography.

- The Fourteenth Amendment did not ban the Pledge of Allegiance or racial segregation, but left those matters to the states.

- The Court's decision in *Brown v. Board of Education* allowed it to assume the moral high ground but had no basis in the Constitution.

The "inarticulate roars" of the Court

In time, and using similar extra-constitutional logic, the Court would hold in a succession of cases that "freedom of expression" was included in the First Amendment. It therefore invalidated, in *Tinker v. Des Moines* (1969), a school dress code prohibition of armbands (which were going to be worn as a political protest). And it enforced its invented right of "freedom of expression" in *Texas v. Johnson* (1989), also known as the *Flag-burning Case*. In that case, a Communist had stolen an American flag, taken it to the site of the 1984 Republican National Convention, and burned it.

Justice William Brennan, for the majority, conceded, "The First Amendment literally forbids the abridgement only of 'speech.'" He then added, "We have long recognized that its protection does not end at the spoken or written word." (Translation: "This Court long ago embarked on a career of striking down state statutes regulating not only speech and the press, but also other kinds of conduct we deem 'expressive.'") Brennan dismissed Texas's argument that its statute—which banned flag burning as a breach of the peace and as the destruction of a sacred object—was valid. Forty-eight other states had similar statutes.

What the Court should have recognized was the simple fact that the First Amendment left these issues to the states. But neither Chief Justice Rehnquist in his dissent nor any other justice offered the correct, originalist arguments. Rehnquist did not argue that the Incorporation Doctrine was wrong or even that burning a flag is not speaking. He instead argued that burning a flag was no more expressive than "an inarticulate grunt or roar." But if inarticulate roars could be banned, we wouldn't be reading many Supreme Court opinions.

Louisiana briefly considered responding to the Court's decision in the *Flag-burning Case* by making it legal to beat up flag-burners. Perhaps such violence is covered by "freedom of expression." In the end,

Louisiana didn't go ahead with the idea: state legislatures often are more restrained in their behavior than the Court is.

Freedom of pornography

If the American people wanted the broadcast media covered under the First Amendment clause that protects "freedom of the press," they could bring the Constitution into line with modern technology through a constitutional amendment. It is not a self-evident truth that "the press" (newspapers, magazines, book publishers) is identical to broadcast media, or that the ratifiers intended, in preventing Congress from abridging freedom of "the press," to prevent state legislatures or local governments from banning cable companies from broadcasting nudity, sex acts, and other indecent material. Nevertheless, in *Wilkinson v. Jones* (1987) the Court protected such "speech" carried by cable companies. Had the First Amendment been interpreted as written, cable TV would not be protected by it—and, of course, the amendment would not cover actions by state and local governments.

Portrait of a Justice

Earl Warren (1891–1974) is second in significance only to John Marshall in the annals of chief justices. Like Marshall, Warren paid notably little attention to the people's understanding in adopting particular legal provisions, but preferred instead to write his own political and social views into "constitutional law." Across a broad range of legal subjects—from racial segregation to state legislatures' apportionment, from criminal procedure to speech and press regulation, from criminal penalties to church-state relations, from obscenity to federalism—Warren left the law markedly different than he had found it. America still suffers as a result.

In addition, the Court has delivered itself of a string of decisions about pornography, which today—thanks to the invention of photography, movies, videos and DVDs, and the Internet—is of a completely different nature from anything known in 1791 or 1868. Yet rather than leaving the regulation of pornography to the states and local governments, which can respond to these changes as the people see fit, the Court has decided that it is the sole judge of the legality—and even the morality—of prurient material.

The starting point in this line of cases was Justice Brennan's decision in *Roth v. United States* (1957). The test for obscenity (sexual material the Court would allow Congress and the states to regulate) was "whether to the average person, applying contemporary community standards, the dominant theme of the material taken as a whole appeals to prurient interest." Here, in one of Brennan's earliest opinions, we find a characteristic sleight of hand: his words cannot mean what they say. After all, if the issue was community standards, why should state and local statutes governing obscenity be reviewed by the Committee of Nine Lawyers in Washington, D.C.?

In *Stanley v. Georgia* (1969), a Court majority overturned a conviction for possession of obscene materials on the grounds that "if the First Amendment means anything, it means that a State has no business telling a man, sitting alone in his own house, what books he may read or what films he may watch."

The Court held that "mere private possession of obscene material" could not be criminalized. The Court did not say, however, which clause of the Constitution protected "private possession of obscene material." Surely it was not freedom of speech or freedom of the press or the Due Process Clause of the Fourteenth Amendment. So what was it? There was nothing in the opinion that one might call "legal reasoning," only a naked—if you'll pardon the word—assertion of judicial power.

Soon enough, in *Miller v. California* (1973), Chief Justice Warren Burger announced new guidelines for permissible regulation of such material. "Obscene material," Burger wrote for the majority, "is unprotected by the First Amendment," and in order to classify particular films as "obscene," the justices instituted regular Court viewings of pornographic material. Works that could be regulated, they said, must "depict or describe sexual conduct," which must be "specifically defined by the applicable state law." Proscription must "be limited to works which, taken as a whole, appeal to the prurient interest in sex, which portray sexual conduct in a patently offensive way, and which, taken as a whole, do not have serious literary, artistic, political, or scientific value."

Here, as in concocting his three-part *Lemon* test for violation of the Establishment Clause, Burger undertook to spare the mere mortals in the legislatures the task of defining these offenses. And who would apply this definition? Why, the Nine Great Personages in Washington, D.C., of course! A law degree and a judicial appointment make one a great expert in "serious literary, artistic, political, or scientific value," so why should we have elections anyway?

In *City of Erie v. Pap's A.M.* (2000), which involved a city ordinance aimed at establishments featuring nude dancing, the Court majority held that "nude dancing of the type at issue here ... falls ... within the outer ambit of the First Amendment's protection." In other words, the Court said that the First Amendment Speech Clause, through the Fourteenth Amendment's Due Process Clause, extended protection (though not absolute protection) against state regulation to nude dancers and their employers.

The Supreme Court has also decided, in a string of cases, that the public has a First Amendment right to attend criminal trials. Somehow, in other words, the Press Clause extends not only to the right to publish, but to a fancied right to attend. Thus, in *Globe Newspaper Company v. Superior Court*

A Book You're Not Supposed to Read

Disaster by Decree: The Supreme Court Decisions on Race and the Schools by Lino Graglia; Ithaca, NY: Cornell University Press, 1976.

for the County of Norfolk (1982), Justice Brennan—(n)ever on the lookout for the interests of crime victims—somehow managed to concede that a state might have an interest in excluding the press and general public from a trial when a minor was testifying as the victim of a sex crime. Yet, nevertheless, he claimed that the First Amendment overruled such an interest. But, you say, the First Amendment restricts only Congress. Ah, yes, but of course the First Amendment is now incorporated into the Fourteenth Amendment's Due Process Clause, so the Massachusetts statute protecting minors who are testifying in sex crime cases is void. Uh-huh.

The Supremes and criminal law

The federal courts have been equally assertive in legislating criminal law. The most notorious and influential case was *Miranda v. Arizona* (1966), in which a five-justice majority established the rule that a suspect may not be questioned without first being informed of his rights. Chief Justice Earl Warren noted that a suspect in custody might be expected to feel compelled to answer, and implicitly claimed that this was to be avoided. Why it would be a bad thing for a suspect to offer up a voluntary confession was unclear then, and it remains unclear now—although, like most such precedents, it has proven impossible to undo.

Chief Justice William Rehnquist railed against *Miranda* for his first three decades on the Court, then joined in upholding it at the very end of his career. As conservative legal commentator Robert Bork once put it, long-standing acceptance of a precedent can lead to the rise of so many expectations on its basis as to rule out its rejection. Lost both to the liberals who supported *Miranda* in the first place and to the conservatives who uphold it now is that it marked yet another instance in which the federal government, through the courts, unconstitutionally arrogated power reserved to the states.

In *Gideon v. Wainwright* (1963) and *Douglas v. California* (1963), the Court imposed upon the states a new requirement that all indigent criminal defendants be given trial and appellate counsel at the public's expense. Supposedly, this requirement flowed from the Due Process Clause—which, apparently, no one had understood correctly in its first ninety-five years.

In *Mapp v. Ohio* (1961), Justice Tom C. Clark (Ramsey's father and a graduate of my law school) held that state courts, like federal courts, must exclude the fruit of illegal searches. Thus, the public was to pay the price for police errors and/or misbehavior, and criminals were to benefit. Clark sanctimoniously noted, "If the Government becomes a lawbreaker, it breeds contempt for law" without asking what the government became if it let criminals off on technicalities. He also declined to consider what the federal judiciary became if it cloaked its own procedural preferences in the garb of "constitutional requirements."

Cruel and unusual punishment

The Supreme Court of the 1950s and 1960s often gave the impression that it had found a new Constitution only marginally related to the old one. The Warren Court of 1954–1969 was the great age of judicial legislation, when American constitutional law was remade in the image of the liberal intellectual. The federal courts have been in the business for many decades now of remaking the American law of criminal punishment. On what basis?

In 1992, Justice Sandra Day O'Connor, a Republican appointee who had absorbed the Warren Court legacy, wrote in *Hudson v. McMillian* that the Court needed to apply not the law, but the "evolving standards of decency that mark the progress of a maturing society." In other words, if the Court's majority opinion differed from the opinion of the elected rubes in state governments, then the Court's "standards of decency" had simply "evolved" beyond theirs. The Court's "advanced" standards needed to be applied, which in the area of criminal law usually meant forcing the states to treat criminals more leniently.

This language of "standards of decency" reverberates most often in the Court's decisions involving the Eighth Amendment's Cruel and Unusual Punishment Clause, especially when the cases touch on capital punishment. (It has also been applied to prison smoking regulations and rules depriving prisoners of television or pornographic magazines.)

Probably the most outrageous trend in the capital punishment area was the determination by Justices William Brennan, Thurgood Marshall, and Harry Blackmun in their last decades on the Court that capital punishment always violated the Eighth Amendment ban on cruel and unusual punishments. These three based this determination on the idea of evolving standards of decency—and, predictably, they did not think that Americans at large were nearly so advanced down the evolutionary trail as they were. Critics pointed out that the Fifth and Fourteenth Amendment bans on depriving anyone of "life, liberty, or property without due process of law" clearly contemplated capital punishment *with* due process of law, but Brennan, in particular, insisted that he saw a better way. No one has ever illustrated the drawbacks of lifetime tenure as well as Brennan, whose entire career represented a constant affront to the average American citizen and his elected representatives.

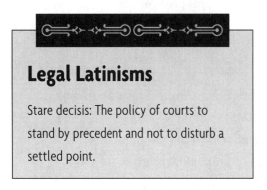

Legal Latinisms

Stare decisis: The policy of courts to stand by precedent and not to disturb a settled point.

For a brief period in the 1970s, Brennan and company succeeded in banning capital punishment altogether.

Brown v. Board of Education and its offspring

The main reason the Court has been able to assert its moral superiority over us lesser mortals is its decision in *Brown v. Board of Education* (1954). It is a historical fact that the Fourteenth Amendment's Equal Protection Clause was not intended to end segregation in public schools. But because the Court ruled that it did, and because the end of segregation is seen as a good thing, the Court covered itself in glory for legislating from the bench.

Intellectuals at large loved the decision. They also knew that such a momentous constitutional amendment, which is what the ruling really was, could never have been won through the constitutional amendment process. How far superior to mere politics, then, was government by judiciary!

But how did *Brown* come to be, and what did it actually accomplish?

The Court's first anti–school segregation decision was 1938's *Missouri ex rel. Gaines v. Canada*. The Court ruled that Missouri had to provide its black citizens who wanted to attend law school the same opportunities it did its white ones. Arguably, this was simply an application of *Plessy*'s "separate but equal" doctrine.

The next notable race discrimination case was *Shelley v. Kraemer* (1948). At issue was a restrictive covenant, an agreement among neighbors that none of them would sell his house to a non-white. The legal issue, according to the Court, was whether the state court system in Missouri could be involved in enforcing such an agreement.

Consider what was really going on in the case: the Court was intervening to consider the validity of a private contract freely entered into among neighbors. Clearly, the Fourteenth Amendment's injunction that no state could deny any person the equal protection of the laws was not at issue; the law involved was simply the law of private contracts. Such agreements are made all the time, and courts—without looking into the motives underlying them—enforce them as a matter of course. So, for example, if someone writes in his will that he will leave more of his property to his sons than to his daughters or more to his Baptist grandchildren than to his Lutheran ones, courts simply do not care.

In *Shelley*, however, the Court ruled that if a state enforced a private agreement discriminating against non-whites, as the restrictive covenants did, it would violate the Fourteenth Amendment. And while no state action had been involved in making these covenants, the state courts were implicated because they enforced them—which supposedly violated the Fourteenth Amendment.

If anyone took this reading of the matter seriously, provisions in wills favoring people or institutions by race, sex, religion, ethnic background, national origin, or any of a score of other suspect classifications would be unenforceable; so would donations to scholarship funds directed to particular sex, racial, ethnic, or religious groups. But the Court majority intended its reasoning to be applied solely to restrictive covenants. In short, the justices had decided that they did not like restrictive covenants, and the Equal Protection Clause offered them plausible—if legally fatuous—grounds for invalidating them. So they did.

Desegregation in the South was already under way by 1948, as various cities considered integrating police forces and sporting events, cities in the upper South started electing blacks to political positions, and the segregation of public transportation was up for debate. At the same time, lawyers from the National Association for the Advancement of Colored People (NAACP) systematically attacked segregation through the courts.

In 1950, the Supreme Court decided in *Sweatt v. Painter* that Texas could not require black law students to attend a different state law school from white students. No matter how many resources were poured into the black school, the justices reasoned, it would never be on par, in terms of prestige, alumni influence, or history, with the University of Texas School of Law in Austin. When it came to legal education, "separate but equal" was impossible, and so separation was unconstitutional.

By this point, as the late Georgia governor and U.S. senator Herman Talmadge conceded, white politicians in the South could see the handwriting on the wall. Yet they rushed to spend money on upgrading facilities in black primary and secondary schools in an attempt to render them truly "separate but equal."

Too late. In 1954, with *Brown v. Board of Education*, the Court served up what Justice Robert H. Jackson admitted was new law for a new day: segregation of the races in public schools would be unconstitutional ever after. The Court based its holding on "modern authority," in Warren's words, in the field of psychology: specifically, on Kenneth Clark's doll experiments.

Clark had shown northern and southern black children a white doll and a black doll and asked them to identify which one they preferred. Many black children from segregated schools chose the white doll. Clark testified that he had demonstrated that "a fundamental effect of segregation is basic confusion in individuals and their concepts about themselves," adding that the black kids had "been definitely harmed in the development of their personalities."

On examination, however, Clark's own data showed that black kids from unsegregated environments were more likely to prefer the white dolls than those from segregated environments. If the experiment proved anything, in other words (which seems doubtful), it was that segregation *improved* children's "concepts about themselves."

In any event, it should go without saying that neither the ratifiers of the Constitution nor the ratifiers of the Fourteenth Amendment imagined that the Supreme Court should analyze doll tests to decide how states must organize their school systems. If the doll tests were relevant to anyone, perhaps they were relevant to teachers, principals, school boards, and maybe even city, county, and state legislators. But the Supreme Court? Why? Where is the "doll test" in the Constitution?

On the same day the Court issued its opinion in *Brown v. Board of Education*, it decided in *Bolling v. Sharpe* that the Fifth Amendment's Due Process Clause banned segregation of public schools in the District of Columbia. This was hardly a tenable reading of the Fifth Amendment, which had been drafted chiefly by James Madison (owner of more than one hundred slaves) and ratified by the states, a majority of which still had legal slavery. Nor was it any more tenable under the Fourteenth Amendment. The Congress that wrote the Fourteenth Amendment had itself established segregated schools in Washington, D.C.

And, of course, the *Brown* ruling violated the Court's own precedent of *Plessy v. Ferguson*, which said that segregation was constitutional. No

Portrait of a Justice

William Brennan (1906–1990) played a leading role in the revolutionary Warren Court of the 1950s and 1960s and then, with the liberal bloc's decline in the Burger and early Rehnquist years, became the Court's chief liberal spokesman.

His approach to judging was captured in his Rule of Five: with five votes, he could do anything. He led the majority that wrote the failed Equal Rights Amendment into "constitutional law," banned capital punishment for a number of years, forced children to submit to school busing for racial balance, restricted legislatures' discretion in punishing criminals, drove Christianity from the public square, and generally made McGovernism the country's ruling legal philosophy. Brennan was to the twentieth century what John Marshall was to the nineteenth: the judge who won for a roundly rejected political impulse a lasting victory in the courts.

amendment had changed the Constitution since. The South, predictably, was outraged by *Brown*. The growing support for desegregation among white southerners fell away. Senator Harry Flood Byrd of Virginia—scion of one of the South's great seventeenth-century families and never a racial bomb-thrower—promised "massive resistance" to desegregation.

Had segregationists known what was going on behind closed doors at the Supreme Court, they would have been even more outraged. One justice had asked his law clerk to research the question of whether the Fourteenth Amendment had been intended to ban racial segregation in schools. The clerk, despite his own predilections, had answered no, and his research was shared among the justices. Some of the nation's leading historians advised the NAACP the same way.

But in his opinion for the Court, Chief Justice Earl Warren said that the Court could not be bound by the understanding of 1868. In short, the Court could not be bound by the Constitution or the clear original understanding of its amendments. Nor did the Court have to show the slightest respect to the laws made by freely elected legislatures in the states. In fact, the Court was bound by nothing at all but the personal policy preferences of nine justices.

How, exactly, could this judicial ukase be enforced? Did school districts across the country, not just the South (the case was *Brown v. Board of Education* of Topeka, Kansas, after all), have to desegregate overnight? The Court said that the parties should come back the next year to talk about it.

So *Brown v. Board of Education* was really a multi-part decision. The ruling in 1954 was only Part I. In *Brown v. Board of Education (II)* (1955), the Court said that schools must be desegregated "with all deliberate speed." Meanwhile, resistance was building. In the end, some southern localities closed their public schools—for years—rather than have black and white students attend school together; whites in some areas, meanwhile, were provided state-supported private schooling while their black neighbors were left with few or no educational options. The issue of desegregation now dominated southern politics

President Dwight Eisenhower thought that *Brown* was incorrect, but he did not say so in public. He essentially kept his hands off the schools issue, although his administration was involved in ongoing litigation concerning other forms of segregation. In 1958, however, when the governor of Arkansas sent in the National Guard rather than allow Little Rock's Central High School to admit a handful of black students, Eisenhower intervened by sending in U.S. Army paratroopers.

Here the Supreme Court saw its opening. In an opinion in *Cooper v. Aaron* (1958) signed by all the justices, the Court declared that it was the final decider of all questions constitutional. It denied that state governors and legislators had anything to say about segregated schools. Calling on

A Book You're Not Supposed to Read

A Time to Lose: Representing Kansas in Brown v. Board of Education by Paul E. Wilson; Lawrence, KS: University Press of Kansas, 1995.

Chief Justice John Marshall's claim of judicial supremacy in *Marbury v. Madison* (1803), the Court insisted that the Supremacy Clause of the Constitution made not only the Constitution, but also the Court's "constitutional law," "the supreme law of the land." State executive and legislative attempts to circumvent Supreme Court decisions, the Court said, were attempts to circumvent the Constitution itself.

With the strong wind of the *Brown* decision at its back, the Court would soon undertake a wide-ranging revolution in American law and government. In time, it would become accustomed to deciding any question it found interesting, despite the absence of constitutional authority to do so. Its critics would have to answer the question, "If you disapprove of the Court's reasoning in this case, does that mean you don't accept *Brown*?"

The Court's frustration with *Brown*'s results did not end in 1958. In fact, between 1954 and 1964, *Brown* had almost no effect on Deep South enrollment patterns. It was only the Civil Rights Act of 1964, with its assignment of limitless federal resources to enforcement of the Fifteenth Amendment, and the Voting Rights Act of 1965, that forced southern Democrats to appeal for black votes, that ended racial segregation in southern education.

The civil rights legislation of the 1960s

One issue that had arisen repeatedly during the debate over the Civil Rights Act of 1964—which, thanks to Democratic opposition, was the longest debate in the history of Congress—concerned the act's constitutionality. After all, the Supreme Court had ruled in the *Civil Rights Cases* of 1883 that the nearly identical Civil Rights Act of 1875 was an unconstitutional attempt by Congress to regulate matters reserved exclusively to the states.

By any fair reading, the *Civil Rights Cases* were correctly decided. But, as justices had made clear in handing down the *Brown (I)* decision in 1954, they did not intend to be bound by history—that is, by the people's intention when they ratified the Fourteenth Amendment. Instead, the Court was in the business of giving America "new law for a new day."

By the end of 1964, then, the Court hurriedly decided the cases of *Heart of Atlanta Motel, Inc. v. United States* and *Katzenbach v. McClung*. In the former case, the motel's owner invoked his private property rights. He said that the Civil Rights Act of 1964 could not compel him to open his motel to blacks, because that would be a violation of his Thirteenth Amendment rights; if Congress could tell him how to run his motel, he was being forced into a state of involuntary servitude. He also denied that renting a hotel room was "interstate commerce," and thus subject to congressional regulation under the Commerce Clause.

The Court, however, held that the Civil Rights Act, which banned racial discrimination in public accommodations, was a valid exercise of Congress's Commerce Clause powers, even if regulating interstate commerce had not been the intent of the act. In his opinion for the Court, Justice Tom Clark said that Congress's powers under the Commerce Clause were "plenary"—i.e., virtually unlimited. This was a momentous curtailment of traditional property rights.

In *Katzenbach*, the Court upheld the Civil Rights Act as applied to restaurants, again using the Commerce Clause (specifically citing the *Wickard v. Filburn* decision, which said that wheat grown for private use could be regulated as "interstate commerce").

The Court's lesson for Congress was that it, like the Court, could do whatever it wanted to do under the guise of regulating commerce. Far from being the protector of the Constitution, the Supreme Court has been a relentless agent of an ever more powerful and unrestrained federal government.

Chapter Twelve

THE COURT'S BRAVE NEW WORLD: FROM AFFIRMATIVE ACTION TO SODOMY

In 1968, the Court decided that "all deliberate speed" was not desegregating the public schools quite fast enough for its liking. In *Green v. County School Board of New Kent County* (1968), the Court ruled that public schools must achieve racial balance immediately. Many school districts had offered parents a choice of two schools for their children, and most parents had preferred to send their children to schools near their homes, with the result being that most black parents sent their children to predominantly black schools and most white parents sent their children to predominantly white schools. Not getting the results it wanted, the Court ruled that voluntary desegregation plans that failed to create substantially integrated schools were unacceptable.

So the Court set new standards. Where *Brown v. Board of Education* had prohibited assigning students to schools on the basis of their race, the Court now insisted on it. So in "implementing" *Brown* the Court actually inverted it, and demanded that school administrators and judges racially divide students to integrate the schools. Since neighborhoods, and thus neighborhood schools, tended to be racially identifiable, busing students—even the youngest students—among neighborhoods became a "constitutional" requirement.

Thus, a racialist assumption—that black students would never receive an equal education so long as they went to school only with other black

Guess what?

- In order to forcibly integrate the public schools, the Supreme Court effectively overturned its landmark anti-segregation ruling in *Brown v. Board of Education.*

- The Fourteenth Amendment did not ban sex discrimination.

- The Bill of Rights, according to the Supreme Court, contains "emanations from penumbras" that guarantee a right to contraception and abortion.

Legal Latinisms

Writ of certiorari: A writ issued from a superior to an inferior court, requesting a certified record of a case. The Supreme Court uses writs of certiorari to choose its cases.

children—yielded racialist assignment. In 1973's *Keyes v. School District No. 1, Denver, Colorado*, the same set of postulates was applied by the Court to public schools in Denver, Colorado—a jurisdiction that had never had formal racial segregation. Soon, Boston, Massachusetts, was rent by turmoil over forced busing of students. Busing became a national political issue in many localities where schools had never been segregated, as parents were outraged that their children were being bused across town in a judicially mandated social experiment.

In Boston, opposition to busing plans was led by a black mother. Across the country, people of all races came to agree that they did not want six-year-olds to ride buses for as much as three hours a day as part of the Supreme Court's "constitutional" "remedy." Wealthy liberals (like Senator Ted Kennedy of Massachusetts) became notorious for their hypocrisy in supporting the Court in this line of cases while sending their own children to private schools. One federal judge responsible for an enormous busing plan explained his own apparent hypocrisy in sending his children to private schools by saying, "When I'm on the bench, I'm a judge, and when I'm at home, I'm a father."

Here we see why formulation of policy was left by the Founding Fathers mainly to the state governments (and also why, within the federal government, Congress, not the Court, is supposed to be the legislative branch). Under no circumstances would this idiocy have been spawned by the republican system of elections. Yet, as since John Marshall's day, life tenure (and wealth) insulated federal judges. They could not be held to account by the electorate, nor did they necessarily feel the full effects of their own actions.

Many cities' court-enforced integration plans have been allowed to lapse in recent years, but this line of precedents has not been overruled—and many Americans still suffer under it. Perhaps its extreme manifestation came in St. Louis, where a federal judge ordered an enormous statewide tax increase to finance construction of a palatial high school intended to spur white enrollment in an essentially black school. King George III's authority in America never rivaled that of a contemporary federal judge.

Affirmative action

Lyndon Johnson, who signed the Civil Rights Act of 1964, also instituted the policy of "affirmative action"—a practice that has come to be called "benign race discrimination." "Affirmative action" first meant finding blacks who might not have applied to a school or for a job because of low expectations rather than lack of ability. But when it did not appear that segregation had created an enormous cohort of black street sweepers who were really frustrated potential brain surgeons, the definition of affirmative action began to mutate.

The Supreme Court got into the affirmative action business in *Griggs v. Duke Power Co.* (1971). The Court ruled that the Duke Power Company, in requiring a high school diploma and high aptitude test scores for employment and promotion, was being racially discriminatory, because proportionately fewer blacks did well on these tests or had diplomas. The Court decided that company employment standards nationwide had to be "reasonably related" to the relevant jobs; companies could not rely on broad educational qualifications in making

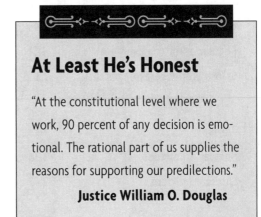

At Least He's Honest

"At the constitutional level where we work, 90 percent of any decision is emotional. The rational part of us supplies the reasons for supporting our predilections."

Justice William O. Douglas

hiring decisions. Having no intent to discriminate was no defense; it was the balance of racial statistics that mattered. Soon enough, businesses throughout the country responded by hiring and promoting staff on a racial basis. The non-discrimination policy enacted by Congress in 1964 had become, in the hands of lawyers and federal judges, a virtual mandate to discriminate.

Quotas also appealed to university administrators as convenient mechanisms for demonstrating that they too were on board the Supreme Court's Civil Rights Express. A flash point in what would become the extended controversy over quotas, goals, timetables, and other measures of "benign" discrimination (discrimination against whites and, later, against men) was the 1978 decision in *University of California Board of Regents v. Bakke.*

Bakke by the Numbers

1973	Overall grade point average	Science grade point average	MCAT scores
Bakke	3.44	3.46	96, 94, 97, 72
Regular admittee averages	3.51	3.49	81, 76, 83, 69
Quota admittee averages	2.62	2.88	46, 24, 35, 33
1974			
Bakke	3.44	3.46	96, 94, 97, 72
Regular admittees	3.36	3.29	69, 67, 82, 72
Quota admittees	2.42	2.62	34, 30, 37, 18

When Allen Bakke first applied to the University of California Medical School in 1973, the school reserved 16 percent of its admissions for minorities. Bakke was denied admission even though his qualifications were better than those of all the minority candidates admitted under the 16 percent quota. In fact, as the Supreme Court conceded (in a footnote), the qualifications of the minority students were pitifully poor.

Would you want your heart surgery performed by a doctor who had scored in the bottom third on the Medical College Admission Test (MCAT)? Note that the MCAT percentiles listed in the box at left are *average* scores of the admittees, which means that some of them scored lower than the bottom third or even below the eighteenth percentile on portions of the MCAT.

The Court's decision was nonsensical: four justices would have upheld the University of California's program as consistent with the Equal Protection Clause, four would have torpedoed it completely, and the ninth—Justice Lewis Powell, who would make a career of decisions like this—voted to force the school to admit Bakke while also stating that schools could give particular races and ethnic groups special privileges to augment "educational diversity." These privileges, however, had to be "on the margins." A forthright quota could not be used.

Of course, given the enormous disparity between the qualifications of most students admitted to the school and those of the preferred minority applicants, marginal "affirmative action" would have admitted few, if any, specially privileged minority students at all.

In *Hopwood v. Texas* (1996), a case similar to *Bakke*, a circuit court of appeals struck down the race-based admissions policy of the University of Texas School of Law. The court stated that the University of Texas could not use racial discrimination now "to make up for past racial wrongs."

The Supreme Court let that case stand, but then in *Gratz v. Bollinger* (2003), it ruled that while the University of Michigan could no longer give blanket preference to members of certain preferred minority groups, its law school could discriminate in the way outlined by Justice Powell in *Bakke*—which presumably made *Hopwood* a dead letter.

Way back in the 1950s, with *Brown*, the Court had announced non-discrimination as "new law for a new day." But when the legislators on the bench didn't like the results of non-discrimination, they told state governments that it was acceptable to discriminate against academically high-achieving racial groups (usually Asians and non-Hispanic whites) in favor of underachievers (blacks, Hispanics, Eskimos, Aleuts, and Indians). Some kinds of race discrimination were better than others.

Do you think the ratifiers would agree? To ask the question is to answer it.

Sex discrimination and the Fourteenth Amendment

The Fourteenth Amendment has nothing at all to say about sex discrimination, and while it was a matter of public debate at the time (the late 1860s and the 1870s) whether women should be granted the rights guaranteed to black men, Congress omitted language from the Fifteenth Amendment guaranteeing women the right to vote. A hundred years later, however, the Court was ready to break new legislative ground.

So in the 1973 case of *Frontiero v. Richardson*, Justice William Brennan offered up an opinion effectively declaring sex discrimination on par with race discrimination. He won three other justices' votes for that opinion, falling one short of a majority. If he had won, the Court would have (yet again and unconstitutionally) passed into law a constitutional amendment. As it was, the public was already discussing an Equal Rights Amendment to the Constitution, which Congress had sent to the states for their ratification. If Brennan's opinion had been the majority opinion, it would have rendered the public debate pointless. And in the end, it would have overturned the result of the states' consideration of the amendment—which was to reject it.

If Justice Brennan did not win that one, he did win in 1976's *Craig v. Boren*, in which the Court invalidated a provision of Oklahoma law setting the male drinking age at twenty-one and the female drinking age at eighteen. Justice Brennan sounded every bit the 1970s feminist in his "reasoning." He used the word "gender" instead of "sex" and invoked the (constitutional?) idea that legis-

Translation: We Can Do Whatever We Want

"We who have the final word can speak softly or angrily. We can seek to challenge and annoy, as we need not stay docile and quiet."

Justice William O. Douglas

lators should seek "more 'germane' bases of classification." He then turned to evidence showing that boys eighteen to twenty were more than eleven times as likely as those twenty-one or older to be arrested for "alcohol-related driving offenses," which he described as an "unpersuasive" justification for such "gender" discrimination.

How wonderful for the people of Oklahoma, then, that Justice Brennan was going to substitute his elevated expertise for that of the local, elected legislators who had determined that a 1,111 percent higher likelihood of alcohol-related offenses was substantial! Need it be added that Brennan's diktat about men and equal protection had no relationship whatsoever to the Supreme Court's own previous definition of the Equal Protection Clause's purpose: protecting recently freed slaves from their masters?

Having invented the idea that sexual classifications fall under the Equal Protection Clause, the Court has since felt itself entitled to strike down various other state statutes distinguishing males from females. In 1982's *Mississippi University for Women v. Hogan* the Court struck down the school's "sexist" admissions policies. The Court ruled that it caused impermissible hardship to a male applicant who lived in Columbus, Mississippi (where

A Book You're Not Supposed to Read

The Southern Essays of Richard Weaver by Richard Weaver (particularly the essay "Life without Discrimination"); Indianapolis: Liberty Press, 1987.

the school is located), to have to travel to Jackson or Hattiesburg, where he could find state-supported nursing schools that allowed men to enroll.

Notoriously, in *United States v. Virginia* (1996), the Court disallowed the all-male admissions policy of the Virginia Military Institute (VMI). The hallowed Virginia school objected that admitting women would change the school's purpose, lower the physical fitness standards the school required, and force it to segregate its traditionally shared housing (essentially a barracks). The Court swept these concerns aside as insignificant. In short, perhaps the people of Virginia had believed for a century and a half that the all-male education offered by VMI was worth public support, but a majority of the Supreme Court came to a different legislative conclusion. The Court used the fig leaf of the Equal Protection Clause as justification to substitute its judgment for the Virginia General Assembly's.

The Supreme Court and "privacy"

Nothing since *Brown* and its "civil rights" interventions has won the Court more plaudits from the liberal intelligentsia than inventing and developing a "right to privacy." Under this rubric, found nowhere in the Constitution—but allegedly hiding there—the courts have created a right to marital contraception, a generalized right to contraception, a right to abortion, and a right to homosexual sodomy; they have even created a right not to have a state constitutional provision banning officials from conferring special privileges upon homosexuals. (No, that is not a typo.)

The Court first turned to this matter in *Griswold v. Connecticut* (1965). In that case, a physician had been convicted of violating Connecticut's ban on prescribing or using contraceptives. He appealed, claiming that the Connecticut law violated the Fourteenth Amendment's Due Process Clause. As the Connecticut law had nothing to do with protecting the rights of freed slaves (which was what the Fourteenth Amendment covered), it was only through the magic of the Supreme Court that this logic could be even remotely tenable.

Justice William O. Douglas should have produced guffaws when, for the majority, he announced, "We do not sit as a super-legislature to determine the wisdom, need, and propriety of laws that touch economic problems, business affairs, or social conditions."

Exceptions, though, inevitably had to be made. As Justice Douglas noted, "This law, however, operates directly on an intimate relation of husband and wife." It was not clear why the Supreme Court was the proper institution to pass upon the desirability of state laws operating "directly on an intimate relation of husband and wife." That role for the Court never came up during the drafting and ratification of the Constitution.

But according to the Court, the Due Process Clause of the Fourteenth Amendment enshrined a right for married couples to use condoms. Perhaps the Constitution

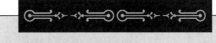

Isn't This a Job for Legislatures?

"We must never lose sight of the fact that the law has a moral foundation, and we must never fail to ask ourselves not only what the law is, but what the law should be."

Justice Anthony Kennedy

did not actually say so, but "the specific guarantees in the Bill of Rights [as purportedly made applicable against the states by the Due Process Clause] have penumbras, formed by emanations from those guarantees that help give them life and substance. Various guarantees create zones of privacy."

Even among academics devoted to the existence of a "right" to contraception, Douglas's "reasoning" here is considered entirely laughable.

Mere mention of the "emanations of penumbras" will draw titters in most legal forums. But, as in the sex discrimination cases, lack of justification has not led to the unraveling of the precedent. Far from it: the Court has built upon *Griswold* and continues to do so.

In *Eisenstadt v. Baird* (1972), the Court extended the newly minted contraception right to unmarried couples. Next, in 1973, it decided that there exists a "constitutional" right to procure an abortion. Purchase of this service, and its provision by strangers, is a component of "privacy," which is a general right enforceable by the federal courts against the states.

With its decision to that effect in *Roe v. Wade*, the Court undid the abortion regulations of all fifty states. Academics and liberal intellectuals helped sell this idea to the public by taking up the word *fetus* (Latin for "very young one") to refer to unborn babies (eventually defined by the Court's precedents as "babies whose heads have not cleared the birth canal completely"). As the Fourteenth Amendment was self-evidently about protecting the civil rights—including the right to life—of former slaves, it took the "reasoning" of a Supreme Court justice to turn it around and use it to establish a right to end the lives of unborn children.

Legal Latinisms

De jure: Fully compliant with the law. It's often, in common parlance, contrasted with de facto, meaning existing in fact, but not necessarily in law.

It seemed likely to many observers that the Court was going to backtrack on its controversial *Roe* decision when it undertook to decide 1992's *Planned Parenthood v. Casey*. A series of appointments to the Court by presidents forthrightly opposed to *Roe*—and opposed to "judicial activism" generally—gave the Court an opportunity to recant.

But it was not to be. The Court not only failed to overturn *Roe*, but it also delivered a breathtakingly silly statement of constitutional philosophy: where the Court "calls the contending sides of a national contro-versy to end their national division by accepting a common mandate rooted in the Constitution," its decision has a special "dimension." The Court claimed to have done this only twice: in *Brown* and in *Roe*. This conveniently overlooked the Court's pro-slavery *Dred Scott* decision, which settled—until it was reversed by an enormous war and the Thir-teenth, Fourteenth, Fifteenth Amendments—a "national controversy" by repealing the Missouri Compromise and declaring that blacks could not be citizens.

The Court ignored this unfortunate history and said it could not reverse its decision of a controversial case. "So to overrule under fire in the absence of the most compelling reason to reexamine a watershed decision would subvert the Court's legitimacy beyond any serious ques-tion."

Justice Sandra Day O'Connor added that *Roe* had been "in confor-mance with the Constitution." What part of the Constitution? Why, the Due Process Clause, of course. The one that guaranteed the recently freed slaves that they would not be punished without a hearing, the right to counsel, the right to call witnesses, the right to cross-examine, and so on.

You can be forgiven for asking, in Professor Lino Graglia's words, whether the right to an abortion was included in the word "due" or in the word "process."

O'Connor opined that the Court was the chief expositor of America's constitutional "ideals," and that continued enforcement of unconstitu-tional "constitutional" decisions such as *Roe* was a necessary attribute of the "rule of law." Of course, it really is just the opposite. The Court has overturned the right of the people of the states to govern themselves, over-turned the Tenth Amendment, and thus overturned the Constitution—and called it the "rule of law."

One of O'Connor's fellows in this exercise, Justice Anthony Kennedy, delivered himself of this pearl: "At the heart of liberty is the right to

Books You're Not Supposed to Read

The New Color Line: How Quotas and Privilege Destroy Democracy by Paul Craig Roberts and Lawrence M. Stratton; Washington, DC: Regnery, 1997.

Civil Rights: Rhetoric or Reality? by Thomas Sowell; New York: William Morrow, 1984.

Preferential Policies: An International Perspective by Thomas Sowell; New York: William Morrow, 1990.

define one's own concept of existence, of meaning, of the universe, and of the mystery of human life." These are among the many rights not enumerated in the Constitution, and best left, as the Constitution leaves them, to the determination of the people and the states, not to an unaccountable Supreme Court majority of five justices.

Not stopping at contraception and abortion, the Court used the *Griswold* precedent to establish a right to engage in homosexual sodomy. In *Bowers v. Hardwick* (1986), the Court ruled with four dissents (including the "evolving standards of decency" trio of Brennan, Thurgood Marshall, and *Roe* author Harry Blackmun) that there was no fundamental right to engage in homosexual sodomy. In light of the long-standing tradition in the English-speaking world of punishing such sodomy severely (including by castration, burning at the stake, and—if Thomas Jefferson had had his way—boring holes in noses), the Court could hardly have ruled to the contrary. Except that four justices would have, and one of the majority justices, Lewis Powell, later said that he regretted his vote.

Of course, the American people have never amended the Constitution to create a right to homosexual sodomy. But the Supreme Court soon did that for them. The Court simply decided there should be such a right, and, as usual, trotted out the Fourteenth Amendment's Due Process Clause to overturn state laws, its own previous ruling (which somehow it couldn't do with *Roe*), and the tradition of English common law.

Romer v. Evans (1996) involved a state constitutional amendment. Approved by the people of Colorado, the amendment stated: "Neither the state of Colorado, through any of its branches or departments, nor any of its agencies, political subdivisions, municipalities or school districts, shall enact, adopt or enforce any statute, regulation, ordinance or policy whereby homosexual, lesbian or bisexual orientation, conduct, practices or relationships shall constitute or otherwise be the basis of, or entitle any person or class of persons to have or claim any minority status, quota preferences, protected status or claim of discrimination. This Section of the Constitution shall be in all respects self-executing." In other words, self-identified homosexuals were to be denied any special minority privileges.

The Supreme Court, however, overturned the right of the people of Colorado to govern themselves, and said that of course the Constitution meant that state officials must be left free to provide special privileges for self-identified homosexuals. The Equal Protection Clause of the Fourteenth Amendment meant, according to Justice Anthony Kennedy, that homosexuals could not be denied the opportunity to seek special privileges from state and local governments. Kennedy said that this policy of disallowing special privileges could only be explained by "animus toward the class that it affects." Here, the Court majority ruled invalid the commonly held position that homosexuality is about conduct, not identity. Kennedy silently rejected the idea—clearly reflected in the Colorado

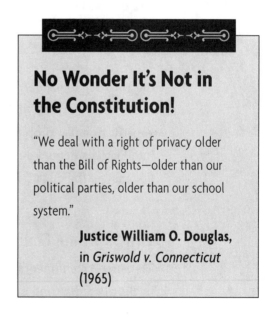

No Wonder It's Not in the Constitution!

"We deal with a right of privacy older than the Bill of Rights—older than our political parties, older than our school system."

Justice William O. Douglas, in *Griswold v. Connecticut* (1965)

amendment—that engaging in sodomy was at issue, not the disposition to do so. The Court, in other words, once again used the Fourteenth Amendment grab-bag as a source of limitless judicial power to disallow state policies with which it disagreed.

As Justice Antonin Scalia noted in dissent, what the Court had done was to say "that opposition to homosexuality is as reprehensible as racial or religious bias." Here, as in *Roe*, the Court simply preempted a legitimate political debate; as in virtually every instance since 1937, it took the side of the leftward-most of the contending forces against the traditional (and coincidentally the Christian) position.

Is this republican government?

A Book You're Not Supposed to Read

Men in Black: How the Supreme Court Is Destroying America by Mark Levin; Washington, DC: Regnery, 2005.

Predictably, the Court followed its *Romer* thinking in *Lawrence v. Texas* (2003), which declared a constitutional right to homosexual sodomy. The intellectual class, in support of the Court's *Lawrence* legislation (and let us call it "legislation," because it was absolutely not founded on any constitutional provision or on any traditional conception of the role of judges and the function of a written federal constitution), hooted down critics who asked why, if private homosexual sodomy was constitutionally protected, bestiality, incest, and group sex were not. Intellectuals hooted down people who asked that question, but they did not answer the question.

The Supreme Court's electoral interventions

The First Amendment Speech and Press Clauses, as John Marshall noted in *Barron v. Baltimore* (1833), originally operated as limitations on the federal government. Their chief purpose, Republicans noted in the dispute over the Alien and Sedition Acts of 1798, was to guarantee that there could be robust political debate.

In recent years, however, the Court has moved in the opposite direction, so that the First Amendment works as a wedge, allowing pornographers to operate their establishments in spite of the preferences of local citizens as reflected by the policies of state and local governments.

At the same time, however, under the guise of "campaign finance reform," Congress is allowed by the Supreme Court to restrict political discussion in a way that mirrors the Sedition Act in its benefits to incumbents. Among other things, the legislation upheld by the Court in *McConnell v. Federal Election Commission* (2003) bans issue advertising in favor of particular candidates within sixty days of an election. Such advertising is one of the most powerful tools for overcoming incumbents' advantage in personal familiarity to voters (what journalists call "name ID"), and it is impossible to see how restricting political speech can possibly be constitutional. Congress's Bipartisan Campaign Act of 2002 (known as the McCain-Feingold Bill) restricted political advertising—that is, the press—in various other ways as well.

What originally had been a guarantee that Congress would not regulate political speech or the political press thus has come to be treated by the Supreme Court as allowing exactly that kind of regulation, on the

Portrait of a Justice

William Rehnquist (1924–2005) was for years the leading proponent of originalist jurisprudence on the twentieth-century Supreme Court. By the end of his tenure, however, he was prone to bow before Court precedent, such as in upholding the *Miranda* decision, even though he had long noted that originalism mandated the opposite result. He presided at the impeachment trial of Bill Clinton before the Senate, generally to positive evaluations, and he did carry the day in favor of federalism and against a broad (even untethered) reading of Congress's Commerce Clause power. Resounding originalist opinions such as his dissent in *Wallace v. Jaffree* (1985) (wherein he exploded the Court's modern church-state jurisprudence) were his most lasting contribution.

grounds that money—the expenditure of which is what is restricted—is property, not speech. And some have argued that Congress should be allowed *greater* latitude in regulating political expenditures (in order, they say, to limit the power of special interests).

This formulation is absurd, of course. The actual effect of the law is not only to protect incumbent politicians but also to protect the incumbent media (and the incumbent corporations that own them), who are free to editorialize, while restricting the right of people who want to purchase air time or advertising space in print.

More egregious than the Court's unfounded decisions in restricting political speech (*McConnell* being only the most important) was its performance in *Bush v. Gore* (2000).

In the 2000 presidential election, Florida's Division of Elections first announced that Governor George Bush of Texas had defeated Vice President Albert Gore, Jr. As the margin was small—fewer than two thousand votes—Florida law required a machine recount. The recount yielded a smaller margin, but the same result: Bush would receive Florida's electoral votes.

When the flurry of suits that demanded recounts or the stoppage of recounts reached the Supreme Court, it responded in a "per curiam" opinion—one, that is, from the whole Court. The Court solemnly intoned, "None are more conscious of the vital limits on judicial authority than are the members of this Court." That was a laugh, but the problem in Florida was that its own state supreme court was interpreting the state constitution as the U.S. Supreme Court usually interprets the federal Constitution—however it pleased, openly dis-

Legal Logic and Affirmative Action

Does anyone outside the Supreme Court really think the ratifiers of the Constitution imagined the Court setting employment policies for the nation's businesses?

regarding the laws governing elections in Florida to allow perpetual recounts until the preferred outcome (a Gore victory) could be arranged.

The proper remedy to the Florida Supreme Court's overreaching lay with the Florida legislature. The legislature was fully empowered by Article II, Section 1 of the federal Constitution to establish the manner of the Florida electors' allocation between Bush and Gore. The popular votes had been counted and recounted and recounted in selected counties, always yielding the same result, and the secretary of state, under the state constitution, had a deadline for certifying the vote tallies. If counties failed to submit their votes by the deadline, she was constitutionally empowered to ignore them. Thus, however one cut it, the issue was clearly decided. Bush was the electoral choice of the state of Florida, under the electoral laws of the state, and the Florida legislature was the constitutional authority—not the Florida Supreme Court—to decide which electors were going to Washington.

Nevertheless, the Supreme Court couldn't restrain itself from commenting on Florida's electoral processes, implicitly disapproving the state's method of counting votes, and expressing the Court's concern that "equal protection" be respected in any recount process (though, as punch-card ballots are not racially or sexually identifiable, it was not clear what "equal protection" could amount to beyond an anodyne counsel of "play fair"). Only Chief Justice Rehnquist (with two associates) pointed out that the Constitution gives state legislatures the power to assign the states' electoral votes.

Surprisingly, while his reasoning did not attract a majority, Rehnquist's vote carried the day. George Bush received Florida's electoral votes, as the Florida legislature intended. The fiasco of the Supreme Court intervening to settle this dispute could only have been made worse by its doing what the dissenters wanted: returning the matter to a nakedly partisan, Democrat-dominated state supreme court. The Court declined to do so by a margin of one vote. That was a one-vote majority in favor of the Constitution over the judicial clique that thinks the law is what it says it is.

CONCLUSION

What, then, can be done to right two centuries' nearly uninterrupted misapplication of the federal Constitution? How might the promises made by Federalists such as James Wilson and Edmund Randolph in the ratification process of 1787–1788 be made to bear fruit? Specifically, how can we stop the Supreme Court from acting as the supreme legislator of the United States?

The prospects are dim. One serious obstacle to reform is the Seventeenth Amendment, which substituted popular election of senators for their original election by state legislatures. This stripped the state governments of their sole significant check on federal overreaching. Also, the modern case method of instructing prospective lawyers in constitutional law, which consists simply of discussing judicial opinions about the Constitution, makes it highly unlikely that American attorneys as a class will ever come to understand that the account of the Constitution judges peddle has little connection to the ratifiers' understanding. Lawyers, then, will not soon know that the Constitution of the judges is not the one the people voted for.

The intellectual class, by and large, has no problem with this. The party line is that Supreme Court rulings are raw exercises of power whether judges purport to be bound by the original understanding or not, so why not admit it? This idea is promoted in academia, the liberal media, and elite opinion generally. These circles treat references to originalist understandings of the Constitution as either disingenuous or irrelevant. The *New York Times*, the *Washington Post*, and, nowadays, most people assess Supreme Court rulings according to their policy preferences, along the lines of "I dislike this policy, so it's 'unconstitutional'" (or the reverse).

What constitutional law is supposed to be is the application of the Constitution's plain meaning to bind judges, presidents, and congresses—all wielders of federal power. If we want to return to Thomas Jefferson's vision of the Republic, if we want the Constitution enforced in the way it was explained to the people at the time of its ratification, then we have to overcome the received wisdom about what constitutional law is. I hope *The Politically Incorrect Guide™ to the Constitution* is one small step in that direction.

There are other steps we can take as well. The main problem with the Supreme Court's rulings over the last seventy years is that they have allowed Congress to do too much and state governments to do too little. In other words, the Supreme Court has ignored the Constitution's division of powers between the state and federal governments. The solution, then, is to provide the states with a new check on federal interference and overreaching.

One idea is to create a constitutional council of the fifty states. The council could consist either of the fifty state chief justices or of fifty members elected to represent the states. The council would be given power to review the federal courts' constitutional decisions. This council could help restore the republican federal government of very limited powers we started off with and undo the unrepublican judgeocracy of limitless powers we have now.

When the Philadelphia Convention of 1787 adjourned from writing the Constitution, a woman was waiting at the door. She asked delegate Benjamin Franklin what they had wrought, and he said a constitution for "a republic, if you can keep it." To the extent that we have not kept the Constitution that Franklin helped to write, it is time we took it back.

THE ARTICLES OF CONFEDERATION

Agreed to by Congress November 15, 1777; ratified and in force, March 1, 1781.

Preamble

To all to whom these Presents shall come, we the undersigned Delegates of the States affixed to our Names send greeting.

Articles of Confederation and perpetual Union between the States of New Hampshire, Massachusetts bay, Rhode Island and Providence Plantations, Connecticut, New York, New Jersey, Pennsylvania, Delaware, Maryland, Virginia, North Carolina, South Carolina and Georgia.

Article I. The Stile of this Confederacy shall be "The United States of America."

Article II. Each state retains its sovereignty, freedom, and independence, and every power, jurisdiction, and right, which is not by this Confederation expressly delegated to the United States, in Congress assembled.

Article III. The said States hereby severally enter into a firm league of friendship with each other, for their common defense, the security of their liberties, and their mutual and general welfare, binding themselves to assist each other, against all force offered to, or attacks made upon them, or any of them, on account of religion, sovereignty, trade, or any other pretense whatever.

Article IV. The better to secure and perpetuate mutual friendship and intercourse among the people of the different States in this Union, the free inhabitants of each of these States, paupers, vagabonds, and fugitives from justice excepted, shall be entitled to all privileges and immunities of free citizens in the several States; and the people of each State shall free ingress and regress to and from any other State, and shall enjoy therein all the privileges of trade and commerce, subject to the same duties, impositions, and restrictions as the inhabitants thereof respectively, provided that such restrictions shall not extend so far as to prevent the removal of property imported into any State, to any other State, of which the owner is an inhabitant; provided also that no imposition, duties or restriction shall be laid by any State, on the property of the United States, or either of them.

If any person guilty of, or charged with, treason, felony, or other high misdemeanor in any State, shall flee from justice, and be found in any of the United States, he shall, upon demand of the Governor or executive power of the State from which he fled, be delivered up and removed to the State having jurisdiction of his offense.

Full faith and credit shall be given in each of these States to the records, acts, and judicial proceedings of the courts and magistrates of every other State.

Article V. For the most convenient management of the general interests of the United States, delegates shall be annually appointed in such manner as the legislatures of each State shall direct, to meet in Congress on the first Monday in November, in every year, with a power reserved to each State to recall its delegates, or any of them, at any time within the year, and to send others in their stead for the remainder of the year.

No State shall be represented in Congress by less than two, nor more than seven members; and no person shall be capable of being a delegate for more than three years in any term of six years; nor shall any person, being a delegate, be capable of holding any office under the United States, for which he, or another for his benefit, receives any salary, fees or emolument of any kind.

Each State shall maintain its own delegates in a meeting of the States, and while they act as members of the committee of the States.

In determining questions in the United States in Congress assembled, each State shall have one vote.

Freedom of speech and debate in Congress shall not be impeached or questioned in any court or place out of Congress, and the members of Congress shall be protected in their persons from arrests or imprisonments, during the time of their going to and from, and attendance on Congress, except for treason, felony, or breach of the peace.

Article VI. No State, without the consent of the United States in Congress assembled, shall send any embassy to, or receive any embassy from, or enter into any conference, agreement, alliance or treaty with any King, Prince or State; nor shall any person holding any office of profit or trust under the United States, or any of them, accept any present, emolument, office or title of any kind whatever from any King, Prince or foreign State; nor shall the United States in Congress assembled, or any of them, grant any title of nobility.

No two or more States shall enter into any treaty, confederation or alliance whatever between them, without the consent of the United States in Congress assembled, specifying accurately the purposes for which the same is to be entered into, and how long it shall continue.

No State shall lay any imposts or duties, which may interfere with any stipulations in treaties, entered into by the United States in Congress assembled, with any King, Prince or State, in pursuance of any treaties already proposed by Congress, to the courts of France and Spain.

No vessel of war shall be kept up in time of peace by any State, except such number only, as shall be deemed necessary by the United States in Congress assembled, for the defense of such State, or its trade; nor shall any body of forces be kept up by any State in time of peace, except such number only, as in the judgement of the United States in Congress assembled, shall be deemed requisite to garrison the forts necessary for the defense of such State; but every State shall always keep up a well-regulated and disciplined militia, sufficiently armed and accoutered, and shall provide and constantly have ready for use, in public stores, a due number of filed pieces and tents, and a proper quantity of arms, ammunition and camp equipage.

No State shall engage in any war without the consent of the United States in Congress assembled, unless such State be actually invaded by enemies, or shall have received certain advice of a resolution being formed by some nation of Indians to invade such State, and the danger is so imminent as not to admit of a delay till the United States in Congress assembled can be consulted; nor shall any State grant commissions to any ships or vessels of war, nor letters of marque or reprisal, except it be after a declaration of war by the United States in Congress assembled, and then only against the Kingdom or State and the subjects thereof, against which war

has been so declared, and under such regulations as shall be established by the United States in Congress assembled, unless such State be infested by pirates, in which case vessels of war may be fitted out for that occasion, and kept so long as the danger shall continue, or until the United States in Congress assembled shall determine otherwise.

Article VII. When land forces are raised by any State for the common defense, all officers of or under the rank of colonel, shall be appointed by the legislature of each State respectively, by whom such forces shall be raised, or in such manner as such State shall direct, and all vacancies shall be filled up by the State which first made the appointment.

Article VIII. All charges of war, and all other expenses that shall be incurred for the common defense or general welfare, and allowed by the United States in Congress assembled, shall be defrayed out of a common treasury, which shall be supplied by the several States in proportion to the value of all land within each State, granted or surveyed for any person, as such land and the buildings and improvements thereon shall be estimated according to such mode as the United States in Congress assembled, shall from time to time direct and appoint.

The taxes for paying that proportion shall be laid and levied by the authority and direction of the legislatures of the several States within the time agreed upon by the United States in Congress assembled.

Article IX. The United States in Congress assembled, shall have the sole and exclusive right and power of determining on peace and war, except in the cases mentioned in the sixth article—of sending and receiving ambassadors—entering into treaties

and alliances, provided that no treaty of commerce shall be made whereby the legislative power of the respective States shall be restrained from imposing such imposts and duties on foreigners, as their own people are subjected to, or from prohibiting the exportation or importation of any species of goods or commodities whatsoever—of establishing rules for deciding in all cases, what captures on land or water shall be legal, and in what manner prizes taken by land or naval forces in the service of the United States shall be divided or appropriated—of granting letters of marque and reprisal in times of peace—appointing courts for the trial of piracies and felonies committed on the high seas and establishing courts for receiving and determining finally appeals in all cases of captures, provided that no member of Congress shall be appointed a judge of any of the said courts.

The United States in Congress assembled shall also be the last resort on appeal in all disputes and differences now subsisting or that hereafter may arise between two or more States concerning boundary, jurisdiction or any other causes whatever; which authority shall always be exercised in the manner following. Whenever the legislative or executive authority or lawful agent of any State in controversy with another shall present a petition to Congress stating the matter in question and praying for a hearing, notice thereof shall be given by order of Congress to the legislative or executive authority of the other State in controversy, and a day assigned for the appearance of the parties by their lawful agents, who shall then be directed to appoint by joint consent, commissioners or judges to constitute a court for hearing and determining the matter in question: but if they cannot agree, Congress shall name three persons out of each of the United States, and from the list of such persons each party shall alternately strike out one, the petitioners beginning, until the number shall be reduced to thirteen; and from that number not less than seven, nor more than nine names as Congress shall direct, shall in the presence of Congress be drawn out by lot, and the persons whose names shall be so drawn or any five of them, shall be commissioners or judges, to hear and finally determine the controversy, so always as a major part of the judges who shall hear the cause shall agree in the determination: and if either party shall neglect to attend at the day appointed, without showing reasons, which Congress shall judge sufficient, or being present shall refuse to strike, the Congress shall proceed to nominate three persons out of each State, and the secretary of Congress shall strike in behalf of such party absent or refusing; and the judgement and sentence of the court to be appointed, in the manner before prescribed, shall be final and conclusive; and if any of the parties shall refuse to submit to the authority of such court, or to appear or defend their claim or cause, the court shall nevertheless proceed to pronounce sentence, or judgement, which shall in like manner be final and decisive, the judgement or sentence and other proceedings being in either case transmitted to Congress, and lodged among the acts of Congress for the security of the parties concerned: provided that every commissioner, before he sits in judgement, shall take an oath to be administered by one of the judges of the supreme or superior court of the State, where the cause shall be tried, 'well and truly to hear and determine the matter in question, according to the best of his judgement, without favor, affection or hope of reward': provided also, that no State shall be deprived of territory for the benefit of the United States.

All controversies concerning the private right of soil claimed under different grants of two or more States, whose jurisdictions as they may respect such lands, and the States which passed such grants are adjusted, the said grants or either of them being at the same time claimed to have originated antecedent to such settlement of jurisdiction, shall on the petition of either party to the Congress of the United States, be finally determined as near as may be in the same manner as is before prescribed for deciding disputes respecting territorial jurisdiction between different States.

The United States in Congress assembled shall also have the sole and exclusive right and power of regulating the alloy and value of coin struck by their own authority, or by that of the respective States—fixing the standards of weights and measures throughout the United States—regulating the trade and managing all affairs with the Indians, not members of any of the States, provided that the legislative right of any State within its own limits be not infringed or violated—establishing or regulating post offices from one State to another, throughout all the United States, and exacting such postage on the papers passing through the same as may be requisite to defray the expenses of the said office—appointing all officers of the land forces, in the service of the United States, excepting regimental officers—appointing all the officers of the naval forces, and commissioning all officers whatever in the service of the United States—making rules for the government and regulation of the said land and naval forces, and directing their operations.

The United States in Congress assembled shall have authority to appoint a committee, to sit in the recess of Congress, to be denominated 'A Committee of the States', and to consist of one delegate from each State; and to appoint such other committees and civil officers as may be necessary for managing the general affairs of the United States under their direction—to appoint one of their members to preside, provided that no person be allowed to serve in the office of president more than one year in any term of three years; to ascertain the necessary sums of money to be raised for the service of the United States, and to appropriate and apply the same for defraying the public expenses—to borrow money, or emit bills on the credit of the United States, transmitting every half-year to the respective States an account of the sums of money so borrowed or emitted—to build and equip a navy—to agree upon the number of land forces, and to make requisitions from each State for its quota, in proportion to the number of white inhabitants in such State; which requisition shall be binding, and thereupon the legislature of each State shall appoint the regimental officers, raise the men and cloath, arm and equip them in a solid-like manner, at the expense of the United States; and the officers and men so cloathed, armed and equipped shall march to the place appointed, and within the time agreed on by the United States in Congress assembled. But if the United States in Congress assembled shall, on consideration of circumstances judge proper that any State should not raise men, or should raise a smaller number of men than the quota thereof, such extra number shall be raised, officered, cloathed, armed and equipped in the same manner as the quota of each State, unless the legislature of such State shall judge that such extra number cannot be safely spread out in the same, in which case they shall raise, officer, cloath, arm and equip as many of such extra number as they judge can be safely spared. And the officers and men so cloathed, armed, and equipped, shall march to the place appointed, and within the time agreed on by the United States in Congress assembled.

The United States in Congress assembled shall never engage in a war, nor grant letters of marque or reprisal in time of peace, nor enter into any treaties or alliances, nor coin money, nor regulate the value thereof, nor ascertain the sums and expenses necessary for the defense and welfare of the United States, or any of them, nor emit bills, nor borrow money on the credit of the United States, nor appropriate money, nor agree upon the number of vessels of war, to be built or purchased, or the number of land or sea forces to be raised, nor appoint a commander in chief of the army or navy, unless nine States assent to the same: nor shall a question on any other point, except for adjourning from day to day be determined, unless by the votes of the majority of the United States in Congress assembled.

The Congress of the United States shall have power to adjourn to any time within the year, and to any place within the United States, so that no period of adjournment be for a longer duration than the space of six months, and shall publish the journal of their proceedings monthly, except such parts thereof relating to treaties, alliances or military operations, as in their judgement require secrecy; and the yeas and nays of the delegates of each State on any question shall be entered on the journal, when it is desired by any delegates of a State, or any of them, at his or their request shall be furnished with a transcript of the said journal, except such parts as are above excepted, to lay before the legislatures of the several States.

Article X. The Committee of the States, or any nine of them, shall be authorized to execute, in the recess of Congress, such of the powers of Congress as the United States in Congress assembled, by the consent of the nine States, shall from time to time think expedient to vest them with; provided that no power be delegated to the said

Committee, for the exercise of which, by the Articles of Confederation, the voice of nine States in the Congress of the United States assembled be requisite.

Article XI. Canada acceding to this confederation, and adjoining in the measures of the United States, shall be admitted into, and entitled to all the advantages of this Union; but no other colony shall be admitted into the same, unless such admission be agreed to by nine States.

Article XII. All bills of credit emitted, monies borrowed, and debts contracted by, or under the authority of Congress, before the assembling of the United States, in pursuance of the present confederation, shall be deemed and considered as a charge against the United States, for payment and satisfaction whereof the said United States, and the public faith are hereby solemnly pledged.

Article XIII. Every State shall abide by the determination of the United States in Congress assembled, on all questions which by this confederation are submitted to them. And the Articles of this Confederation shall be inviolably observed by every State, and the Union shall be perpetual; nor shall any alteration at any time hereafter be made in any of them; unless such alteration be agreed to in a Congress of the United States, and be afterwards confirmed by the legislatures of every State.

And Whereas it hath pleased the Great Governor of the World to incline the hearts of the legislatures we respectively represent in Congress, to approve of, and to authorize us to ratify the said Articles of Confederation and perpetual Union. Know Ye that we the undersigned delegates, by virtue of the power and authority to us given for that purpose, do by these presents, in the name and in behalf of our respective constituents, fully and entirely ratify and

confirm each and every of the said Articles of Confederation and perpetual Union, and all and singular the matters and things therein contained: And we do further solemnly plight and engage the faith of our respective constituents, that they shall abide by the determinations of the United States in Congress assembled, on all questions, which by the said Confederation are submitted to them. And that the Articles thereof shall be inviolably observed by the States we respectively represent, and that the Union shall be perpetual.

In Witness whereof we have hereunto set our hands in Congress. Done at Philadelphia in the State of Pennsylvania the ninth day of July in the Year of our Lord One Thousand Seven Hundred and Seventy-Eight, and in the Third Year of the independence of America.

On the part and behalf of the State of New Hampshire:
Josiah Bartlett
John Wentworth Junr. August 8th 1778

On the part and behalf of the State of Massachusetts Bay:
John Hancock
Samuel Adams
Elbridge Gerry
Francis Dana
James Lovell
Samuel Holten

On the part and behalf of the State of Rhode Island and Providence Plantations:
William Ellery
Henry Marchant
John Collins

On the part and behalf of the State of Connecticut:
Roger Sherman
Samuel Huntington
Oliver Wolcott
Titus Hosmer
Andrew Adams

On the part and behalf of the State of New York:
James Duane
Francis Lewis
Wm Duer
Gouv Morris

On the part and behalf of the State of New Jersey, November 26, 1778:
Jno Witherspoon
Nath. Scudder

On the part and behalf of the State of Pennsylvania:
Robt Morris
Daniel Roberdeau
John Bayard Smith
William Clingan
Joseph Reed 22nd July 1778

On the part and behalf of the State of Delaware:
Tho Mckean February 12, 1779
John Dickinson May 5th 1779
Nicholas Van Dyke

On the part and behalf of the State of Maryland:
John Hanson March 1 1781
Daniel Carroll

On the part and behalf of the State of Virginia:
Richard Henry Lee
John Banister
Thomas Adams
Jno Harvie
Francis Lightfoot Lee

On the part and behalf of the State of No Carolina:
John Penn July 21st 1778
Corns Harnett
Jno Williams

On the part and behalf of the State of South Carolina:
Henry Laurens
William Henry Drayton
Jno Mathews
Richd Hutson
Thos Heyward Junr

On the part and behalf of the State of Georgia:
Jno Walton 24th July 1778
Edwd Telfair
Edwd Langworthy

THE DECLARATION OF INDEPENDENCE

IN CONGRESS, July 4, 1776.

The unanimous Declaration of the thirteen united States of America,

When in the Course of human events, it becomes necessary for one people to dissolve the political bands which have connected them with another, and to assume among the powers of the earth, the separate and equal station to which the Laws of Nature and of Nature's God entitle them, a decent respect to the opinions of mankind requires that they should declare the causes which impel them to the separation.

We hold these truths to be self-evident, that all men are created equal, that they are endowed by their Creator with certain unalienable Rights, that among these are Life, Liberty and the pursuit of Happiness.—That to secure these rights, Governments are instituted among Men, deriving their just powers from the consent of the governed,—That whenever any Form of Government becomes destructive of these ends, it is the Right of the People to alter or to abolish it, and to institute new Government, laying its foundation on such principles and organizing its powers in such form, as to them shall seem most likely to effect their Safety and Happiness. Prudence, indeed, will dictate that Governments long established should not be changed for light and transient causes; and accordingly all experience hath shewn, that mankind are more disposed to suffer, while evils are sufferable, than to right themselves by abolishing the forms to which they are accustomed. But when a long train of abuses and usurpations, pursuing invariably the same Object evinces a design to reduce them under absolute Despotism, it is their right, it is their duty, to throw off such Government, and to provide new Guards for their future security.—Such has been the patient sufferance of these Colonies; and such is now the necessity which constrains them to alter their former Systems of Government. The history of the present King of Great Britain is a history of repeated injuries and usurpations, all having in direct object the establishment of an absolute Tyranny over these States. To prove this, let Facts be submitted to a candid world.

He has refused his Assent to Laws, the most wholesome and necessary for the public good.

He has forbidden his Governors to pass Laws of immediate and pressing importance, unless suspended in their operation till his Assent should be obtained; and when so suspended, he has utterly neglected to attend to them.

He has refused to pass other Laws for the accommodation of large districts of people, unless those people would relinquish the right of Representation in the Legislature, a right inestimable to them and formidable to tyrants only.

He has called together legislative bodies at places unusual, uncomfortable, and distant from the depository of their public Records, for the sole purpose of fatiguing them into compliance with his measures.

He has dissolved Representative Houses repeatedly, for opposing with manly firmness his invasions on the rights of the people.

He has refused for a long time, after such dissolutions, to cause others to be elected; whereby the Legislative powers, incapable of Annihilation, have returned to the People at large for their exercise; the State remaining in the mean time exposed to all the dangers of invasion from without, and convulsions within.

He has endeavoured to prevent the population of these States; for that purpose obstructing the Laws for Naturalization of Foreigners; refusing to pass others to encourage their migrations hither, and raising the conditions of new Appropriations of Lands.

He has obstructed the Administration of Justice, by refusing his Assent to Laws for establishing Judiciary powers.

He has made Judges dependent on his Will alone, for the tenure of their offices, and the amount and payment of their salaries.

He has erected a multitude of New Offices, and sent hither swarms of Officers to harrass our people, and eat out their substance.

He has kept among us, in times of peace, Standing Armies without the Consent of our legislatures.

He has affected to render the Military independent of and superior to the Civil power.

He has combined with others to subject us to a jurisdiction foreign to our constitution, and unacknowledged by our laws; giving his Assent to their Acts of pretended Legislation:

For Quartering large bodies of armed troops among us:

For protecting them, by a mock Trial, from punishment for any Murders which they should commit on the Inhabitants of these States:

For cutting off our Trade with all parts of the world:

For imposing Taxes on us without our Consent:

For depriving us in many cases, of the benefits of Trial by Jury:

For transporting us beyond Seas to be tried for pretended offences

For abolishing the free System of English Laws in a neighbouring Province, establishing therein an Arbitrary government, and enlarging its Boundaries so as to render it at once an example and fit instrument for introducing the same absolute rule into these Colonies:

For taking away our Charters, abolishing our most valuable Laws, and altering fundamentally the Forms of our Governments:

For suspending our own Legislatures, and declaring themselves invested with power to legislate for us in all cases whatsoever.

He has abdicated Government here, by declaring us out of his Protection and waging War against us.

He has plundered our seas, ravaged our Coasts, burnt our towns, and destroyed the lives of our people.

He is at this time transporting large Armies of foreign Mercenaries to compleat the works of death, desolation and tyranny, already begun with circumstances of Cruelty & perfidy scarcely paralleled in the most barbarous ages, and totally unworthy the Head of a civilized nation.

He has constrained our fellow Citizens taken Captive on the high Seas to bear Arms against their Country, to become the executioners of their friends and Brethren, or to fall themselves by their Hands.

He has excited domestic insurrections amongst us, and has endeavoured to bring on the inhabitants of our frontiers, the merciless Indian Savages, whose known rule of warfare, is an undistinguished destruction of all ages, sexes and conditions.

In every stage of these Oppressions We have Petitioned for Redress in the most humble terms: Our repeated Petitions have been answered only by repeated injury. A Prince whose character is thus marked by every act which may define a Tyrant, is unfit to be the ruler of a free people.

Nor have We been wanting in attentions to our Brittish brethren. We have warned them from time to time of attempts by their legislature to extend an unwarrantable jurisdiction over us. We have reminded them of the circumstances of our emigration and settlement here. We have appealed to their native justice and magnanimity, and we have conjured them by the ties of our common kindred to disavow these usurpations, which, would inevitably interrupt our connections and correspondence. They too have been deaf to the voice of justice and of consanguinity. We must, therefore, acquiesce in the necessity, which denounces our Separation, and hold them, as we hold the rest of mankind, Enemies in War, in Peace Friends.

We, therefore, the Representatives of the united States of America, in General Congress, Assembled, appealing to the Supreme Judge of the world for the rectitude of our intentions, do, in the Name, and by Authority of the good People of these Colonies, solemnly publish and declare, That these United Colonies are, and of Right ought to be Free and Independent States; that they are Absolved from all Allegiance to the British Crown, and that all political connection between them and the State of Great Britain, is and ought to be totally dissolved; and that as Free and Independent States, they have full Power to levy War, conclude Peace, contract Alliances, establish Commerce, and to do all other Acts and Things which Independent States may of right do. And for the support of this Declaration, with a firm reliance on the protection of divine Providence, we mutually pledge to each other our Lives, our Fortunes and our sacred Honor.

Georgia
Button Gwinnett
Lyman Hall
George Walton

North Carolina
William Hooper
Joseph Hewes
John Penn

South Carolina
Edward Rutledge
Thomas Heyward, Jr.
Thomas Lynch, Jr.
Arthur Middleton

Massachusetts
John Hancock

Maryland
Samuel Chase
William Paca
Thomas Stone
Charles Carroll of Carrollton

Virginia
George Wythe
Richard Henry Lee

Thomas Jefferson
Benjamin Harrison
Thomas Nelson, Jr.
Francis Lightfoot Lee
Carter Braxton

Pennsylvania
Robert Morris
Benjamin Rush
Benjamin Franklin
John Morton
George Clymer
James Smith
George Taylor
James Wilson
George Ross

Delaware
Caesar Rodney
George Read
Thomas McKean

New York
William Floyd
Philip Livingston
Francis Lewis
Lewis Morris

New Jersey
Richard Stockton
John Witherspoon
Francis Hopkinson
John Hart
Abraham Clark

New Hampshire
Josiah Bartlett
William Whipple
Matthew Thornton

Massachusetts
Samuel Adams
John Adams
Robert Treat Paine
Elbridge Gerry

Rhode Island
Stephen Hopkins
William Ellery

Connecticut
Roger Sherman
Samuel Huntington
William Williams
Oliver Wolcott

THE CONSTITUTION OF THE UNITED STATES

We the People of the United States, in Order to form a more perfect Union, establish Justice, insure domestic Tranquility, provide for the common defence, promote the general Welfare, and secure the Blessings of Liberty to ourselves and our Posterity, do ordain and establish this Constitution for the United States of America.

ARTICLE I
Section 1

All legislative Powers herein granted shall be vested in a Congress of the United States, which shall consist of a Senate and House of Representatives.

Section 2

The House of Representatives shall be composed of Members chosen every second Year by the People of the several States, and the Electors in each State shall have the Qualifications requisite for Electors of the most numerous Branch of the State Legislature.

No Person shall be a Representative who shall not have attained to the Age of twenty five Years, and been seven Years a Citizen of the United States, and who shall not, when elected, be an Inhabitant of that State in which he shall be chosen.

Representatives and direct Taxes shall be apportioned among the several States which may be included within this Union, according to their respective Numbers, which shall be determined by adding to the whole Number of free Persons, including those bound to Service for a Term of Years, and excluding Indians not taxed, three fifths of all other Persons. The actual Enumeration shall be made within three Years after the first Meeting of the Congress of the United States, and within every subsequent

Term of ten Years, in such Manner as they shall by Law direct. The Number of Representatives shall not exceed one for every thirty Thousand, but each State shall have at Least one Representative; and until such enumeration shall be made, the State of New Hampshire shall be entitled to chuse three, Massachusetts eight, Rhode-Island and Providence Plantations one, Connecticut five, New-York six, New Jersey four, Pennsylvania eight, Delaware one, Maryland six, Virginia ten, North Carolina five, South Carolina five, and Georgia three.

When vacancies happen in the Representation from any State, the Executive Authority thereof shall issue Writs of Election to fill such Vacancies.

The House of Representatives shall chuse their Speaker and other Officers; and shall have the sole Power of Impeachment.

Section 3

The Senate of the United States shall be composed of two Senators from each State, chosen by the Legislature thereof for six Years; and each Senator shall have one Vote.

Immediately after they shall be assembled in Consequence of the first Election, they shall be divided as equally as may be into three Classes. The Seats of the Senators of the first Class shall be vacated at the Expiration of the second Year, of the second Class at the Expiration of the fourth Year, and of the third Class at the Expiration of the sixth Year, so that one third may be chosen every second Year; and if Vacancies happen by Resignation, or otherwise, during the Recess of the Legislature of any State, the Executive thereof may make temporary Appointments until the next

Meeting of the Legislature, which shall then fill such Vacancies.

No Person shall be a Senator who shall not have attained to the Age of thirty Years, and been nine Years a Citizen of the United States, and who shall not, when elected, be an Inhabitant of that State for which he shall be chosen.

The Vice President of the United States shall be President of the Senate, but shall have no Vote, unless they be equally divided.

The Senate shall chuse their other Officers, and also a President pro tempore, in the Absence of the Vice President, or when he shall exercise the Office of President of the United States.

The Senate shall have the sole Power to try all Impeachments. When sitting for that Purpose, they shall be on Oath or Affirmation. When the President of the United States is tried, the Chief Justice shall preside: And no Person shall be convicted without the Concurrence of two thirds of the Members present.

Judgment in Cases of Impeachment shall not extend further than to removal from Office, and disqualification to hold and enjoy any Office of honor, Trust or Profit under the United States: but the Party convicted shall nevertheless be liable and subject to Indictment, Trial, Judgment and Punishment, according to Law.

Section 4

The Times, Places and Manner of holding Elections for Senators and Representatives, shall be prescribed in each State by the Legislature thereof; but the Congress may at any time by Law make or alter such Regulations, except as to the Places of chusing Senators.

The Congress shall assemble at least once in every Year, and such Meeting shall be on the first Monday in December, unless they shall by Law appoint a different Day.

Section 5

Each House shall be the Judge of the Elections, Returns and Qualifications of its own Members, and a Majority of each shall constitute a Quorum to do Business; but a smaller Number may adjourn from day to day, and may be authorized to compel the Attendance of absent Members, in such Manner, and under such Penalties as each House may provide.

Each House may determine the Rules of its Proceedings, punish its Members for disorderly Behaviour, and, with the Concurrence of two thirds, expel a Member.

Each House shall keep a Journal of its Proceedings, and from time to time publish the same, excepting such Parts as may in their Judgment require Secrecy; and the Yeas and Nays of the Members of either House on any question shall, at the Desire of one fifth of those Present, be entered on the Journal.

Neither House, during the Session of Congress, shall, without the Consent of the other, adjourn for more than three days, nor to any other Place than that in which the two Houses shall be sitting.

Section 6

The Senators and Representatives shall receive a Compensation for their Services, to be ascertained by Law, and paid out of the Treasury of the United States. They shall in all Cases, except Treason, Felony and Breach of the Peace, be privileged from Arrest during their Attendance at the Session of their respective Houses, and in going to and returning from the same; and for any Speech or Debate in either House, they shall not be questioned in any other Place.

No Senator or Representative shall, during the Time for which he was elected, be appointed to any civil Office under the Authority of the United States, which shall have been created, or the Emoluments whereof shall have been encreased during such time; and no Person holding any Office under the United States, shall be a Member of either House during his Continuance in Office.

Section 7

All Bills for raising Revenue shall originate in the House of Representatives; but the Senate may propose or concur with Amendments as on other Bills.

Every Bill which shall have passed the House of Representatives and the Senate, shall, before it become a Law, be presented to the President of the United States: If he approve he shall sign it, but if not he shall return it, with his Objections to that House in which it shall have originated, who shall enter the Objections at large on their Journal, and proceed to reconsider it. If after such Reconsideration two thirds of that House shall agree to pass the Bill, it shall be sent, together with the Objections, to the other House, by which it shall likewise be reconsidered, and if approved by two thirds of that House, it shall become a Law. But in all such Cases the Votes of both Houses shall be determined by yeas and Nays, and the Names of the Persons voting for and against the Bill shall be entered on the Journal of each House respectively. If any Bill shall not be returned by the President within ten Days (Sundays excepted) after it shall have been presented to him, the Same shall be a Law, in like Manner as if he had signed it, unless the Congress by their Adjournment prevent its Return, in which Case it shall not be a Law.

Every Order, Resolution, or Vote to which the Concurrence of the Senate and House of Representatives may be necessary (except on a question of Adjournment) shall be presented to the President of the United States; and before the Same shall take Effect, shall be approved by him, or being disapproved by him, shall be repassed by two thirds of the Senate and House of Representatives, according to the Rules and Limitations prescribed in the Case of a Bill.

Section 8

The Congress shall have Power To lay and collect Taxes, Duties, Imposts and Excises, to pay the Debts and provide for the common Defence and general Welfare of the United States; but all Duties, Imposts and Excises shall be uniform throughout the United States;

To borrow Money on the credit of the United States;

To regulate Commerce with foreign Nations, and among the several States, and with the Indian Tribes;

To establish an uniform Rule of Naturalization, and uniform Laws on the subject of Bankruptcies throughout the United States;

To coin Money, regulate the Value thereof, and of foreign Coin, and fix the Standard of Weights and Measures;

To provide for the Punishment of counterfeiting the Securities and current Coin of the United States;

To establish Post Offices and Post Roads;

To promote the Progress of Science and useful Arts, by securing for limited Times to Authors and Inventors the exclusive Right to their respective Writings and Discoveries;

To constitute Tribunals inferior to the supreme Court;

To define and punish Piracies and Felonies committed on the high Seas, and Offences against the Law of Nations;

To declare War, grant Letters of Marque and Reprisal, and make Rules concerning Captures on Land and Water;

To raise and support Armies, but no Appropriation of Money to that

Use shall be for a longer Term than two Years;

To provide and maintain a Navy;

To make Rules for the Government and Regulation of the land and naval Forces;

To provide for calling forth the Militia to execute the Laws of the Union, suppress Insurrections and repel Invasions;

To provide for organizing, arming, and disciplining, the Militia, and for governing such Part of them as may be employed in the Service of the United States, reserving to the States respectively, the Appointment of the Officers, and the Authority of training the Militia according to the discipline prescribed by Congress;

To exercise exclusive Legislation in all Cases whatsoever, over such District (not exceeding ten Miles square) as may, by Cession of particular States, and the Acceptance of Congress, become the Seat of the Government of the United States, and to exercise like Authority over all Places purchased by the Consent of the Legislature of the State in which the Same shall be, for the Erection of Forts, Magazines, Arsenals, dock-Yards, and other needful Buildings;—And

To make all Laws which shall be necessary and proper for carrying into Execution the foregoing Powers, and all other Powers vested by this Constitution in the Government of the United States, or in any Department or Officer thereof.

Section 9

The Migration or Importation of such Persons as any of the States now existing shall think proper to admit, shall not be prohibited by the Congress prior to the Year one thousand eight hundred and eight, but a Tax or duty may be imposed on such Importation, not exceeding ten dollars for each Person.

The Privilege of the Writ of Habeas Corpus shall not be suspended, unless when in Cases of Rebellion or Invasion the public Safety may require it.

No Bill of Attainder or ex post facto Law shall be passed.

No Capitation, or other direct, Tax shall be laid, unless in Proportion to the Census or enumeration herein before directed to be taken.

No Tax or Duty shall be laid on Articles exported from any State.

No Preference shall be given by any Regulation of Commerce or Revenue to the Ports of one State over those of another; nor shall Vessels bound to, or from, one State, be obliged to enter, clear, or pay Duties in another.

No Money shall be drawn from the Treasury, but in Consequence of Appropriations made by Law; and a regular Statement and Account of the Receipts and Expenditures of all public Money shall be published from time to time.

No Title of Nobility shall be granted by the United States: And no Person holding any Office of Profit or Trust under them, shall, without the Consent of the Congress, accept of any present, Emolument, Office, or Title, of any kind whatever, from any King, Prince, or foreign State.

Section 10

No State shall enter into any Treaty, Alliance, or Confederation; grant Letters of Marque and Reprisal; coin Money; emit Bills of Credit; make any Thing but gold and silver Coin a Tender in Payment of Debts; pass any Bill of Attainder, ex post facto Law, or Law impairing the Obligation of Contracts, or grant any Title of Nobility.

No State shall, without the Consent of the Congress, lay any Imposts or Duties on Imports or Exports, except what may be absolutely necessary for executing it's inspection Laws: and the net Produce of all Duties and Imposts, laid by any State on Imports or Exports, shall be for the Use of the Treasury of the United States; and all such Laws shall be subject to the Revision and Controul of the Congress.

No State shall, without the Consent of Congress, lay any Duty of Tonnage, keep Troops, or Ships of War in time of Peace, enter into any Agreement or Compact with another State, or with a foreign Power, or engage in War, unless actually invaded, or in such imminent Danger as will not admit of delay.

ARTICLE II
Section 1

The executive Power shall be vested in a President of the United States of America. He shall hold his Office during the Term of four Years, and, together with the Vice President, chosen for the same Term, be elected, as follows:

Each State shall appoint, in such Manner as the Legislature thereof may direct, a Number of Electors, equal to the whole Number of Senators and Representatives to which the State may be entitled in the Congress: but no Senator or Representative, or Person holding an Office of Trust or Profit under the United States, shall be appointed an Elector.

The Electors shall meet in their respective States, and vote by Ballot for two Persons, of whom one at least shall not be an Inhabitant of the same State with themselves. And they shall make a List of all the Persons voted for, and of the Number of Votes for each; which List they shall sign and certify, and transmit sealed to the Seat of the Government of the United States, directed to the President of the Senate. The President of the Senate shall, in the Presence of the Senate and House of Representatives, open all the Certificates, and the Votes shall then be counted. The Person having the greatest Number of Votes shall be the President, if such Number be a Majority of the whole Number of Electors appointed; and if there be more than one who have such Majority, and have an equal Number of Votes, then the House of Representatives shall immediately chuse by Ballot one of them for President; and if no Person have a Majority, then from the five highest on the List the said House shall in like Manner chuse the President. But in chusing the President, the Votes shall be taken by States, the Representation from each State having one Vote; A quorum for this purpose shall consist of a Member or Members from two thirds of the States, and a Majority of all the States shall be necessary to a Choice. In every Case, after the Choice of the President, the Person having the greatest Number of Votes of the Electors shall be the Vice President. But if there should remain two or more who have equal Votes, the Senate shall chuse from them by Ballot the Vice President.

The Congress may determine the Time of chusing the Electors, and the Day on which they shall give their Votes; which Day shall be the same throughout the United States.

No Person except a natural born Citizen, or a Citizen of the United States, at the time of the Adoption of this Constitution, shall be eligible to the Office of President; neither shall any Person be eligible to that Office who shall not have attained to the Age of thirty five Years, and been fourteen Years a Resident within the United States.

In Case of the Removal of the President from Office, or of his Death, Resignation, or Inability to discharge the Powers and Duties of the said Office, the Same shall devolve on the Vice President, and the Congress may by Law provide for the Case of Removal, Death, Resignation or Inability, both of the President and Vice President, declaring what Officer shall then act as President, and such Officer shall act accordingly, until the Disability be removed, or a President shall be elected.

The President shall, at stated Times, receive for his Services, a Compensation, which shall neither be increased nor diminished during the Period for which he shall have been elected, and he shall not receive within that Period any other Emolument from the United States, or any of them.

Before he enter on the Execution of his Office, he shall take the following Oath or Affirmation:—"I do solemnly swear (or affirm) that I will faithfully execute the Office of President of the United States, and will to the best of my Ability, preserve, protect and defend the Constitution of the United States."

Section 2

The President shall be Commander in Chief of the Army and Navy of the United States, and of the Militia of the several States, when called into the actual Service of the United States; he may require the Opinion, in writing, of the principal Officer in each of the executive Departments, upon any Subject relating to the Duties of their respective Offices, and he shall have Power to grant Reprieves and Pardons for Offences against the United States, except in Cases of Impeachment.

He shall have Power, by and with the Advice and Consent of the Senate, to make Treaties, provided two thirds of the Senators present concur; and he shall nominate, and by and with the Advice and Consent of the Senate, shall appoint Ambassadors, other public Ministers and Consuls, Judges of the supreme Court, and all other Officers of the United States, whose Appointments are not herein otherwise provided for, and which shall be established by Law: but the Congress may by Law vest the Appointment of such inferior Officers, as they think proper, in the President alone, in the Courts of Law, or in the Heads of Departments.

The President shall have Power to fill up all Vacancies that may happen during the Recess of the Senate, by granting Commissions which shall expire at the End of their next Session.

Section 3

He shall from time to time give to the Congress Information of the State of the Union, and recommend to their Consideration such Measures as he shall judge necessary and expedient; he may, on extraordinary Occasions, convene both Houses, or either of them, and in Case of Disagreement between them, with Respect to the Time of Adjournment, he may adjourn them to such Time as he shall think proper; he shall receive Ambassadors and other public Ministers; he shall take Care that the Laws be faithfully executed, and shall Commission all the Officers of the United States.

Section 4

The President, Vice President and all civil Officers of the United States, shall be removed from Office on Impeachment for, and Conviction of, Treason, Bribery, or other high Crimes and Misdemeanors.

Article III
Section 1

The judicial Power of the United States shall be vested in one supreme Court, and in such inferior Courts as the Congress may from time to time ordain and establish. The Judges, both of the supreme and inferior Courts, shall hold their Offices during good Behaviour, and shall, at stated Times, receive for their Services a Compensation, which shall not be diminished during their Continuance in Office.

Section 2

The judicial Power shall extend to all Cases, in Law and Equity, arising under this Constitution, the Laws of the United States, and Treaties made, or which shall be made, under their Authority;—to all Cases affecting Ambassadors, other public Ministers and Consuls;—to all Cases of admiralty and maritime Jurisdiction;—to Controversies to which the United States shall be a Party;—to Controversies between two or more States;—between a State and Citizens of another State;—between Citizens of different States;—between Citizens of the same State claiming Lands under Grants of different States, and between a State, or the Citizens thereof, and foreign States, Citizens or Subjects.

In all Cases affecting Ambassadors, other public Ministers and Consuls, and those in which a State shall be Party, the supreme Court shall have original Jurisdiction. In all the other Cases before mentioned, the supreme Court shall have appellate Jurisdiction, both as to Law and Fact, with such Exceptions, and under such Regulations as the Congress shall make.

The Trial of all Crimes, except in Cases of Impeachment, shall be by Jury; and such Trial shall be held in the State where the said Crimes shall have been committed; but when not committed within any State, the Trial shall be at such Place or Places as the Congress may by Law have directed.

Section 3

Treason against the United States, shall consist only in levying War against them, or in adhering to their Enemies, giving them Aid and Comfort. No Person shall be convicted of Treason unless on the Testimony of two Witnesses to the same overt Act, or on Confession in open Court.

The Congress shall have Power to declare the Punishment of Treason, but no Attainder of Treason shall work Corruption of Blood, or Forfeiture except during the Life of the Person attainted.

ARTICLE IV
Section 1

Full Faith and Credit shall be given in each State to the public Acts, Records, and judicial Proceedings of every other State. And the Congress may by general Laws prescribe the Manner in which such Acts, Records and Proceedings shall be proved, and the Effect thereof.

Section 2

The Citizens of each State shall be entitled to all Privileges and Immunities of Citizens in the several States.

A Person charged in any State with Treason, Felony, or other Crime, who shall flee from Justice, and be found in another State, shall on Demand of the executive Authority of the State from which he fled, be delivered up, to be removed to the State having Jurisdiction of the Crime.

No Person held to Service or Labour in one State, under the Laws thereof, escaping into another, shall, in Consequence of any Law or Regulation therein, be discharged from such Service or Labour, but shall be delivered up on Claim of the Party to whom such Service or Labour may be due.

Section 3

New States may be admitted by the Congress into this Union; but no new State shall be formed or erected within the Jurisdiction of any other State; nor any State be formed by the Junction of two or more States, or Parts of States, without the Consent of the Legislatures of the States concerned as well as of the Congress.

The Congress shall have Power to dispose of and make all needful Rules and Regulations respecting the Territory or other Property belonging to the United States; and nothing in this Constitution shall be so construed as to Prejudice any Claims of the United States, or of any particular State.

Section 4

The United States shall guarantee to every State in this Union a Republican Form of Government, and shall protect each of them against Invasion; and on Application of the Legislature, or of the Executive (when the Legislature cannot be convened), against domestic Violence.

ARTICLE V

The Congress, whenever two thirds of both Houses shall deem it necessary, shall propose Amendments to this Constitution, or, on the Application of the Legislatures of two thirds of the several States, shall call a Convention for proposing Amendments, which, in either Case, shall be valid to all Intents and Purposes, as Part of this Constitution, when ratified by the Legislatures of three fourths of the several States, or by Conventions in three fourths thereof, as the one or the other Mode of Ratification may be proposed by the Congress; Provided that no Amendment which may be made prior to the Year One thousand eight hundred and eight shall in any Manner affect the first and fourth Clauses in the Ninth Section of the first Article; and that no State, without its Consent, shall be deprived of its equal Suffrage in the Senate.

ARTICLE VI

All Debts contracted and Engagements entered into, before the Adoption of this Constitution, shall be as valid against the United States under this Constitution, as under the Confederation.

This Constitution, and the Laws of the United States which shall be made in Pursuance thereof; and all Treaties made, or which shall be made, under the Authority of the United States, shall be the supreme Law of the Land; and the Judges in every State shall be bound thereby, any Thing in the Constitution or Laws of any State to the Contrary notwithstanding.

The Senators and Representatives before mentioned, and the Members of the several State Legislatures, and all executive and judicial Officers, both of the United States and of the several States, shall be bound by Oath or Affirmation, to support this Constitution; but no religious Test shall ever be required as a Qualification to any

Office or public Trust under the United States.

ARTICLE VII

The Ratification of the Conventions of nine States, shall be sufficient for the Establishment of this Constitution between the States so ratifying the Same.

The Word, "the," being interlined between the seventh and eighth Lines of the first Page, the Word "Thirty" being partly written on an Erazure in the fifteenth Line of the first Page, The Words "is tried" being interlined between the thirty second and thirty third Lines of the first Page and the Word "the" being interlined between the forty third and forty fourth Lines of the second Page.

Attest William Jackson Secretary

Done in Convention by the Unanimous Consent of the States present the Seventeenth Day of September in the Year of our Lord one thousand seven hundred and Eighty seven and of the Independence of the United States of America the Twelfth In witness whereof We have hereunto subscribed our Names,

G°. Washington
Presidt and deputy from Virginia

Delaware
Geo: Read
Gunning Bedford jun
John Dickinson
Richard Bassett
Jaco: Broom

Maryland
James McHenry
Dan of St Thos. Jenifer
Danl. Carroll

Virginia
John Blair
James Madison Jr.

North Carolina
Wm. Blount

Richd. Dobbs Spaight
Hu Williamson

South Carolina
J. Rutledge
Charles Cotesworth Pinckney
Charles Pinckney
Pierce Butler

Georgia
William Few
Abr Baldwin

New Hampshire
John Langdon
Nicholas Gilman

Massachusetts
Nathaniel Gorham
Rufus King

Connecticut
Wm. Saml. Johnson
Roger Sherman

New York
Alexander Hamilton

New Jersey
Wil: Livingston
David Brearley
Wm. Paterson
Jona: Dayton

Pennsylvania
B Franklin
Thomas Mifflin
Robt. Morris
Geo. Clymer
Thos. FitzSimons
Jared Ingersoll
James Wilson
Gouv Morris

AMENDMENT I

Congress shall make no law respecting an establishment of religion, or prohibiting the free exercise thereof; or abridging the freedom of speech, or of the press; or the right of the people peaceably to assemble, and to petition the Government for a redress of grievances.

AMENDMENT II

A well regulated Militia, being necessary to the security of a free State, the right of the people to keep and bear Arms, shall not be infringed.

AMENDMENT III

No Soldier shall, in time of peace be quartered in any house, without the consent of the Owner, nor in time of war, but in a manner to be prescribed by law.

AMENDMENT IV

The right of the people to be secure in their persons, houses, papers, and effects, against unreasonable searches and seizures, shall not be violated, and no Warrants shall issue, but upon probable cause, supported by Oath or affirmation, and particularly describing the place to be searched, and the persons or things to be seized.

AMENDMENT V

No person shall be held to answer for a capital, or otherwise infamous crime, unless on a presentment or indictment of a Grand Jury, except in cases arising in the land or naval forces, or in the Militia, when in actual service in time of War or public danger; nor shall any person be subject for the same offence to be twice put in jeopardy of life or limb; nor shall be compelled in any criminal case to be a witness against himself, nor be deprived of life, liberty, or property, without due process of law; nor shall private property be taken for public use, without just compensation.

AMENDMENT VI

In all criminal prosecutions, the accused shall enjoy the right to a speedy and public trial, by an impartial jury of the State and district wherein the crime shall have been committed, which district shall have been previously ascertained by law, and to be informed of the nature and cause of the accusation; to be confronted with the witnesses against him; to have compulsory process for obtaining witnesses in his favor, and to have the Assistance of Counsel for his defence.

AMENDMENT VII

In Suits at common law, where the value in controversy shall exceed twenty dollars, the right of trial by jury shall be preserved, and no fact tried by a jury, shall be otherwise re-examined in any Court of the United States, than according to the rules of the common law.

AMENDMENT VIII

Excessive bail shall not be required, nor excessive fines imposed, nor cruel and unusual punishments inflicted.

AMENDMENT IX

The enumeration in the Constitution, of certain rights, shall not be construed to deny or disparage others retained by the people.

AMENDMENT X

The powers not delegated to the United States by the Constitution, nor prohibited by it to the States, are reserved to the States respectively, or to the people.

AMENDMENT XI

Passed by Congress March 4, 1794. Ratified February 7, 1795.

The Judicial power of the United States shall not be construed to extend to any suit in law or equity, commenced or prosecuted against one of the United States by Citizens of another State, or by Citizens or Subjects of any Foreign State.

AMENDMENT XII

Passed by Congress December 9, 1803. Ratified June 15, 1804.

The Electors shall meet in their respective states and vote by ballot for President and Vice-President, one of whom, at least, shall not be an inhabitant of the same state with themselves; they shall name in their ballots the person voted for as President, and in distinct ballots the person voted for as Vice-President, and they shall make distinct lists of all persons voted for as President, and of all persons voted for as Vice-President, and of the number of votes for each, which lists they shall sign and certify, and transmit sealed to the seat of the government of the United States, directed to the President of the Senate;—the President of the Senate shall, in the presence of the Senate and House of Representatives, open all the certificates and the votes shall then be counted;—The person having the greatest number of votes for President, shall be the President, if such number be a majority of the whole number of Electors appointed; and if no person have such majority, then from the persons having the highest numbers not exceeding three on the list of those voted for as President, the House of Representatives shall choose immediately, by ballot, the President. But in choosing the President, the votes shall be taken by states, the representation from each state having one vote; a quorum for this purpose shall consist of a member or members from two-thirds of the states, and a majority of all the states shall be necessary to a choice. [And if the House of Representatives shall not choose a President whenever the right of choice shall devolve upon them, before the fourth day of March next following, then the Vice-President shall act as President, as in case of the death or other constitutional disability of the President.] The person having the greatest number of votes as Vice-President, shall be the Vice-President,

if such number be a majority of the whole number of Electors appointed, and if no person have a majority, then from the two highest numbers on the list, the Senate shall choose the Vice-President; a quorum for the purpose shall consist of two-thirds of the whole number of Senators, and a majority of the whole number shall be necessary to a choice. But no person constitutionally ineligible to the office of President shall be eligible to that of Vice-President of the United States.

AMENDMENT XIII

Passed by Congress January 31, 1865. Ratified December 6, 1865.

Section 1

Neither slavery nor involuntary servitude, except as a punishment for crime whereof the party shall have been duly convicted, shall exist within the United States, or any place subject to their jurisdiction.

Section 2

Congress shall have power to enforce this article by appropriate legislation.

AMENDMENT XIV

Passed by Congress June 13, 1866. Ratified July 9, 1868.

Section 1

All persons born or naturalized in the United States, and subject to the jurisdiction thereof, are citizens of the United States and of the State wherein they reside. No State shall make or enforce any law which shall abridge the privileges or immunities of citizens of the United States; nor shall any State deprive any person of life, liberty, or property, without due process of law; nor deny to any person within its jurisdiction the equal protection of the laws.

Section 2

Representatives shall be apportioned among the several States according to their respective numbers, counting the whole number of persons in each State, excluding Indians not taxed. But when the right to vote at any election for the choice of electors for President and Vice-President of the United States, Representatives in Congress, the Executive and Judicial officers of a State, or the members of the Legislature thereof, is denied to any of the male inhabitants of such State, being twenty-one years of age, and citizens of the United States, or in any way abridged, except for participation in rebellion, or other crime, the basis of representation therein shall be reduced in the proportion which the number of such male citizens shall bear to the whole number of male citizens twenty-one years of age in such State.

Section 3

No person shall be a Senator or Representative in Congress, or elector of President and Vice-President, or hold any office, civil or military, under the United States, or under any State, who, having previously taken an oath, as a member of Congress, or as an officer of the United States, or as a member of any State legislature, or as an executive or judicial officer of any State, to support the Constitution of the United States, shall have engaged in insurrection or rebellion against the same, or given aid or comfort to the enemies thereof. But Congress may by a vote of two-thirds of each House, remove such disability.

Section 4

The validity of the public debt of the United States, authorized by law, including debts incurred for payment of pensions and bounties for services in suppressing insurrection or rebellion, shall not be questioned. But neither the United States nor any State shall assume or pay any debt or obligation incurred in aid of insurrection or rebellion against the United States, or any claim for the loss or emancipation of any slave; but all such debts, obligations and claims shall be held illegal and void.

Section 5

The Congress shall have the power to enforce, by appropriate legislation, the provisions of this article.

AMENDMENT XV

Passed by Congress February 26, 1869. Ratified February 3, 1870.

Section 1

The right of citizens of the United States to vote shall not be denied or abridged by the United States or by any State on account of race, color, or previous condition of servitude.

Section 2

The Congress shall have the power to enforce this article by appropriate legislation.

AMENDMENT XVI

Passed by Congress July 2, 1909. Ratified February 3, 1913.

The Congress shall have power to lay and collect taxes on incomes, from whatever source derived, without apportionment among the several States, and without regard to any census or enumeration.

AMENDMENT XVII

Passed by Congress May 13, 1912. Ratified April 8, 1913.

The Senate of the United States shall be composed of two Senators from each State, elected by the people thereof, for six years; and each Senator shall have one vote. The electors in each State shall have the qualifications requisite for electors of the most numerous branch of the State legislatures.

When vacancies happen in the representation of any State in the Senate, the executive authority of such State shall issue writs of election to fill such vacancies: Provided, That the legislature of any State may empower the executive thereof to make temporary appointments until the people fill the vacancies by election as the legislature may direct.

This amendment shall not be so construed as to affect the election or term of any Senator chosen before it becomes valid as part of the Constitution.

AMENDMENT XVIII

Passed by Congress December 18, 1917. Ratified January 16, 1919.

Section 1

After one year from the ratification of this article the manufacture, sale, or transportation of intoxicating liquors within, the importation thereof into, or the exportation thereof from the United States and all territory subject to the jurisdiction thereof for beverage purposes is hereby prohibited.

Section 2

The Congress and the several States shall have concurrent power to enforce this article by appropriate legislation.

Section 3

This article shall be inoperative unless it shall have been ratified as an amendment to the Constitution by the legislatures of the several States, as provided in the Constitution, within seven years from the date of the submission hereof to the States by the Congress.

AMENDMENT XIX

Passed by Congress June 4, 1919. Ratified August 18, 1920.

The right of citizens of the United States to vote shall not be denied or abridged by the United States or by any State on account of sex.

Congress shall have power to enforce this article by appropriate legislation.

AMENDMENT XX

Passed by Congress March 2, 1932. Ratified January 23, 1933.

Section 1

The terms of the President and the Vice President shall end at noon on the 20th day of January, and the terms of Senators and Representatives at noon on the 3d day of January, of the years in which such terms would have ended if this article had not been ratified; and the terms of their successors shall then begin.

Section 2

The Congress shall assemble at least once in every year, and such meeting shall begin at noon on the 3d day of January, unless they shall by law appoint a different day.

Section 3

If, at the time fixed for the beginning of the term of the President, the President elect shall have died, the Vice President elect shall become President. If a President shall not have been chosen before the time fixed for the beginning of his term, or if the President elect shall have failed to qualify, then the Vice President elect shall act as President until a President shall have qualified; and the Congress may by law provide for the case wherein neither a President elect nor a Vice President shall have qualified, declaring who shall then act as President, or the manner in which one who is to act shall be selected, and such person shall act accordingly until a President or Vice President shall have qualified.

Section 4

The Congress may by law provide for the case of the death of any of the persons from whom the House of Representatives may choose a President whenever the right of choice shall have devolved upon them, and for the case of the death of any of the persons from whom the Senate may choose a Vice President whenever the right of choice shall have devolved upon them.

Section 5

Sections 1 and 2 shall take effect on the 15th day of October following the ratification of this article.

Section 6

This article shall be inoperative unless it shall have been ratified as an amendment to the Constitution by the legislatures of three-fourths of the several States within seven years from the date of its submission.

AMENDMENT XXI

Passed by Congress February 20, 1933. Ratified December 5, 1933.

Section 1

The eighteenth article of amendment to the Constitution of the United States is hereby repealed.

Section 2

The transportation or importation into any State, Territory, or Possession of the United States for delivery or use therein of intoxicating liquors, in violation of the laws thereof, is hereby prohibited.

Section 3

This article shall be inoperative unless it shall have been ratified as an amendment to the Constitution by conventions in the several States, as provided in the Constitution, within seven years from the date of the submission hereof to the States by Congress.

AMENDMENT XXII

Passed by Congress March 21, 1947. Ratified February 27, 1951.

Section 1

No person shall be elected to the office of the President more than twice, and no person who has held the office of President, or acted as President, for more than two years of a term to which some other person was elected President shall be elected to the office of President more than once. But this Article shall not apply to any person holding the office of President when this Article was proposed by Congress, and shall not prevent any person who may be holding the office of President, or acting as President, during the term within which this Article becomes operative from holding the office of President or acting as President during the remainder of such term.

Section 2

This article shall be inoperative unless it shall have been ratified as an amendment to the Constitution by the legislatures of three-fourths of the several States within seven years from the date of its submission to the States by the Congress.

AMENDMENT XXIII

Passed by Congress June 16, 1960. Ratified March 29, 1961.

Section 1

The District constituting the seat of Government of the United States shall appoint in such manner as Congress may direct:

A number of electors of President and Vice President equal to the whole number of Senators and Representatives in Congress to which the District would be entitled if it were a State, but in no event more than the least populous State; they shall be in addition to those appointed by the States, but they shall be considered, for the purposes of the election of President and Vice President, to be electors appointed by a State; and they shall meet in the District and perform such duties as provided by the twelfth article of amendment.

Section 2

The Congress shall have power to enforce this article by appropriate legislation.

AMENDMENT XXIV

Passed by Congress August 27, 1962. Ratified January 23, 1964.

Section 1

The right of citizens of the United States to vote in any primary or other election for President or Vice President, for electors for President or Vice President, or for Senator or Representative in Congress, shall not be denied or abridged by the United States or any State by reason of failure to pay poll tax or other tax.

Section 2

The Congress shall have power to enforce this article by appropriate legislation.

AMENDMENT XXV

Passed by Congress July 6, 1965. Ratified February 10, 1967.

Section 1

In case of the removal of the President from office or of his death or resignation, the Vice President shall become President.

Section 2

Whenever there is a vacancy in the office of the Vice President, the President shall nominate a Vice President who shall take office upon confirmation by a majority vote of both Houses of Congress.

Section 3

Whenever the President transmits to the President pro tempore of the Senate and the Speaker of the House of Representatives his written declaration that he is unable to discharge the powers and duties of his office, and until he transmits to them a written declaration to the contrary, such powers and duties shall be discharged by the Vice President as Acting President.

Section 4

Whenever the Vice President and a majority of either the principal officers of the executive departments or of such other body as Congress may by law provide, transmit to the President pro tempore of the Senate and the Speaker of the House of Representatives their written declaration that the President is unable to discharge the powers and duties of his office, the Vice President shall immediately assume the powers and duties of the office as Acting President.

Thereafter, when the President transmits to the President pro tempore of the Senate and the Speaker of the House of Representatives his written declaration that no inability exists, he shall resume the powers and duties of his office unless the Vice President and a majority of either the principal officers of the executive department or of such other body as Congress may by law provide, transmit within four days to the President pro tempore of the Senate and the Speaker of the House of Representatives their written declaration that the President is unable to discharge the powers and duties of his office. Thereupon Congress shall decide the issue, assembling within forty-eight hours for that purpose if not in session. If the Congress, within twenty-one days after receipt of the latter written declaration, or, if Congress is not in session, within twenty-one days after Congress is required to assemble, determines by two-thirds vote of both Houses that the President is unable to discharge the powers and duties of his office, the Vice President shall continue to discharge the same as Acting President; otherwise, the President shall resume the powers and duties of his office.

AMENDMENT XXVI

Passed by Congress March 23, 1971. Ratified July 1, 1971.

Section 1

The right of citizens of the United States, who are eighteen years of age or older, to vote shall not be denied or abridged by the United States or by any State on account of age.

Section 2

The Congress shall have power to enforce this article by appropriate legislation.

AMENDMENT XXVII

Originally proposed Sept. 25, 1789. Ratified May 7, 1992.

No law, varying the compensation for the services of the Senators and Representatives, shall take effect, until an election of representatives shall have intervened.

ACKNOWLEDGMENTS

I must thank Mr. Wayne Carpenter, formerly honors government teacher of Belton, Texas, High School, for his enthusiasm for his subject. Tom Woods of the Ludwig von Mises Institute played a key role in this book's conception and its execution, and is generally a "hail fellow well met." Lee Cheek, a true friend in academia if ever there was such a thing, merits thanks for steadfast encouragement of all my scholarly endeavors.

Peter Onuf will perhaps wince to see his name here. Credit, I answer, is not the same as blame—and yet, the Virginian Jeffersonian pulse of this book owes much to his inspiration.

Forrest McDonald and R. Kent Newmyer, senior scholars in no need of my gratitude, encouraged me in my work, both personally and through their fine crafting of historical narratives. Clyde Wilson, too, has been in my corner for years.

Lino Graglia, without whom the University of Texas School of Law would have been an intellectual wasteland for me, may wonder why he needs my praise, but it is rather more in the form of an appreciation than a personal encomium.

My parents, Chuck and Linda Gutzman, stressed the significance of education, books, and general cussedness. Blame them!

Trianna, Marika, and Cyril support their daddy whatever he does. I could not do it without them.

Lorie, to whom this tome is dedicated, knows that the dedication only scratches the surface of what I mean to say.

NOTES

Chapter One: What Made the Constitution: Revolution and Confederation

1. Harold B. Gill Jr., "The Model of an American Whig," *Colonial Williamsburg Journal*, Autumn 2002.

Chapter Two: Federalism vs. Nationalism at the Philadelphia Convention

1. I have relied for information on Philadelphia Convention participants on M. E. Bradford, *Founding Fathers* (Lawrence: University Press of Kansas, 1994).

2. *Black's Law Dictionary*, 5th edition (St. Paul, MN: West Publishing Company, 1979) has been of great help in compiling the definitions of Legal Latinisms throughout this book.

Chapter Four: Judges: Power-Hungry from the Beginning

1. Julius Goebel, Jr., *The Oliver Wendell Holmes Devise History of the Supreme Court of the United States, Volume I: Antecedents and Beginnings to 1801* (New York: Macmillan, 1971), 732.

2. Letter to John G. Jackson, December 27, 1821.

3. *The Documentary History of the Ratification of the Constitution: Virginia*, ed. John Kaminski, et al. (Madison, WI: State Historical Society of Wisconsin, 1993), 808.

Chapter Seven: The War for Southern Independence as a Constitutional Crisis

1. Forrest McDonald, "Was the Fourteenth Amendment Constitutionally Adopted?" *Georgia Journal of Southern Legal History* 1, Spring/Summer 199, 15. This article is the basis of the following discussion of the Fourteenth Amendment's (non-)ratification.

INDEX